The Boreal Gourmet

The Boreal Gourmet
Adventures in Northern Cooking

Michele Genest

Photographs by Cathie Archbould

Illustrations by Laurel Parry

LOST MOOSE

To my parents, Janet and Pierre Genest, for their love of good food and good times.

Harbour Publishing Co. Ltd.
P.O. Box 219, Madeira Park, BC, V0N 2H0
www.harbourpublishing.com

Front cover: Fish Lake, Yukon Territory. Styled by Tara Kolla-Hale and Michele Genest, photographed by Cathie Archbould.
All interior photography by Cathie Archbould, www.archbould.com, with the following exceptions: iStockphoto, pp. 16, 35, 37, 68, 71, 83, 87, 103, 206, 226, 242; Michele Genest, p. 199, 200; Paul Gowdie, pp.157, 160; Hector MacKenzie, p. 28, 76, 185, 247; Photocase, 34, 84.
All illustrations by Laurel Parry, except p. 95 by Teresa Karbashewski.
Earlier versions of some recipes and stories appeared in *Yukon, North of Ordinary* and *Up Here* magazines.

Edited by Anna Comfort
Text design by Roger Handling, Terra Firma Digital Arts
Cover design by Anna Comfort
Printed and bound in China

Harbour Publishing acknowledges financial support from the Government of Canada through the Book Publishing Industry Development Program and the Canada Council for the Arts, and from the Province of British Columbia through the BC Arts Council and the Book Publishing Tax Credit.

Library and Archives Canada Cataloguing in Publication

Genest, Michele
The boreal gourmet : adventures in northern cooking / Michele Genest.

ISBN 978-1-55017-475-5

1. Cookery, Canadian—Yukon style. 2. Local foods—Yukon.

TX715.6.G395 2010   641.59719'1   C2010-900053-6

Table of **Contents**

Introduction

In the Yukon, wild or "country" foods—moose, salmon, caribou, berries, mushrooms, plants, herbs and flowers—are part of our everyday diet. Lucky us! At the same time, the growing number of organic farmers and small producers in the Yukon has resulted in a diverse selection of Yukon-made farm and cottage-industry products available on the market. *The Boreal Gourmet* combines a portrait of northern life with an exploration of indigenous foods foraged in the boreal forest and locally produced foodstuffs in gourmet recipes for the home cook.

I grew up in Toronto in a family of five kids. My father was a lawyer who worked long hours, my mother was a gourmet cook. Every night she prepared supper for two different tables, one for the kids, one for the adults; meatloaf for one, sautéed lamb chops finished with a red wine reduction for the other. These two tables taught me that good food was everyday and it was special; that sharing food was boisterous, competitive and unpredictable and that it was matrimonial, loving and private.

The two tables collided when enough of us had reached the age of reason that my parents thought it suitable to introduce us to wine and induct us into the fellowship of really good cooking; the complicated, rich and subtle dishes my mother prepared for their dinner parties: coq au vin, brown sauce that took two days to make, her fabulous silky cheesecake. Mealtimes became the centre of raucous argument, hilarity and excellent food based in the classic French tradition.

My first summer job was in the kitchen at a resort in Western Canada, a revved-up, testosterone-fired place where rage simmered and tempers erupted—once I walked into the larder to find the entire staff staring in shocked silence at the wall, where a chopping knife was embedded an inch deep. A Swiss *chef de partie* came forward to retrieve the implement, and everybody went back to work.

Later, I lived on a Greek island, where I really learned to cook. My boyfriend was the youngest in his family and his mother's favourite. As a child he spent much of his time with his mother and learned all about the things women do, such as gather wild greens and mushrooms from the fields, pick winkles and limpets from the rocks, preserve tuna, process olives and roll out homemade phyllo pastry to three feet in diameter for traditional cheese pies, and he taught it all to me. Soon after I met him he bought a fishing boat, and our repertoire expanded to include squid, sea urchins, lobster (sometimes) and a dozen different kinds of fish. Cooking together was our entertainment, especially in the winter when the weather closed in and there were few visitors to the island.

When I returned to Toronto I wrote for magazines on the subject of entertainment and dining, and became dining editor for *enRoute* magazine, editing copy about restaurants from across the country, and occasionally reviewing a restaurant myself (though I never mastered the art of sneaking out with a menu tucked under my shirt).

Then I moved to Whitehorse—the classic story: came to visit my sister, fell in love with the North and never left. Here I was struck by the enthusiasm with which Yukoners embraced the outdoor life; they hiked and paddled, they whooshed through the wintry landscape on skis and Ski-Doos, and they were always going for walks in the woods, where they engaged in learned discourse about birds, flowers and edible plants. And, I discovered, they were mad hunters, fishers and foragers, supplementing a store-bought diet with the indigenous food First Nations people had subsisted on for thousands of years. Here was the approach I had first encountered in Greece, transposed to a northern landscape. I fell in, with enthusiasm.

I got to know the Yukon during those early years by going out into the bush and picking berries (not very successfully at first), by helping to field dress a moose (with even less success), by canning and cooking and trading recipes and telling stories about cooking. I found a job in the kitchen of the Chocolate Claim, a Whitehorse café and catering company that pioneered imaginative cooking with northern flair, where the collaborative atmosphere encouraged learning and experimentation, and where the cooks went foraging at every opportunity. Later, I wrote cooking columns for two northern magazines, *Up Here* and *Yukon, North of Ordinary*, where my column "The Boreal Chef" currently appears.

I wanted to write *The Boreal Gourmet* in order to share these adventures in northern cooking—the experiments, the disasters, the triumphs, the recipes that evolved and the stories behind them—with Yukon cooks and cooks across the country, and with visitors who may never lift a finger in the kitchen, but who love the North and want to remember what they ate here. Many of the wild ingredients in this book grow in the circumpolar boreal forest and I hope Canadian and other northern cooks will be inspired to explore their own boreal backyards and experiment with what they find.

The recipes are a personal collection reflecting my own background and experience, influenced by my favourite cooks (many of whom contributed recipes) and cookbooks, both the old classics and the exciting newcomers. The emphasis on "gourmet" is intentional, but in this case the writer is not the gourmet, the reader is: curious, appreciative of new tastes and combinations and eager to find new ways to cook with the berries, herbs, plants, mushrooms, fish and game that live and grow in the North. The recipes were developed through trial and error; they borrow a bit from here and a bite from there, and represent an approach that has worked for me and my many collaborators. Some require a bit of time and forethought (I'm a great believer in slow cooking), but I think you'll find your efforts will be rewarded. Each recipe has been tested and tasted by me and by a gang of tasters who contributed their opinions and suggestions with generosity, and (a bonus!) provided lively descriptors for a writer on the lookout for good copy.

I wish you happy reading, happy eating and especially, many excellent adventures in gourmet boreal cooking.

Michele Genest
Whitehorse, Yukon Territory
February 2010

Acknowledgements

The writing of this cookbook has been a wonderful, collaborative experience from start to finish. I'm happy to have this opportunity to thank all those who've contributed everything from wild meat to recipes to sage advice at crucial moments.

To my true and steady companions on this cooking odyssey, Cathie Archbould, photographer, stalwart friend, goddess of the hunt and generous provider of moose, grouse and goat, and Laurel Parry, illustrator, goddess of the hearth and mistress of sourdough, dear friend, recipe-tester and advisor, thank you.

Thanks to all the great women whom I've met, cooked with and learned from through the Chocolate Claim in Whitehorse: Glenys Baltimore, Karon Danks, Lyn Fabio, Mary-El Kerr and Josée Janssen.

To Anne Louise Genest, lifelong accomplice, baker extraordinaire and dispensor of love and wisdom, thank you.

To the cooks who have contributed recipes and ideas, whose names you will find sprinkled throughout the book, thank you. To all the cooks I've ever shared a chopping board with, thank you. To the tasters, for your bravery and your discernment, thank you.

To Priscilla Clarkin, dear friend and number one sous chef, thank you.

Thanks to the lovely Sophia and Nick Marnik for the caribou and the blue chicken's eggs.

To Bev Gray, for moral support and expertise on indigenous herbs, berries and wildflowers, thank you.

To Ward McKimm, for the gift of Margo McKimm's cookbook and permission to share her recipe, thank you.

Thanks to the farmers, fishers and gardeners of the Yukon, who supply us with home-grown, healthy meats, fish, produce and boreal pantry ingredients.

Thanks to the 14 Yukon First Nations for sharing the bounty of their traditional territories.

To my co-workers, thanks for your support.

To Marcelle Dubé and Barbara Dunlop, thank you for your support of northern writers.

To Margaret Webb, thanks for the early years of cooking, talking and writing, and now for the later years.

Thanks to the publishers and editors of *Up Here* magazine and *Yukon, North of Ordinary* magazine, especially Liz Crompton, Mifi Purvis, Jasmine Budak and Elaine Corden. Special thanks to Lily Gontard, founding editor of *Yukon, North of Ordinary*, for launching and helping me shape "The Boreal Chef" cooking column that led to this book.

To Guiniveve Lalena and Tara Kolla-Hale, stylish, talented and generous, thank you for beautifying displays, materials and me.

Thanks to everyone at Harbour Publishing for their support of Pacific Northwest and Yukon writers, and for keeping excellence in Canadian publishing alive. And special thanks to Anna Comfort, editor, fellow cook and trusty guide, for her sharp eye, logical mind and enthusiastic taste-testing. It's been a great trip.

To my family, the Genests and the MacKenzies, for their excitement about the book, their contributions, their Scottish cookbooks, their phone calls with suggestions and questions and their frequent bulletins on triumphant moments in cookery, thank you.

Thanks to Hector, for everything.

Author's Note

The recipes in this book were composed using volume measurements based on the American teaspoon, tablespoon, ounce and cup for both dry and liquid ingredients. Their rounded metric equivalents are included in each recipe.

In these recipes, olive oil is always virgin, vegetables are organic wherever possible, and butter is salted unless stated otherwise.

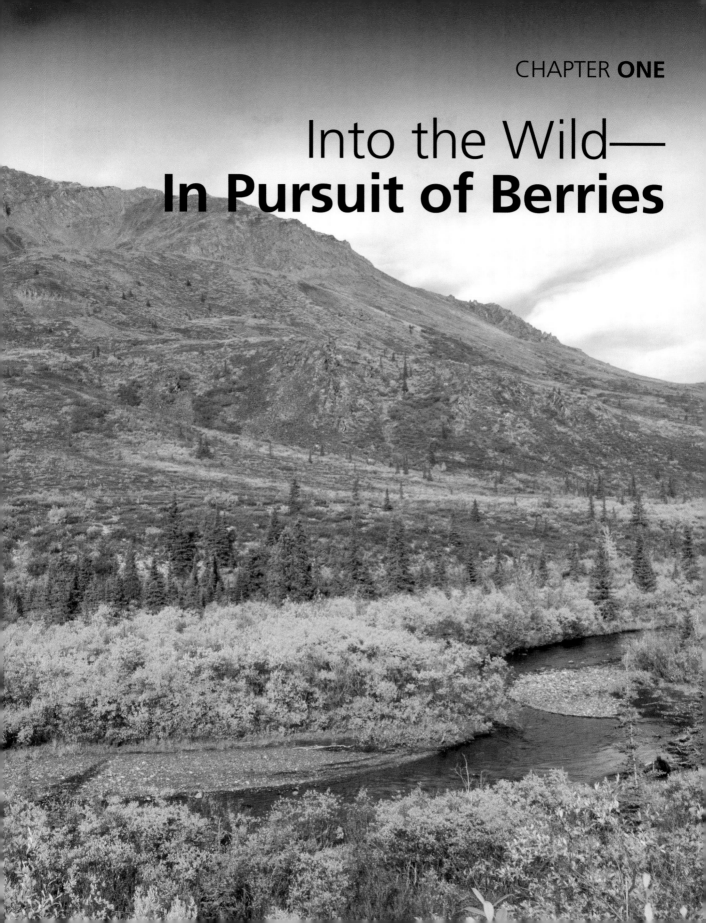

CHAPTER ONE

Into the Wild—
In Pursuit of Berries

Lowbush Cranberries

In the North, the first sign of fall brings on an irresistible urge to forage for berries. How could it not? All around you folks are heading out into the bush or the alpine with empty yogurt containers and ancient Tupperware, coming back with stained fingers, sore backs and a wild look in their eyes. They are evasive when asked where the picking is good this year; they wave a hand in the air and name a lake or a road, but never the exact spot. They stack bags full of cranberries or blueberries or saskatoons three-deep in the freezer, and sometimes open the freezer door just to look at them, so beautiful, so satisfying.

Long before I understood the lure of wild berries, my friend Linda told me a story I found quite odd. She went cranberry picking with some new friends because they'd invited her and because she thought it would be nice to spend a crisp fall day among the fabulous colours. The berries were a mildly interesting by-product. But this was 1993, a bumper year for lowbush cranberries, and they hit the jackpot on a treed and mossy hillside somewhere south of Whitehorse. Linda picked a few berries in a desultory way, but then the plants drew her in, the little shiny leaves (so similar to kinnikinnick, until you get to know the difference) and the red berries tucked amongst the leaves in bunches of two or three or five. The more berries she found, the more she wanted to find. She walked on her knees into damp hollows, following the berries, going deeper and deeper, forgetting her friends, forgetting everything but the feel of berries tumbling into her hand when she tugged them from the stem with the right gentle, rolling motion, the sound of the first berries rattling into the empty container, and then the tiny satisfying thunks as the container filled up.

She soon became a berry fiend; she picked cranberries in the woods outside her rented cabin on Squatter's Row, she picked cranberries on the pathways to her friends' houses when she went visiting, she picked cranberries in every spare minute until the snow came and hid them from sight.

She kept her hoard in a silver bowl in the root cellar underneath the kitchen floor, accessible by a trap door. One night she woke up suddenly with an urgent need to see her

Opposite: Lowbush cranberries, about to become chutney.

Berry picking etiquette

Etiquette is largely unspoken, but you'll figure it out as you go. Some pickers are fiercely private about their patches, others share freely. But there are some basic "rules" when you're out in the berry patch:

- If someone brings you to their favourite patch, don't tell anyone else where it is unless you have their permission.

- If your companion finds a little corner of abundance as you're picking, don't horn in unless you're invited.

- If you find a tiny cache of berries in the lichen or the earth when you're picking, leave it undisturbed. It belongs to a mouse or some other small creature who has plans for it later.

Sharon Shorty, a Yukoner of Teslin Tlingit and Southern Tutchone descent, learned as a child not to eat berries while she was picking. "This was our Elders' way of teaching us patience," she says. If she's picking berries for a potlatch, it's doubly important not to eat them; they are for the community. But when they're turned into jam or sauce and sitting on the groaning board, the berry picker is free to partake, with suitable restraint.

berries. She lit a candle and felt her way down the ladder from the loft into the kitchen, opened the root cellar door and lifted the bowl of cranberries out into the candlelight. She gazed at them, red and shining in their silver bowl, and picked out a leaf or two. Then she slid her hands in amongst the berries, lifted them into the air and let them fall, over and over again, until she was soothed and could go back to bed. "I felt as though I had a treasure, tucked away," she said. Later she turned the berries into jam and chutney and lined up the jars in her kitchen window. But what she liked best, and what she always remembered, were the bright red berries in the silver bowl, hidden in a hole in the floor.

My first berry-picking experiences felt like imitations of the real thing. I didn't know where to go, I didn't know what to look for, and I didn't really believe I would be able to collect enough to make jam or jelly or even a batch of muffins. I had no faith and no luck. At the time I worked in the kitchen of the Chocolate Claim with a couple of wonderful cooks who were expert berry pickers. They went out picking every other day, and stayed late after work putting up jars and jars of preserves and jams and chutneys. They created a lowbush cranberry chutney recipe that is still used by the Chocolate Claim today. To be honest, they intimidated me, and I didn't have the nerve to ask if I could join them. Instead I limped along by myself year after year, picking a cup here and a cup there, never hitting the jackpot, never feeling quite legitimate—what kind of northern cook was I, with no berries of my own, no gleaming jars on my shelves?

Then, in the fall of 2001, Karon Danks, one of those marvelous cooks, called me up and invited me to go on an expedition for lowbush cranberries. Lyn Fabio and Mary-El Kerr (the other marvelous cooks) were coming too, she said. I acted casual: "Sure, I'm not doing anything on Saturday, I'd love to come." But when I got off the phone I jumped around the kitchen: my luck had changed. I was going to pick berries with the pros.

Mary-El picked me up on Saturday morning. In the back seat was a basket of warm cranberry scones under a tea towel. "In order to find cranberries, you must first eat cranberries," she said. We collected Lyn and drove out to the Annie Lake Road, where Karon waited for us by the side of the road. We pulled over and tucked into cranberry scones spread with thin slices of cold butter, accompanied by tea from Lyn's thermos. The necessary ritual observed, we got back into the vehicles and drove until we found a spot the three pros said looked good: lots of spruce and moss, kind of damp, not many bushes, a few rotten stumps.

They nailed it. That damp hollow in the woods was carpeted with berries; it was a bonanza. There were berries everywhere, and big ones, too. "Grapes! Grapes!" cried the pros, and their calls rang through the bush. Lyn and Mary-El both used a berry picker, a device that looks like a dustpan with teeth. Karon and I called it the "the clear-cutter" and said we much preferred picking by hand, the feel of berries in our fingers, the intimate connection with the plant! The other two rolled their eyes. We picked berries for the whole morning, and by the time we stopped I had gathered enough berries to fill four large yogurt containers. The others had more, which was fitting, because they were pros.

We lunched by Annie Lake on cheese and bread and caribou sausage. Karon spotted Dall sheep on the hillside across the lake. After lunch, giddy from the clear air and the berries and a nip of brandy, we covered our faces with green dust from the trunks of trembling aspens, stuck berries on our teeth and took pictures, which Lyn circulated later. The caption on the back says, "The Cranberry Witches."

When I went to bed and closed my eyes that night, I saw something my friend with the silver bowl had told me about all those years ago: cranberries, red and shining, scrolling down my eyelids in an endless, moving pattern.

SIMPLE CRANBERRY SAUCE

8 cups (2 L) lowbush cranberries

3 cups (700 mL) sugar

Combine cranberries and sugar in a pot; cook over medium heat until the cranberries pop and the mixture thickens—30 to 45 minutes. Check for doneness by pouring a drop of the mixture into a saucer and letting it sit for 2 or 3 minutes. Then tilt the saucer to see if the drop runs. If not, it's ready.

Pour into sterilized jars and seal with two-piece metal lids. Leave a ¼-inch headspace in the jar, and wipe any spills from the rim with a clean damp cloth. (Jam or jelly caught between the rim and the lid quickly becomes mouldy, and will spoil the whole jar.) Place the jars in a pot of boiling water and leave them there for 5 minutes. Remove from the bath and let cool to room temperature; you'll know that the seal has been successful when you hear a loud metallic popping sound, and there is a slight indent in the middle of the lid. Store in a cool, dark place.

Makes six to seven 1-cup (250-mL) jars

THE CHOCOLATE CLAIM
CRANBERRY CHUTNEY

This is my all-time favourite cranberry chutney recipe. (Sometimes I add two chopped jalapeno peppers for heat.) Many thanks to Glenys Baltimore, proprietor of the Chocolate Claim, for sharing her recipe here.

Sauté onion until translucent (if you're using jalapenos, cook with the onions), add garlic and spices, combine well and sauté another couple of minutes. Add cranberries and stir until the cranberries begin to pop. Add sugar and vinegar. Cover and simmer for an hour, stirring often.

Pour into sterilized jars, seal with two-piece metal lids, and immerse in a boiling water bath for 5 minutes. Remove and let cool to room temperature. Store in a cool, dark place.

Makes five to six 1-cup (250-mL) jars

1 cup (250 mL) chopped onion

½ Tbsp (7.5 mL) chopped garlic

¼ cup (60 mL) olive oil

1 tsp (5 mL) cinnamon

½ tsp (2.5 mL) ground cardamom

¼ tsp (1 mL) ground cloves

7 cups (1.65 L) whole lowbush cranberries

1 cup (250 mL) white sugar

5 Tbsp (75 mL) balsamic or raspberry vinegar

Pinch of salt

KARON DANKS'S
CRANBERRY ORANGE PRESERVE

2 whole oranges

3 cups (700 mL) white sugar

1 cup (250 mL) orange juice

8 cups (2 L) lowbush cranberries

1 inch (3 cm) fresh ginger, peeled and grated

1 tsp (5 mL) ground cardamom

Wash the oranges well. Cut the oranges into quarters, cut each quarter in half or into thirds, and chop each segment crosswise into thin wedges. Place the chopped oranges, sugar and orange juice in a heavy saucepan and bring to a boil. Reduce heat and simmer for about 20 minutes, or until oranges are soft. Add the cranberries, ginger and cardamom, and return mixture to the heat. Continue to simmer on low heat until the mixture thickens, about 45 minutes to an hour.

Pour into sterilized jars and seal with two-piece metal lids. Immerse in boiling water bath for 5 minutes, remove and let cool to room temperature. Store in a cool, dark place.

Makes ten to twelve 1-cup (250-mL) jars

SPIRITED CRANBERRY SAUCE
WITH SPEYSIDE WHISKY

Speyside is a place rather than a brand name; in whisky terms, it refers to the single malts made with water from the burns (creeks) that run down the hills into the Spey River in the northeast of Scotland. The whisky enthusiast at my house characterizes the Speyside flavours as "gentle, warm and brown." The Speysides include Glenfiddich, Aberlour and Balvenie, as well as numerous others that for some reason take the definite article: the Glenlivet, the Glenrothes, the Macallan—why is this? In any case, go for the 10-year-olds for use in this recipe, rather than the hoarier, more expensive vintages.

Combine all ingredients and cook on medium heat for 30 minutes. Pour into hot, sterilized jars, and boil in a boiling water bath for 5 minutes. Serve at room temperature, with roasted turkey, chicken or duck. It's also good as a dessert sauce for cheesecake or homemade ice cream.

Makes five to six 1-cup (250-mL) jars

8 cups (2 L) lowbush cranberries

¾ cup (180 mL) sugar

2 tsp (10 mL) fireweed honey

Juice and rind of two oranges

1 cup (250 mL) Speyside whisky

2 Tbsp (30 mL) Drambuie

Bees transform fireweed into fireweed honey—"the champagne of honeys."

APPLE AND CRANBERRY TART

1½ cups (300 mL) all-purpose flour

3 Tbsp (45 mL) granulated sugar

½ cup (125 mL) cold unsalted butter, cut into small pieces

Pinch of salt

1 egg yolk

1 tsp (5 mL) vanilla extract, or ½ tsp (2.5 mL) vanilla and ½ tsp (2.5 mL) lemon juice

2 Tbsp (30 mL) cold water plus 1 Tbsp (15 mL) cold water, in reserve

Short-crust Tart Shell

Blend flour, sugar, salt and half the butter in a bowl with your fingertips or a pastry cutter, or pulse in a food processor, until the mixture resembles corn meal. Add the rest of the butter and blend until there are only pea-sized lumps remaining. Beat together the yolk, vanilla/lemon juice with 2 tablespoons (30 mL) water, and add to the mixture a tablespoon at a time, blending or pulsing briefly after each addition, until the mixture comes together. Add the final tablespoon (15 mL) of water only if necessary.

Dump onto a lightly floured work surface and, working quickly, form the mixture into a ball, knead briefly and press into a 5-inch (13-cm) disk.

Have ready a 10-inch (25-cm) tart pan with a removable bottom (or a cake pan, in a pinch).

Roll out the dough between two pieces of waxed paper to a 12-inch (30-cm) diameter, fold it in half, place it in the pan and unfold, pressing lightly into the base and the sides of the pan.

Or cover the round with a sheet of plastic wrap, place it in the bottom of the pan and gradually press it with a flat-bottomed glass across the base and up the sides of the pan.

Patch any holes in the shell with dough from fat sections of the rim, then even out the rim by pushing down lightly with your thumb. Prick the base all over with a fork, freeze for 10 minutes or refrigerate for a couple of hours or overnight.

When you're ready to bake the shell preheat the oven to 375F (190C). Line the shell with tinfoil weighted with dried beans or rice, and bake for 10 minutes. Remove and let cool to room temperature.

Filling

Combine the cranberries, sugar, lemon rind and juice in a saucepan and cook for 30 minutes. Check for sweetness about half-way through, and add more sugar if necessary. But don't go too far—the tartness of the cranberries and lemon is a foil for the sweet apples. Let the mixture cool slightly.

Brush the bottom of the cooled tart shell with melted butter. Layer the apples in the shell, then spoon the still-warm cranberry mixture over top. Bake at 350F (175C) for about 40 minutes, until the cranberry mixture bubbles in the centre and the crust is golden brown. Let cool in the pan to room temperature, take off the removable rim, and serve the tart with **Crème Fraîche** (see page 150), sour cream or vanilla ice cream.

Makes one 10-inch (25-cm) tart

4 cups (1 L) lowbush cranberries

⅓ cup (80 mL) sugar

Juice and rind of one lemon

1 Tbsp (15 mL) melted butter

3 organic BC Ambrosia apples, peeled, cored and sliced

Low-bush cranberries—the leaves are much like kinnikinnick, until you see the difference. Then it's obvious. Persevere!

Highbush Cranberries

By their stink shall ye know them: a fine epithet for the highbush cranberry, or *Viburnum edule,* a member of the honeysuckle family that flourishes in the boreal forests and river valleys of the Yukon, as well as much of northern Canada and the more northerly reaches of the United States. The highbush cranberry is infamously stinky; the ripe berries and indeed the leaves and bark at harvest time give off a smell akin to that of old socks or, some say, rotting meat. This quality is apparently a reproductive strategy designed to attract the big carnivores—grizzlies and black bear, the highbush cranberry's greatest fans—who eat the berry in one spot and excrete its large and indigestible seed in another, thereby ensuring its widespread distribution.

If you live in the boreal forest, you may already be a convert to the virtues of this pungent fruit, whose piquance adds interest to salad dressings, marinades and barbecue sauces as well as the more usual jellies and syrups. Many of you delight in the distinctive aroma, and rely upon it to track the berry each fall. The highbush cranberry is an acquired taste, but once acquired quickly becomes addiction. I ate highbush jelly at a potluck music party at Pete and Mary Beattie's house on Lake Laberge when I first arrived in the Yukon—the wild and never-before-experienced flavour

Testing highbush cranberry jelly with Mary Beattie.

was right in keeping with being thrown a moose jawbone and a stick and told to join the rhythm section.

The highbush cranberry is great accompaniment to wild game—moose, elk, sheep or caribou. The strong flavour needs other strong flavours that will stand up to it, though that said, there's nothing wrong with highbush jelly on toast, or highbush syrup poured over pancakes, or sliding down vanilla ice cream. Mary Beattie, a transplanted California girl locally famous for her syrup, likes to make a warming drink in winter with a couple of tablespoons of syrup mixed into hot water.

A highbush cranberry bush in the back yard is a visual treat all year long, producing white flowers in the spring and gorgeous, nearly translucent red berries in the fall. The leaves, too, do their bit, turning the classic fall colours in September and October, and the ruddy bark is striking against the snow. Although bears love the berries best, the highbush cranberry is also attractive to wildlife such as moose, deer, foxes, squirrels, mice, rabbits, grouse, robins, bohemian waxwings and other songbirds.

There's no question that the neighbours will know when you're cooking up a batch of highbush jelly. That distinctive aroma becomes more intense when the berries are processed, and some members of the family may exit the home, to return only when the cooking session is finished. This is good, because they will be spared the string of curses emanating from the kitchen—it is notoriously difficult to get highbush cranberry jelly to set, if you don't use commercial pectin, which purists eschew. Most cookbooks are not helpful, saying things like the jelly is ready when the hot liquid coats the spoon—one of those perplexing subjective tests useful only if the author is in the kitchen with you. Mary Beattie uses her ears. She says, "You can tell the jelly's ready by the way it pops"—that would be the pop of the slow, deep bubbles breaking the surface. Mary also says the secret to getting jelly to set is to cook small batches at a time, and use a high proportion of sugar to juice. When Mary makes jelly she gets two or three batches boiling on her wood cook stove and, "I have it going all morning long." But the good news is that failed highbush jelly makes excellent highbush syrup, and no one has to know you were aiming for jelly.

A note on nomenclature, just to confuse us

The preferred common name of *Viburnum edule*, or what Yukoners call highbush cranberry, is actually "squashberry." *V. edule* occurs across Canada and the northern United States. Highbush cranberry is the common name for what was formerly called *Viburnum trilobum*, now *V. opulus americanum*, which is also distributed across Canada, but doesn't occur in the wild in the three territories. To the botanist, (Yukon expert Bruce Bennett), looking at pictures of *V. opulus* and *V. edule* side by side, the easiest way to tell the difference is *V. opulus* has deeply lobed leaves (a.k.a. *trilobum*), larger flowers and exerted stamens (you can see the pollen on the anthers). *V. edule* has shallowly lobed leaves, small flowers and stamens that don't stick out of the flowers. To the layperson (me) the easy way to tell the difference is *V. opulus* berries grow in bunches of 30 or more, whereas *V. edule*'s berries grow singly or in very small bunches.

MARY BEATTIE'S HIGHBUSH CRANBERRY JELLY

6 cups (1.4 L) highbush cranberries

water to cover

Boil the berries until they look like they're getting ready to burst, let them cool slightly, and then strain them through a jelly bag. (You can break them with a potato masher or pastry cutter before straining. And don't be afraid to squeeze the jelly bag, unless you want the classic super-clear jelly that the old-fashioned jelly makers like.) Then combine:

> 4 cups (1 L) juice
>
> 3 cups (700 mL) white sugar

Bring to a boil and then simmer the jelly until it pops, or coats a spoon, or both: anywhere from 45 minutes to an hour on the electric or gas stove, and up to 3 hours on a slow wood stove. Pour into sterilized jars, seal with two-piece metal lids, and immerse in a boiling water bath for 5 minutes. Let cool to room temperature and store in a cool, dark place.

Makes three to four 1-cup (250-mL) jars

Highbush Syrup

Mary Beattie makes her syrup by covering the strained fruit and seed pulp with water, boiling and straining again, and combining the resulting juice with honey to taste. I tried her method, and it worked: after boiling and straining the pulp a second time, I had 4 cups (1 L) of juice, to which I added 1 cup (250 mL) of honey. I boiled them together for 20 minutes, put the syrup in sterilized jars, then sealed and immersed in a hot water bath as usual.

Highbush Cranberry Jelly—its pungent flavour quickly becomes addictive.

RED WINE, ROSEMARY AND HIGHBUSH CRANBERRY SAUCE FOR MOOSE ROAST

This recipe works equally well with jelly or syrup, though the flavour is more intense with jelly.

Brush the roast with 2 tablespoons (30 mL) jelly or syrup, then sprinkle with salt, pepper and rosemary. Cook the roast—15 minutes at 425F (220C), then 15 minutes a pound at 350F (175F) for medium rare. Keep the roast warm. Deglaze the pan with the hot water.

Meanwhile, in a saucepan, melt the butter at low heat, add the garlic and rosemary and cook for 5 minutes. Don't let the garlic brown. Add the flour and cook for 1 minute. Add the pan juices, stirring constantly, then gradually add the beef stock, the red wine and finally the highbush cranberry jelly or syrup, allowing the sauce to thicken each time. Let the sauce simmer for a good 20 minutes to allow the flavours to blend. Serve warm with the roast.

Makes six to eight servings

4 to 5 pound (2 to 2.5 kg) moose roast

2 Tbsp (30 mL) highbush cranberry jelly or syrup

Salt, pepper and rosemary to taste

2 Tbsp (30 mL) butter

2 Tbsp (30 mL) flour

1 clove garlic, minced

1 tsp (5 mL) rosemary

½ cup (125 mL) hot water

½ cup (125 mL) strong meat stock

½ cup (125 mL) red wine

¼ cup (60 mL) highbush cranberry jelly or syrup

HIGHBUSH CRANBERRY TRUFFLES

8 ounces (225 gr) dark chocolate
(I use 70 percent cocoa), chopped

¾ cup (180 mL) 35 percent cream

2 Tbsp (30 gr) unsalted butter

2 Tbsp (30 mL) cognac or whisky

2 Tbsp (30 mL) highbush cranberry jelly

Cocoa powder, sifted

Optional:

1 lb (454 gr) dipping chocolate
(white or milk) wafers or good
quality bars

How to temper chocolate

Melt the chocolate in the top of a double boiler over simmering water on very low heat, stirring frequently. Allow it to reach 110F (43C) on a candy thermometer (no higher), then remove from heat and stir with a spatula until the chocolate cools to about 90F (32C). If the chocolate becomes too stiff for dipping, put it back over the hot water again until it thins out enough to coat the truffles easily. You can do this throughout the process. Be careful not to let water or steam get into the chocolate or it will seize.

Put the chopped chocolate in a bowl. Heat the cream and butter in a small saucepan over medium heat. Bring just to a boil. Pour the boiling cream over the chocolate and allow to stand for 5 minutes. Stir until smooth. Add the cognac or whisky and the highbush jelly. Chill 2 to 3 hours, until you can form into balls that will hold their shape. Use a mini ice-cream scooper or a melon baller to form the truffles.

Roll in cocoa powder and store in a cool, dark place.

Or, chill the formed truffles again in the freezer for an hour; outside if the temperature is below freezing. Dip the cold truffles in tempered chocolate: drop a truffle into the chocolate, roll it gently with a couple of forks and then lift it out, letting the excess chocolate drip through the tines of one fork, while scraping underneath with the other. Place the truffle on a baking sheet lined with parchment paper. Near the end of the dipping process the chocolate inevitably gets thicker, and those last truffles will be messier than the first. However, they will taste just as good.

Makes about 50 truffles

Blueberries

When my husband Hector and I go berry-picking our dog Bella, a 10-year-old Lab-shepherd cross, is an essential part of the expedition. She entertains us, shows us where the berries are by her enthusiastic grazing and keeps the program moving at a quick pace. In August of 2009 the three of us drove down the South Klondike Highway to Fraser, BC to pick blueberries. The South Klondike Highway winds through gorgeous country from the Carcross cut-off 20 kilometres south of Whitehorse, through Carcross to Skagway, Alaska. The highway climbs up into an alpine moonscape of tundra and small lakes as you approach where the blueberries are, on a high plateau near the summit, before the road plunges down to sea level at Skagway. Bella sat between us with her nose thrust forward into the air-intake vent, picking up all kinds of information about the landscape we could not discern: bears, moose, squirrels, someone's campfire, someone's *lunch*! When we arrived at our favourite patch between the highway and the Tutshi River, usually so rewarding, we discovered it was all picked out, so we scrambled down the bank and walked over the railway bridge to check out the cliff tops on the other side of the river.

The cliff face is a bank of granite going straight up from the gravel, and the only way we could climb up was over a heap of broken stone and through a steep and narrow cleft. Bella, usually so game, didn't like it. At the bottom of the cleft she tried to turn around and nearly knocked me over, turned to face uphill, balked, and tried to come down again, whimpering and shaking. I wedged myself into the rock, put my hands on her hindquarters and shoved while Hector reached from above, hanging from a bush with one hand, and hauled on her collar. Bella's claws scrabbled on the rock, I pushed, Hector pulled and together we got her through the cleft and up onto the top. Poor Bella. But dogs forget, and soon she was grinning and wagging her tail as we pushed our way through willow and dwarf bush looking for berries. Humans don't forget so quickly, and I wasn't looking forward to the return journey.

The berries were not plentiful, but they were big, and we followed them up small hills and into tiny valleys with pools of water at the bottom, picking here and there, enjoying the long view north towards Teepee Mountain

Blueberries.

Bella, the Mountain Squealer.

and the cold September air. The White Pass and Yukon Route tourist train from Skagway racketed by below us and we waved from the cliff top to the folks at the windows: "Look at us, way up here, picking berries with our dog!" Then it was time to go. When we reached the edge of the cliff Bella sat down and shook. The butterflies started up in my stomach. Hector stepped neatly over the edge and danced from one foothold to another like a mountain goat. At the bottom he turned around to encourage us. I inched downwards on my bottom and Bella followed, pressed against my back with her nose in my ear, whimpering. She pushed ahead of me, panicked, tried to come back up, couldn't, turned around and took a huge leap, scrambling down the cliff wall as the rocks tumbled and flew around her. At the bottom she raced along the gravel, stopped, shook herself and turned to face us, with a big grin on her face. But Hector didn't let her off the hook. "What was all that about, Bella? Eh, you tough mountain guide? Do you charge extra for the squealing, or is it part of the package? Shall we call you the Mountain Squealer, Bell? I think so!" I saw no point in telling him that I'd felt like squealing too, so good old Bella took all the heat. The following chutney is named in her honour.

MOUNTAIN SQUEALER BLUEBERRY CHUTNEY

¼ cup (60 mL) olive oil

1 medium onion, chopped

2 cloves garlic, chopped

2 jalapeno peppers, seeded and chopped

1 Tbsp (15 mL) toasted cumin seed

1 tsp (5 mL) salt

8 cups (2 L) wild blueberries

3 cups (700 mL) sugar

Zest and juice of 2 limes

Sauté the onion in the olive oil until translucent, add the garlic, jalapenos, cumin and salt and sauté a few minutes more. Add the blueberries, sugar and lime zest and juice, stir well to combine, bring to a boil, turn heat down and simmer for 30 to 45 minutes, until the mixture passes the saucer test: pour a drop of the mixture into a saucer and let it sit for 2 or 3 minutes. Then tilt the saucer to see if the drop runs. If not, it's ready. Pour into sterilized jars and seal with a two-piece metal lid. Immerse in a boiling water bath for 5 minutes. Remove from the water and let cool to room temperature. Store in a cool dark place.

Makes about six 1-cup (250-mL) jars

SIMPLE BLUEBERRY JAM

Do we ever lose our hankering for a basic blueberry jam, one that tastes of berries and not much else? Here there's just enough sugar to take the sour edge off and help the jam set.

Mix berries and sugar in a saucepan, bring to a boil and simmer over medium heat for 30 to 45 minutes, or until the jam sets. Pour into sterilized jars, seal, and immerse in a boiling water bath for 5 minutes. Remove, cool to room temperature and store in a cool dark place.

8 cups (2 L) wild blueberries

2 cups (475 mL) sugar

Makes five to six 1-cup (250-mL) jars

Wild berry jams, jellies, chutneys and an artefact: Ione Christensen's Blueberry Jam, circa 1958. Not for consumption! (Food safety tip: consume preserves within two years of canning.)

Raspberries

When I first moved from a cabin on the Mayo Road to my tiny rented house in downtown Whitehorse the backyard was full of raspberry bushes. I killed them. I didn't mean to. It was early spring, I thought they were leftover weeds and I weed-whacked them. I eventually bought the property, and Hector and I built a new house. Next year we will turn our attention to the garden, and raspberry bushes are number one on the list.

Raspberries flourish, though, in the back alleys of downtown Whitehorse, and in the hedges outside the Downtown Urban Gardeners Society community gardens underneath the clay cliffs. There's a sign there that says, "You're welcome to a handful of raspberries, but please leave enough for everyone to share." Last year my friend Priscilla and I scoured the neighbourhood and ended up at the gardens, where we followed the rule, and only supplemented what we already had. It was a bit like trick or treating, only with yogurt containers, and no costumes. We ended up with 16 cups between us. Not bad for urban berry-picking.

Here you'll find a recipe for raspberry vinegar, because the commercial version is so disappointing, and one for a fabulous raspberry and lemon layer cake, created by Yukoner Sarah Hamilton, who is 18, sings and plays fiddle in Done Gone Stringband, works at the Chocolate Claim and one day will go to cooking school.

RASPBERRY VINEGAR

This recipe makes an intense, pink, raspberry-flavoured vinegar that is great in summer and winter salads. Old-fashioned recipes advise us to boil equal parts raspberry vinegar and sugar together, bottle, and then use as the base for a refreshing summer drink.

Pour the vinegar over the raspberries and store in a glass jar with waxed paper under the lid in a cool dark place (not the fridge) for 48 hours. Strain, bottle and refrigerate.

Makes about 3 cups (700 mL)

4 cups (1 L) fresh or frozen wild raspberries

2 cups (475 mL) organic apple cider vinegar

Olive oil and Raspberry Vinegar
(time to make another batch…).

SARAH HAMILTON'S LEMON LAYER CAKE WITH WILD RASPBERRY AND WHITE CHOCOLATE MOUSSE

You can really taste the raspberries, so if you only get a few this year, save them up for this pretty pink number.

2 cups (475 mL) all-purpose flour

2 tsp (10 mL) baking powder

½ tsp (2.5 mL) salt

6 eggs

2 cups (475 mL) sugar

⅔ cup (160 mL) water

2 tsp (10 mL) vanilla extract

This is a perfect cake for a summer celebration, but not in a heat wave. The raspberry and lemon are tart and fresh and the white chocolate adds a delicious, smooth underpinning. The secret to success is to have all the ingredients for the mousse really cold. To this end make the white chocolate ganache the day before and chill it overnight, make sure the whipping cream is super-cold, and chill the bowl and the beaters before whipping.

½ cup (125 mL) water

½ cup (125 mL) sugar

⅓ cup (80 mL) lemon juice, freshly squeezed

Sponge Cake

Grease two 9-inch (23-cm) pans, line with parchment paper, then grease the parchment paper and coat with flour. Preheat oven to 350F (175C).

Sift together the flour, baking powder, and salt in a medium bowl and set aside.

Beat eggs in a stand mixer at medium speed until lemon-coloured, then slowly add sugar while continuing to beat. Once all the sugar is added beat the egg mixture 2 minutes more until it is light-coloured and fluffy. Next, on low speed, add the water and vanilla to the egg mixture. Still on low speed, add the flour mixture to the egg mixture in two parts, scraping the sides of the bowl after each addition.

Pour the batter into prepared pans and drop each onto the counter from a few inches height, to get rid of any large air pockets.

Bake for 25 to 35 minutes until cakes spring back slightly when lightly pressed. Let cakes cool in the pan for 10 minutes, then invert onto a cooling rack. Be sure to let the cakes cool completely before icing.

Lemon Simple Syrup

Combine all ingredients in a small saucepan. Bring to a boil, stirring occasionally. Let cool. Set aside.

White Chocolate Raspberry Mousse

The day before you bake, make the ganache: place the chocolate in a medium-sized bowl. Bring the ½ cup of cream to a boil over medium high heat and remove as soon as it has frothed up. Pour over the chocolate, cover the bowl with a plate and let sit for 5 minutes to melt then beat thoroughly until smooth. Let cool to room temperature, then refrigerate overnight.

When you are ready to assemble the cake, put the bowl and beaters for the whipped cream in the freezer for 15 minutes. Meanwhile, take the now-hardened ganache from the fridge and beat by hand to soften it somewhat. Add the raspberry purée a spoonful at a time at first, then in bigger dollops as the purée and ganache incorporate. Put the mixture back in the fridge while you whip the cream.

If it's a warm summer day, find a cool spot in the house for whipping the cream. If you're using a stand mixer, don't let your attention wander while the cream whips, lest it become over-beaten. A hand-held electric mixer or a balloon whisk will give you more control. Whip the cream until it forms stiff peaks.

Now it's time to incorporate the cream into the ganache. This step is best done by hand to keep as much air in the whipped cream as possible. Fold cream gently into the ganache with a spatula, a cup at a time until all the cream is incorporated. Don't worry about a few streaks, they will lend a marbled effect, and better a few streaks than collapsed cream.

To Assemble the Cake

Cut both cakes in half horizontally with a serrated knife. Place a top half of cake, top-side down, on a serving plate. Dab the simple syrup with a brush onto the exposed side. Ice with a liberal amount of mousse. Place the next layer, a bottom half, on top of the first, cut-side up, and repeat, followed by the next bottom half. Place the last layer, a top half, top-side up and brush with the syrup. The mousse will have oozed out the sides a bit. Smooth with a spatula, then ice the sides with a small amount of mousse at a time, smoothing as you go, and working with a light hand until the cake is entirely covered. Garnish with a circle of raspberries on top and another around the base of the cake. Refrigerate until ready to serve. Add birthday candles and you're ready for the party.

Makes one 9-inch (23-cm) layer cake

½ cup 35 percent cream

6 oz (170 g) white chocolate, chopped

2 cups (475 mL) wild raspberries (fresh or frozen), puréed, pressed through a sieve to remove seeds and chilled for at least 2 hours

2 cups (475 mL) 35 percent cream

Note: Sarah prefers a very moist texture, and uses a quarter of the syrup for each layer; I am more restrained, and end up with leftover syrup.

Strawberries

I've only ever found strawberries in the Yukon twice—once in Faro, a town of 300 in the Central Yukon, on the weekend of the last ever Farrago Music Festival in July 2005, when Sweeney Todd and The Stampeders were the headliners. My friend Suzanne's 10-year-old niece Charlie picked them in our campground, a former trailer park on a wind-blown hilltop surrounded by deserted row houses—remnants of Faro's past, when it was a booming mining town. Just when Charlie had filled a container with about two cups of berries, someone accidentally kicked it over, and Charlie was devastated. She scraped the strawberries back into the container as best she could, but they were covered in dirt and gravel. Later, when we were ready to go down to the festival, Charlie's dad went missing. We found him in the kitchen of the family RV, his hands busy with something in the sink. "What are you doing?" we asked. "I'm cleaning the grit out of Charlie's strawberries," he replied.

That night the tech crew from the festival celebrated by shooting a round of golf on the wacky nine-hole course that winds through the Town of Faro. You tee off on Douglas Avenue near the pump house, meander through town, taking in all the major sights like the school and the Visitor's Centre and end up on the ninth tee beside the old trailer park, where our tent was set up. If you are the tech crew from Farrago in 2005, and it is three o'clock in the morning, you blast Led Zeppelin through the truck stereo and exclaim "Yee-hah!" and "Yeah!" in loud voices before you tee off. If you're ever in Faro, check out the golf course. You can rent clubs at the Visitor's Centre.

Wild strawberries, or *Fragaria virginiana*, subspecies *glauca*, are distributed throughout Central and Southern Yukon, and as far north as Dawson. They tend to like clearings, roadsides and open forests. The only other time I found them was on the Alaska Highway south of Teslin, when my 16-year-old niece Emma was visiting from Richmond Hill, Ontario. She had never picked a wild berry. We gobbled them up.

A niece-like strawberry barrette.

STRAWBERRY MASCARPONE TART, FOR THE NIECES

I adapted this recipe from *Gourmet* magazine, April 2009, using two cups of frozen wild strawberries, picked for me by my friend Sophia in July 2009, while I was away in Ontario. It was all I had. The original recipe calls for six cups of domestic berries; domestic berries would certainly work well, so would the greater volume.

If you have fresh wild strawberries, I wouldn't coat them in sugar, but just make the separate reduction of port and balsamic vinegar and pour it over at the last minute, or serve it on the side. You don't want to fool around with the flavour of wild strawberries when they're fresh. This recipe would also work well with frozen wild raspberries or blueberries.

Make a **Short-crust Tart Shell** (page 20). When you're ready to bake the shell preheat the oven to 375F (190C). Line the shell with tinfoil weighted with dried beans or rice, and bake until the side is set and the edge is pale golden, about 20 minutes. Remove the tinfoil and weights, and bake for 10 minutes more or until the crust is deep golden all over. Cool the crust in the pan for 45 minutes.

While the crust is cooling make the filling:

Wild strawberries, the most delicate of summer treats.

2 to 4 cups (475 mL to 1 L) frozen wild strawberries or *fresh wild strawberries

2 Tbsp (30 mL) granulated sugar (if using frozen berries)

⅓ cup (80 mL) port

⅓ cup (80 mL) balsamic vinegar

1 lb (454 gr) mascarpone cheese

2 Tbsp (30 mL) maple or birch syrup, or fireweed or other honey

Juice of half a lemon

1 tsp (5 mL) grated lemon rind

½ tsp (2.5 mL) vanilla

*If you're using fresh wild strawberries, don't toss them with sugar. Simply combine the balsamic vinegar and the port and reduce to ¼ cup.

Filling

Toss the frozen wild berries with the sugar and let stand for about 30 minutes, stirring occasionally. Strain juice into a small saucepan, and set the berries aside. Combine the juice with the port and balsamic vinegar. Boil until the liquid has reduced to a quarter cup. Transfer to a small bowl and let cool.

Meanwhile, whisk together the mascarpone, sweetener, lemon juice, zest and vanilla until light and fluffy, and spread evenly over the cooled shell. Top with strawberries and drizzle the port glaze over the top, or serve the glaze on the side if your wild strawberries are fresh.

Makes one 10-inch (25-cm) tart

Juniper Berries

The juniper bush, both *Juniperus communis* and *Juniperus horizontalis*, grows prolifically in the Canadian North, *J. communis* reaching right up to the 70th parallel. Martini drinkers know the juniper berry; it flavours their gin. Northern cooks know the purply-blue fruit too, and use it mostly in its dried form, for marinating game. Gwich'in peoples boil the berries for a medicinal tea, good for colds and congestion. I used them as a party trick with the recipe below, and asked people to name the secret ingredient in the sauce. The sauce is a dazzler; it starts out sweet on the tongue and ends on a mysterious savoury note. Nobody guessed the secret ingredient, but they kept coming back for more.

Juniperus communis.

SALMON OR ARCTIC CHAR POACHED IN WHITE WINE, GIN AND JUNIPER BERRIES

2 Tbsp (30 mL) dried juniper berries

2 cups (475 mL) white wine

⅓ cup (80 mL) gin

Salt to taste

Whole sockeye salmon or Arctic char, 3 to 4 lbs, (1.5 to 2 kg) head and tail removed

Roast the juniper berries in a dry cast-iron frying pan over medium heat for 5 minutes, being careful not to let the berries brown. Let cool, then crush with a mortar and pestle.

Prepare a whole fish for poaching: mix white wine, gin and juniper berries and pour into a greased roasting pan or a fish poacher. Make a lid of parchment paper with a vent-hole cut in the middle so the steam can escape. Place the fish in the pan and baste inside and out with the wine-gin-juniper berry mixture.

Bake in a 350F (175C) oven for 15 minutes per inch of thickness—a 3 to 4 pound fish will take about 45 minutes to an hour. (Remember the fish will keep cooking after you take it out of the oven.)

Remove the fish to a platter and make the sauce.

Sauce

1 cup (250 mL) white wine

¼ cup (60 mL) gin

1 cup (240 mL) 35 percent cream

Strain the poaching liquid into a small saucepan, add white wine and gin and boil rapidly at high heat until the liquid is reduced by half. Add the cream and reduce again until the sauce is thick enough to coat a spoon. (I know; another one of those perplexing subjective tests; let's say, when the drops fall off the spoon with reluctance.)

Let the fish cool and remove the skin and bones, leaving the shape of the fish intact—you might have to finesse this part with a couple of spatulas and a sharp knife.

Garnish the fish with lemons and cucumber, and serve the sauce separately, cold or at room temperature.

Makes 10 servings

Soapberry Ice Cream and Other Chilly Adventures

The Yukon spring is a puzzler for the cook in search of indigenous ingredients. New leaves, flowers and berries are a long way off. Moose stews and salmon chowders seem so heavy and wintery when the cottonwood buds release their fragrance, the swans sweep overhead and the sky fills with a delicious new light.

In this season we need something exciting and zingy to match our mood, something like…ice cream! Gelato! Inspired by tales of green tea, garlic and beetroot ice cream, I went shopping for some local ingredients and brought them home: Aroma Borealis teas, Lendrum-Ross Farms goat ricotta cheese and Yukon Wild Things soapberry jelly.

I experimented with eggs, cream and milk, with freezing times and time needed to soften before serving. When I was pretty sure I'd nailed it, I invited a panel of experts over for a sampling: Bev Gray from Aroma Borealis, because she made the teas, Brian Lendrum and Susan Ross, because it was their ricotta, and Elaine Shorty, executive director of the Yukon First Nations Heritage Group, because she grew up on "Indian ice cream," the soapberry and sugar treat so loved by Yukon First Nation people.

The panel assessed flavour and texture. Brian said the Flower Power Tea ice cream was "like a summer garden in full bloom," which made sense, Bev said, because the tea contains dried fireweed, wild roses, elder flower and other local flora.

The Hip Tea smelled strongly of chamomile. Bev told us chamomile was her first smell memory, from her grandmother's home in the fields near the Bay de Chaleur, Nova Scotia. Brian said if Flower Power was summer, then Hip Tea was fall—"a harvest flavour, more mellow. A bit reserved." Elaine thought you could eat this ice cream just before bed.

The tasters loved the creamy texture of the soapberry ice cream, its rosy colour and its tart aftertaste, which Susan described as "not bitter, just sharp. Punchy." They agreed you just can't eliminate that tartness from soapberry—nor would you want to. Elaine said, "We *like* the bitterness." Bev described this one as mouthwatering, literally. "The saponins are enzyme activators and stimulate the saliva glands." For this reason, the gang observed, soapberry

Top: Ripe soapberries, a treat for bears and fans of boreal ice cream.

Bottom: Ice cream begins here: Aroma Borealis herbal tea, lemon and cinnamon.

ice cream would be an excellent palate cleanser between courses.

Alas, the ricotta gelato didn't fare as well as the others. The tasters judged the flavour "not distinctive" and the texture too grainy. The cheese made the gelato "substantial, like part of the meal, rather than a dessert," said Susan. I was partial to the ricotta; I liked the subtle combination of birch syrup, lemon and cinnamon, and for me the cheesiness was a bonus—imagine frozen cheesecake, and you'll get the idea.

During my research, I found the terms gelato and ice cream used pretty well interchangeably. Though everyone has an opinion, there's no consensus. (No eggs in gelato? More air in ice cream?) But it really doesn't matter. Homemade ice cream or gelato is so much tastier than the commercial product under any name.

Also, I was frustrated that many promising recipes ended with "freeze in your ice-cream maker following the manufacturer's instructions." I don't own an ice-cream maker and am not sure that I would make ice cream enough to invest in one—you might be in the same position. The *Joy of Cooking* and good old Jamie Oliver provided the freezing instructions below.

Some caveats and special instructions:

- The custard is ready when it has noticeably thickened. When you raise the spoon the custard obscures the spoon and drops fall slowly and heavily off the tip.
- The ice-cream mixture should be good and cold before freezing. Use a shallow bowl. Take it out of the freezer every half hour and break up the ice crystals with a whisk, making sure the mixture is completely smooth before you return it to the freezer. (Brian, who owns an old-fashioned crank ice-cream maker, says the important thing is to incorporate lots of air as the ice cream freezes.) Do this five times and leave the mixture to harden.
- Pack the ice cream into a tub with a lid for long-term storage. Remember to take it out half an hour before you're ready to serve—the ricotta gelato in particular needs time to soften.

Traditional Ice Cream Recipe from Elder Emma Shorty of Marsh Lake

For enough ice cream for six people, put a half cup (125 mL) of frozen or cooked soapberries into a large bowl. Mix by hand or with an electric beater until it rises in the bowl, about five to seven minutes with an electric beater. If it's not rising quickly enough, add 1 teaspoon to 1 tablespoon of water (5–15 mL). Once the berries are frothy, add sugar to your taste, 1 tablespoon (15 mL) at a time and beat until the sugar is dissolved before adding the next tablespoon. Keep mixing until no drops fall off the beater when you raise the beater from the mixture. When the ice cream is ready it will look smooth, with no bubbles, and will be a beautiful pinkish colour.

AROMA BOREALIS TEA ICE CREAMS

Ice cream makers outside of the Whitehorse area can see Sources at the end of the book for information on ordering Aroma Borealis tea. But if you can't wait, try experimenting with your own favourite herbal tisane.

Warm milk, cream and sugar in a saucepan. Remove from heat. Separate into two equal batches. Add two tablespoons (30 mL) of Hip Tea to one batch and two tablespoons (30 mL) of Flower Power to the other. Cover and steep at room temperature for one hour. Strain each mixture through a sieve into clean saucepans; warm to just below boiling point. The Hip Tea mixture might curdle: don't worry. The eggs will save it.

Whisk egg yolks in separate bowls. Slowly pour the milk mixture into egg yolks, whisking constantly. Pour the two milk-and-egg mixtures into clean saucepans and cook over medium heat, stirring constantly until the mixtures have the consistency of custard. Chill and freeze according to the instructions on page 40.

Makes 3 cups (700 mL) ice cream

1 cup (250 mL) whole milk

2 cups (475 mL) 10 percent cream

¾ cup (180 mL) sugar

2 Tbsp (30 mL) Aroma Borealis Flower Power Tea

2 Tbsp (30 mL) Aroma Borealis Hip Tea

6 egg yolks, 3 to a bowl

SOAPBERRY JELLY ICE CREAM

See Sources at the end of the book for information on ordering soapberry jelly.

1¾ cups (415 mL) 35 percent cream

3-inch (8-cm) strip fresh lemon zest

Pinch of salt

2 large eggs

¾ cup (180 mL) sugar

⅔ cup (160 mL) soapberry jelly

Combine cream, zest and salt in a heavy saucepan and bring to a boil; remove from heat immediately. Discard zest. Whisk eggs with sugar, then add hot cream in a slow stream while whisking. Pour back into saucepan and cook over medium heat, stirring constantly until thick. Don't boil. Pour custard through a fine sieve into a shallow bowl, then cool to room temperature, stirring occasionally. Chill, covered.

When custard is chilled, blend in the soapberry jelly, mixing until the colour is uniform. Follow freezing directions on page 40.

Makes about 2½ cups (600 mL) ice cream

RICOTTA GELATO

1¼ cups (300 mL) 10 percent cream

1¼ cups (300 mL) milk

2 cups (475 mL) whole goat-milk ricotta

½ cup (125 mL) sugar

3-inch (8-cm) cinnamon stick

2-inch (5-cm) strip fresh lemon zest

2 Tbsp (30 mL) birch syrup

½ tsp (2.5 mL) vanilla extract

Mix the ricotta in a food processor with the milk and cream to smooth the texture. Pour into a saucepan, add sugar and cinnamon stick; bring mixture just to a boil while stirring. Remove immediately from heat, add zest, and let the mixture stand, covered, for 10 minutes. Force mixture through a fine sieve set over a bowl and stir in birch syrup and vanilla. Chill mixture, covered, and follow freezing instructions on page 40.

Makes about 4 cups (1 L) ice cream

Ricotta Gelato, softened and ready to serve.

CHAPTER TWO

The Boreal **Pantry**

Essential items for the Boreal Gourmet

The boreal sweeteners: birch syrup, spruce tip syrup, fireweed honey and rose petal jelly.

The boreal staples: spruce tips, rose petals, sage, mushrooms and rosehips.

Boreal Sweeteners

Birch and Spruce Tip Syrups

S ometimes it takes a visitor to alert you to the delicacies in your own backyard. In the fall of 2004 when my childhood friend Filomena Di Ceglie visited from Ontario she scoured the shops in Whitehorse, Haines Junction and Haines Alaska for exotic northern ingredients. In each locale she found some alimentary tidbit I had never noticed before. At Paradise Alley in Whitehorse she found birch syrup, at Madley's General Store in Haines Junction she discovered candied peppered salmon. She spotted spruce tip syrup on a shelf in the Pioneer Inn in Haines, and shot out of her seat to investigate while the waitress waited, pencil in hand, to take her breakfast order.

Fil gathered up all these treasures and took them back to Ontario with her, and I didn't think about syrups again until August 2005 when I came across a young guy selling birch syrup at the agricultural fair in Whitehorse. He was charming and enthusiastic, and he told an amazing story about the process of transforming birch-tree sap into syrup in his home-grown, labour-of-love operation in the woods in the Central Yukon. He said he burned about a cord of wood a day for 15 days to process vast quantities of sap; it took 80 litres of sap, *80 litres,* to produce 1 litre of syrup.

The charming and enthusiastic young man went by the goofily romantic name of Uncle Berwyn. Who could resist? I bought a half-litre of the dark liquid and proceeded to experiment over the next few months, armed with Uncle Berwyn's advice to think of birch syrup not as a sweet to pour over pancakes, but rather a savoury addition to salad dressings or marinades.

I made salad dressing combining birch syrup with walnut oil, pumpkin oil and cider vinegar; I made a birch syrup marinade with soya sauce, balsamic vinegar and olive oil, and a birch syrup stir-fry sauce with lemon juice, garlic and ginger. All were intriguing and to some degree successful. But I'm still searching for the perfect combination of ingredients that will allow the birch syrup to really shine—the unadulterated flavour is unique, reminiscent of molasses but sweeter and almost citrus-y. Currently, one of my favourite treatments is to brush salmon fillets with plain birch syrup, bake them on a tray for 8 to 10 minutes at

Top: Downtown Whitehorse, with Grey Mountain in the background.

Bottom: It takes 80 litres of sap to produce a single litre of birch syrup.

350F (175C), then run them under the broiler for a minute to caramelize the syrup–simple and delicious.

After the birch syrup experiments I turned my attention to spruce tip syrup. I bought a precious half-litre of Birch Boy Private Reserve Alaskan Spruce Tip Syrup at the now-defunct Gold Panner Gift Shop in downtown Whitehorse. Once again I started with savoury foods, combining the syrup with different vinegars and oils for salad dressings and marinades. Each time, the other ingredients overpowered the elusive spruce flavour, which was too subtle to stand up to the stronger, heavier flavours. Even mild rice vinegar was too much—the acid somehow cut the spruce off at the knees.

So I called Fil for help. She rummaged in her cupboard for her spruce tip syrup, and tried a drop on her finger. "I've got it," she said, "Baklava!" Of course—baklava, the Middle Eastern sweet traditionally assembled with phyllo pastry, melted butter and some combination of almonds, walnuts or pistachios, baked and then drenched with sweet syrup when it's hot out of the oven. We agreed baklava would highlight the aromatic tang of the syrup, a taste exactly like the smell of damp spruce in late winter. (There are only a few foods I can think of that taste like a scent; this is one of them.)

I substituted pine and macadamia nuts for the more usual walnuts, in the theory that their mild flavour would give the spruce a better chance to shine. Normally, baklava syrup is made with sugar and honey (the honey provides the flavour); I substituted spruce tip syrup for the honey. I agonized over whether to add cinnamon, but finally threw it in. (Next time I'll leave it out.)

Now, here's the curious part. Once again, the elusive spruce flavour disappeared in the mix. But for the first time in a lifetime of eating pine nuts, I could taste the pine. Somehow the spruce tip syrup lost its own unique character but intensified the flavour of the pine. It was as though the two conifers had duked it out in the oven, and spruce finally threw its weight behind pine, like the second-place delegate in a tight leadership race. (Remember the 1968 Liberal Leadership Convention, when Mitchell Sharp withdrew and put all of his people behind Pierre Elliot Trudeau?)

In the end, though, delicious as the baklava was, I wanted to taste the spruce all on its own, and so came up with the brilliant and unusual idea of hot cakes. Yup. **Sourdough Hot Cakes** (page 189), without fruit or flavouring, won the spruce tip syrup taste-test prize.

Both Uncle Berwyn, based in Dawson City, Yukon, and the Haines, Alaska-based Birch Boy Products are home-grown cottage industries run by people who love what they do; bush artisans in the old-fashioned family tradition. See Sources at the end of the book for more information on both businesses.

BIRCH SYRUP MARINADE OR GLAZE FOR SALMON OR ARCTIC CHAR

Marinade

¼ cup (60 mL) birch syrup

¼ cup (60 mL) olive oil

2 Tbsp (30 mL) balsamic vinegar

1 Tbsp (15 mL) soya sauce

Marinate two pounds of salmon or Arctic char fillets or steaks in birch syrup mixture for 2 to 3 hours, turning every hour or so. Cook at 350F (175C), 15 minutes per inch of thickness. Err on the side of underdone, because the fish will keep cooking once it's out of the oven. Let cool slightly so it re-absorbs the juices, and serve with simple green vegetables and boiled, buttered potatoes.

Makes about ⅔ cup (160 mL) of marinade

If I don't have time to marinate the fish, I reduce the marinade proportions and use it as a glaze:

Glaze

2 Tbsp (30 mL) birch syrup

2 Tbsp (30 mL) olive oil

1 Tbsp (15 mL) balsamic vinegar

½ Tbsp (7.5 mL) soya sauce

In this case, brush a third of the glaze on the fish fillets or steaks, place them in a 400F (205C) oven and glaze every few minutes until the fish is done, about 4 minutes each side for a 1-inch thick steak, 7 minutes for a skinned fillet and 12 minutes for a whole, skin-on, 2-lb (900 gr) fillet, 1½ inches (4 cm) thick.

Makes about ⅓ cup (80 mL) of glaze

PINE AND MACADAMIA NUT BAKLAVA WITH SPRUCE TIP SYRUP

Toast the pine nuts and macadamia nuts in the oven for 10 minutes at 350F (175C). Let cool. Coarsely chop the macadamia nuts, but leave the pine nuts whole. Toss nuts with 2 tablespoons (30 mL) of sugar and cinnamon, if using. While the nuts are in the oven, start the syrup: place ½ cup (125 mL) sugar, water and spruce tip syrup in a saucepan and bring to a boil. Reduce heat and simmer until the syrup is thick enough to coat the back of a spoon. Let cool and place in refrigerator.

To assemble the baklava, unwrap the phyllo sheets and unroll them to their full size on a piece of plastic wrap and cover the sheets with a tea towel—this will keep them from drying out.

Layer 12 sheets of phyllo, brushing each one with melted butter to the edges, in a large baking pan with a rim—a small roasting pan also works well. The pan should be large enough to fit the phyllo but not so big that the syrup will run all over and burn. Sprinkle the nut mixture evenly over the pastry pile and cover with the remaining 12 sheets, buttering each one. If your layers overlap the sides of the pan, at the sixth or seventh top sheet, fold the bottom sheets over the top sheets, and continue layering the remainder. If the butter cools, add a couple of tablespoons and melt again.

Cut the top layers and filling into diamond shapes, leaving the bottom layers intact. Bake at 350F (175C) for 30 minutes, then raise oven temperature to 475F (245C) and bake about 15 minutes longer, or until golden.

Remove from oven and pour the refrigerated syrup over the puffed dough. Cut along the existing lines, let cool and serve.

Makes thirty-six 2-inch (5-cm) pieces

1 cup (250 mL) toasted chopped macadamia nuts

1 cup (250 mL) toasted pine nuts

½ cup (125 mL) plus 2 Tbsp (30 mL) white sugar

1 tsp (5 mL) cinnamon (optional)

1 cup (250 mL) water

½ cup (125 mL) spruce tip syrup

1 cup (250 mL) melted butter

24 sheets (1 lb, 454 gr) phyllo pastry

Halloumi Cheese and Fireweed Honey

Melted cheese and honey is a classic Italian combo I had never encountered until September 2007, when I visited Tuscany. At a tiny restaurant in the hilltop town of Torita di Siena, the daughter of the house served our table of four a plate of melted cheese drizzled with honey and sprinkled with pine nuts. The combination of temperature, flavour and texture was captivating—the honey drew a sweet, lemony thread through the warm animal taste of the cheese, and the pine nuts provided a crunchy, buttery contrast. A couple of nights later, in the Umbrian city of Spoleto, this simple but engaging dish appeared again, only with black truffles this time instead of pine nuts—completely different, equally intriguing.

I came back to the Yukon determined to recreate the experience in my own kitchen and—upping the ante somewhat—using locally produced cheese and honey, because part of the appeal of those Tuscan and Umbrian dishes was that the ingredients came from the green valleys and high mountain pastures. I discovered by chance that Whitehorse graphic designer Patricia Halladay had just returned from a walking tour through the Umbrian mountains and had also sampled cheese and honey, so I signed her up on the search for the local version of those warm and earthy flavours.

Together we set out to find the ingredients for a full-on, melted cheese and honey taste-test session, trying to stay true to the theme of local products. Despite the impressive and diverse yield of Yukon farms and gardens, Yukon-made cheese is still hard to find; the clear choice was the halloumi goat cheese Brian Lendrum and Susan Ross produce on their farm on Lake Laberge, 30 minutes north of Whitehorse. (Brian calls their goats "the girls," as in "come and meet the girls who make the cheese," when he invites you to the farm.)

Halloumi originated on Cyprus, where it is equally loved by Turkish and Greek Cypriots, and often substitutes for the more usual *kasseri* or *kefalograviera* cheese in the famous Greek dish, *saganaki*. Brian and Susan's halloumi comes with a recipe for saganaki; Brian says, "I do hope the Greeks would find this an acceptable version." To compare melting characteristics and flavours we selected a number of mild Italian cheeses: *fontina*, *friulano*, *provolone* and goat *mozzarella*.

For the honey we turned to Eric and Ying Allen's Wild Things Fireweed Honey. Their million or so bees, imported originally from Hawaii, Russia and Europe, feed on the nectar of the fireweed that proliferates near the Allens' Little Fox Lake property. In a good year the bees produce 3,000 pounds of delicate, champagne-coloured honey.

The final preparation for the taste-testing was to gather the nuts and fungi—another mix of the local and imported—roasted pine nuts, hazelnuts and almonds, dried porcini mushrooms and preserved black truffles from the Umbrian city of Norcia, sautéed with garlic and butter, and finally, sautéed Yukon morels, picked after the fire season in 2004.

On the big night we laid out dishes of nuts and mushrooms, a basket of sliced baguette, glasses and a bottle of Montepulciano d'Abruzzo, and instructed our three guest tasters: experiment with as many different combinations as possible—goat mozzarella with almonds and honey, fontina with just honey, halloumi with morels, and so on.

And then, working fast, we began the toasting: we arranged squares of fontina, provolone, mozzarella and friuliano in heat-proof ramekins and broiled them on the top shelf of the oven at high for three to five minutes, then hauled them out when they were bubbling and gooey. The testers dove in with forks and hunks of bread, passing nuts and mushrooms and honey hand over hand down the bar. Meanwhile I slid slices of halloumi into a frying pan where a tablespoon of olive oil had been heating at medium, let it brown on one side for two minutes, then flipped it over for another two minutes, as directed by Brian and Susan's instructions, and slapped it on a plate.

In the end, though different tasters preferred different combinations of ingredients, we all agreed: the honey contributed an unexpected note of interest to the cheese; subtle, sweet and entirely right. In all, it was a great way to experience, think and talk about taste and texture.

Now here's the thing: halloumi was not the best choice for recreating this Tuscan/Umbrian delicacy, because it doesn't melt, it softens. Halloumi is a great choice for frying and grilling precisely because it keeps its shape, unlike the Italian cheeses we sampled, which turned deliciously

Melted fontina with sautéed morels.

Wilted arugula salad with halloumi and BC blackberries from the organic produce club.

goopy. Brian and Susan's halloumi is perfect for other uses: for breakfast, fried and placed on toast spread with fireweed honey; for a summer lunch, on shish kebabs with baby tomatoes and shrimp brushed with lime and fireweed honey; for an appetizer of *saganaki* (highly acceptable!) and in this wilted arugula salad adapted from a recipe for wilted spinach and feta. To those of you who cruise the Fireweed Market in Shipyards Park in Whitehorse on a summer Thursday evening: you could create this dish almost entirely from Yukon-grown products, plus some local blueberries, picked by you. For the nuts and the wine to accompany, well, you might have to search farther afield.

WILTED ARUGULA SALAD WITH FIREWEED HONEY VINAIGRETTE

This recipe is very forgiving of substitutions—the important thing is to keep the balance of tart fruit, crunchy nuts, vinegar and honey.

½ pound (225 gr) of arugula leaves, washed

Handful of pine nuts (or almonds, or hazelnuts)

½ cup (125 mL) blueberries (or raspberries, or wild strawberries, blackberries or even cranberries)

5 Tbsp (75 mL) olive oil

1 red onion, halved and sliced

1 package of Lendrum-Ross halloumi cheese, (about 7 ounces/200 gr) cut into bite-sized pieces.

2 Tbsp (30 mL) sherry vinegar or balsamic vinegar

1 tsp (5 mL) fireweed honey

Salt and pepper to taste

Place arugula, fruit and nuts in large bowl. Heat 2 tablespoons (30 mL) oil in iron frying pan over medium high heat. Add onion; sauté until brown and softened, about 7 minutes. Transfer to bowl with arugula.

Fry halloumi pieces in the same oil, turning when one side is brown, about 2 minutes. Cook for a further 2 minutes; add to arugula.

Add vinegar to pan, let bubble briefly until it loses its sharp aroma, remove pan from heat, add honey and remaining oil. Season with salt and pepper. Pour over arugula; toss to coat and wilt slightly. Serve immediately.

Makes four servings

Magic Food

Before going any further on the subject of spruce tips and rose petals, I must warn the reader. Here you enter the territory of fairy tale. Spruce tips and rose petals are the food of Narnia, of Lorien, of the garden before the fall. To pluck ripe pears and peaches from the orchards in the abundant south is one thing; to pluck spruce tips from the forest in the Pioneer Cemetery at the corner of Sixth and Wood Street in Whitehorse is to be in a childhood dream, where the earth and everything that grows on it is benign and if you feel like eating buds from conifer trees or blossoms from the rose bushes that climb the clay cliffs, well, you can, they won't harm you. For a city girl raised in the populated south, wild berries are a revelation, but spruce tips and rose petals are magic food; they are kind of unbelievable.

There is something else to say about these two items from the boreal forest. Their flavour is elusive. The idea of eating spruce tips or rosebuds is enchanting, and the food itself becomes delicious because of the idea. Your imagination and your senses, eager to discern the flavour of rose petals or spruce tips in the dish you've prepared, work together to help you find it. With rose petals especially, you must train your palate; rather than acquiring the taste for rosebuds, you acquire the ability to taste them.

Spruce Tips

It's important to pick spruce tips at the right time, when the tips are small and tender. The right time happens quickly and lasts only a couple of days for any given tree— the south side might be finished while the north is only starting. Brand-new spruce tips grow at the end of the branch, are a bright green, and are capped with a small, brown, papery husk. The needles are soft, almost silky, and bunched closely together like the hairs of a paintbrush. Once the brown husk falls off and the needles spring outwards the resiny taste becomes pronounced and bitter, and you've missed the boat. But the good news is you can start at lower altitudes and move up into the mountains, following the warmth as it climbs. From my extremely amateur and entirely subjective experience, in the southern Yukon you have about two weeks to harvest spruce tips

Spruce tips must be gathered at just the right time, but they can be frozen for year-round use.

in the month of May; when that period starts and ends depends on temperature and sunlight.

I learned much about spruce tips from Alaskan cook Laurie Helen Constantino, who writes a blog called "Mediterranean Cooking in Alaska" and is a fearless and inventive forager. Ms. Constantino lives sometimes on an unidentified island in the Northern Aegean and sometimes in Anchorage. She has recipes for spruce tip syrup, candied spruce tips, spruce tip vinegar and more. The recipes here for spruce tip salt and spruce tip shortbread were adapted from hers. Alaskans make beer with spruce tips, and so do breweries in Ontario, Newfoundland and Quebec; in Northern Europe the spruce beer tradition is august.

SPRUCE TIP SALT

2 Tbsp (30 mL) kosher salt

2 Tbsp (30 mL) spruce tips

Chop the spruce tips or grind them in a food processor until fine. Mix with salt, bottle and store in the spice cupboard, where they will keep indefinitely. Some uses: a rub for **Cedar-Planked Salmon** (page 233), a flavouring for spreads or dips or an accent for **Broiled Salmon**, next page.

Spruce Tip Salt—the perfect accent for Broiled Salmon.

BROILED SALMON WITH SPRUCE TIP SALT, CRUSHED JUNIPER BERRIES AND SPRUCE TIP SYRUP

Here the spruce and juniper emphasize the earthy flavour of the fish, reminding us of its birth place and its last journey in fresh water, rather than its life at sea.

Grind the juniper berries with a mortar and pestle, combine them with the spruce tip salt and press into the flesh of the salmon, both sides, then brush the top side with spruce tip syrup. Broil at high for 3 minutes, turn the steaks over, brush the top with syrup and broil again for 3 to 4 minutes.

Makes four servings

4 salmon steaks, 1½ inches (4 cm) thick

1½ tsp (7.5 mL) spruce tip salt

1 tsp (5 mL) juniper berries

2 Tbsp (30 mL) spruce tip syrup

SPRUCE TIP AND CHÈVRE SPREAD

Combine all ingredients, mixing well. Spread on crackers and top with a piece of **Smoked Arctic Char with Grappa** (page 158).

Makes 1 cup (250 mL) spread

2 Tbsp (30 mL) fresh spruce tips, chopped

Grated rind of 1 small lemon

1 cup (250 mL) smooth chèvre

Sprucetips, *just* past the best-before date for picking.

SPRUCE TIP SHORTBREAD

Adapted from Laurie Helen Constantino, with help from Laurel Parry. Laurel's recipe results in shortbread that is a bit soft and slightly undercooked, for my taste, if eaten right away. However after two or three months of being stored in a cookie tin, Laurel's shortbread is divine: rich, hard and crumbly. The spruce tip flavour stays strong. These spruce tip shortbreads are surely the quintessential northern pantry item, in the sweets department.

Laurel's Recipe
(Let season for a couple of months)

½ cup plus 1 Tbsp (140 mL) granulated sugar

2 Tbsp (30 mL) chopped spruce tips

1 cup (250 mL) unsalted butter, at room temperature

¼ cup (60 mL) rice flour

1¾ cup (430 mL) all-purpose flour

⅛ tsp (0.5 mL) baking powder

¼ tsp (1 mL) salt

Follow method, below.

Boreal Gourmet Version
(No seasoning necessary)

½ cup plus 1 Tbsp (140 mL) granulated sugar

2 Tbsp (30 mL) chopped spruce tips

1 cup (250 mL) unsalted butter, at room temperature

2¼ cups (530 mL) all-purpose flour

¼ tsp (1 mL) salt

Combine sugar with the chopped spruce tips and set aside 1 tablespoon (15 mL) of the mixture for garnish. Cream the butter until light and fluffy, add the remaining sugar/spruce tip mix and cream together. Add the remaining dry ingredients and mix well.

Gather the dough into a ball and press into an 8-inch (20-cm) shortbread mold or pat into an 8-inch circle and place on a baking sheet.

Bake at 325F (160C) for 30 to 35 minutes, or until edges begin to brown slightly.

When shortbread is ready, remove from the oven and set on a rack for 10 minutes. If using a press, run a knife along the edge to loosen. Sprinkle half the reserved sugar/spruce tip mix onto the counter, and place shortbread upper-side down on the sugar. Sprinkle the remaining sugar over the other side, turn the shortbread over and slice into wedges while still warm.

Makes 8 or 16 wedges

1. SPRING pick spruce tips

2. Summer gather rose petals

3 CHRISTMAS make shortbread

4. serve.

Rose Petals

We have an abundance of wild roses in the Yukon, where the distribution of *Rosa acicularis*, by far the most common type, is territory-wide, extending from the BC–Yukon border right to the North Slope and the shores of the Beaufort Sea. The flowers range in shade from light pink to deep rosy red, and the scent of many pink and red roses on many bushes is mildly intoxicating when you're in amongst them and the wind is blowing. The petals are velvety soft, and to pluck the petals from the stem and let them drift down into the container at your feet is a dual sensual pleasure, both tactile and olfactory. At first I picked the whole flower, until my picking partner told me not to, because then there would be no rosehip. It's better to bunch the fingers of one hand around the flower and pull gently, leaving the pistils and stamens behind.

Caution: Wild roses growing in the bush have generally not been treated with pesticides or herbicides, but if you're picking in a garden or other cultivated area, do make sure the roses haven't been sprayed.

To dry rose petals

Bev Gray of Aroma Borealis Herb Shop in Whitehorse advises that the best time to pick roses is in the morning after the dew has dried, or during the long northern evening. Spread the petals in a single layer on a towel or on screens, if you have them, out of direct sunlight in a place where the air will circulate freely. I learned this too late: I spread the petals out in a sunny room and I think they lost a good deal of the oil, where the fragrance and flavour is, to evaporation. (The house smelled fabulous.) But the dried petals retained their fragrance enough that the scent is strong as soon as I open the container, the colour is lovely, and the taste is discernibly roses. I confess I invested $3 in a bottle of Cortas rosewater, widely available in supermarkets and specialty shops, and have added small amounts for extra flavour in the recipes here.

ROSE PETAL SUGAR

Grind rose petals in a food processor or pound them in a mortar until the pieces are small and powdery, then pulse briefly or mix by hand with sugar. Store in an airtight container in a dark place. Sprinkle on cookies, pancakes or rice pudding; try adding to salad dressings made with raspberry vinaigrette.

Makes a scant ½ cup (125 mL) of sugar

¼ cup (60 mL) dried rose petals

¼ cup (60 mL) granulated sugar

Rose Petal Sugar, pink and pretty.

ROSE PETAL SHORTBREAD

Follow the recipe for **Spruce Tip Shortbread, *Boreal Gourmet* version** (page 54), but substitute 2 tablespoons (30 mL) rose petals for the spruce tips, and grind the rose petals and sugar together in a food processor. (Reserve 1 tablespoon for garnish.)

To the butter and sugar, add

> 1 tsp (15 mL) rosewater

then add the flour and salt and proceed as recipe directs.

Makes 8 or 16 wedges

ALMOND MILK, SAFFRON AND ROSE PETAL SAUCE FOR FISH

A very subtle, light sauce suitable for trout, chum, or other delicate-fleshed fish, derived from a medieval recipe in *A Fifteenth Century Cookry Boke.*

2 cups (475 mL) Almond Milk (recipe follows)

¼ medium-sized onion or 1 whole shallot stuck with a clove

A good pinch of saffron

1 tsp (5 mL) **Rose Petal Sugar** (page 57)

1 tsp (5 mL) rosewater

1 tsp (5 mL) port

1 tsp (5 mL) cornstarch dissolved in 1 Tbsp (15 mL) water

Place onion or shallot in almond milk, place in a saucepan over medium high heat and heat until boiling. Watch carefully, the milk will foam up. There's no need to skim the sauce, just stir the foam back into the liquid. Simmer at medium low until the milk is reduced by half—about 20 minutes. Strain into a clean pot, add the rose petal sugar, rosewater, saffron and port, and simmer together for another 3 or 4 minutes. Make a slurry of the cornstarch and water, add to the sauce and stir until the sauce has thickened, another 1 to 2 minutes. Serve warm with baked, broiled or poached fish.

Makes about 1 cup (250 mL) sauce

The 15th-Century Version

Take Almaunde Mylke and flowre of Rys, & Sugre, an Safroun, an boyle hem y-fere; than take Red Rosys, and grynd fayre in a morter with Almaunde mylke; than take Loches, an toyle hem with Flowre, an frye hem, & ley him in dysshys; than take gode pouder, and do in the Sewe, & caste the Sewe a-bouyn the lochys, & serve forth.

ALMOND MILK

Work in batches when grinding the almonds—my food processor couldn't handle four cups of water at once and leaked.

Soak the almonds overnight. Place a saucer on the almonds to keep them submerged. The next day drain almonds and, in batches, grind them as fine as possible in a blender or food processor with fresh water. Set a strainer over a bowl and strain each batch as it's finished. Don't be afraid to press the liquid out of the pulp with the back of a wooden spoon. The ground almonds that are left in the strainer won't have much flavour, but you can use them in muffins or bread; just remember to adjust the flour and liquid. Store the almond milk in the fridge; use the extra on cereal, or to make rice pudding or risotto.

An alternative is to grind the almonds after soaking in fish or chicken stock. Then you'll have the beginning of a nice soup, with the two cups (475 mL) you don't use for the recipe on the previous page.

Makes about 4 cups (1 L) milk

1 cup (250 mL) almonds, plus water to cover

4 cups (1 L) water

CHESTNUT, ROSE PETAL SAUCE

Another adaptation, this time from the recipe for Quail in Rose Petal Sauce in Laura Esquivel's *Like Water for Chocolate*. Many versions are in circulation out there. This one substitutes plums or seedless grapes for the usual pitaya (dragon fruit), and rose petal jelly for the honey. Be forewarned that preparing the chestnuts is a bit time-consuming; it's handy to have a sous-chef.

12 fresh chestnuts

3 cups (700 mL) water

2 Tbsp (30 mL) butter

2 cloves of garlic, minced

1½ tsp (7.5 mL) anise seed

1 cup (250 mL) dried rose petals or 4 cups (1 L) fresh

2 ripe plums, chopped, or 1 cup (250 mL) seedless red grapes or 1 pitaya, peeled and chopped

2 Tbsp **Rose Petal Jelly** (page 61) or fireweed honey

1 tsp (5 mL) rosewater, or more to taste

Salt and freshly ground black pepper

Prepare the chestnuts. Cut a cross in the base of each chestnut—easier said than done, we found. Try a small serrated knife to cut the cross then put the point of a paring knife at the crux and twist. Cook the chestnuts for 5 minutes in a cast iron frying pan at medium heat. They should open, but if they don't, don't worry.

Bring 2 cups (475 mL) of water to a boil, add the chestnuts and cook over medium heat for 15 minutes. Let cool and then peel off the shells. We found that giving the ones that hadn't opened a good hit with a mallet helped. Discard any that aren't a creamy white or look spoiled.

Grind the rose petals and chestnuts in the food processor and purée until fairly smooth. (If you're going to use chilies, add them now.) At this point the rose petals will be quite fragrant. Add the plums, grapes or pitaya, pulse once or twice and slowly pour in 1 cup (250 mL) of water. Now, the intensity of the rose fragrance diminishes.

Melt butter over medium low heat in the same pan you used for the chestnuts, add the garlic and anise seed and cook for 5 minutes. Add the chestnut and pose petal mixture, and simmer for 10 minutes, then stir in the rose petal jelly, salt and pepper, and rosewater to taste. Serve warm or at room temperature to accompany grilled meat.

Makes about 2 cups (475 mL) sauce

Priscilla Clarkin, a Yukon friend who lived for five years in Mexico, was the sous chef when we tested this recipe. She said the result was *muy auténtico* and suggests adding some ground chilies. Why not? At my house we served it at room temperature in a bowl as a sort of chutney, with lamb chops one night and grilled moose steaks the next. Delicious.

ROSE PETAL JELLY

I tried to make this jelly set without pectin, but it just wouldn't. Ying Allen of Yukon Wild Things warned me about this—she said that if you didn't use pectin the jelly would take so long to set it would lose all its flavour. She was right. My second batch, with pectin, was more successful in retaining its delicate perfumed flavour, so elusive as to be more a scent than a taste. I found after six months that the rose flavour in the jelly had almost disappeared, though the colour was as enchanting as ever. Use your jelly right away, on toast, on crackers and cream cheese, as a glaze on roasted meat, or as a filling for homemade cookies.

Combine the rose petals and water in a stainless steel saucepan, bring to the boil and simmer for 15 minutes. Strain into a glass bowl and discard the petals. Add lemon juice to the liquid, measure and return to the saucepan. For every cup of liquid add ¾ cup (180 mL) of sugar. Bring to a boil over high heat, and boil for 1 minute. Remove from heat and stir in liquid pectin. Pour into sterilized jars, seal and immerse in a boiling water bath for 5 minutes. Let cool to room temperature and store in a cool, dark place. The jelly will be quite firm, holding its shape when spooned onto a plate.

4 cups (1 L) fresh rose petals, loosely packed

4 cups (1 L) water

juice of 2 lemons

3–4 cups (0.7–1 L) sugar

85 mL pouch of liquid pectin

Wild rose, food of fairy tale and legend.

Sage

A couple of years ago, Whitehorse chef Mary-El Kerr told me a fabulous Yukon food story: she tasted wild sage in the meat of a Fannin sheep caught in the mountains outside Faro. Yes: she meant the sage the sheep had eaten. One of her hunter friends cooked a sheep steak for her on the barbecue, seasoned with nothing but pepper. And there it was, the taste of sage, in the meat, unmistakable.

I've been excited about wild sage ever since.

Northern sage is not related to the European *Salvia* sold in supermarkets and garden centres, but a member of the sunflower family; the genus is *Artemisia*. One of our most common sages is *Artemisia frigida*, or "pasture sage" in the vernacular (but as Yukon botanist Jennifer Line says, "here we just call it sage"), which grows all over the clay cliffs on the western edge of Whitehorse. There are 14 varieties of *Artemisia* in the Yukon, some of them quite rare. *Artemisia absinthium* (common wormwood), which we don't have here, was once used in the manufacture of absinthe. An excess can cause "giddiness and attacks of epileptiform convulsions" according to *British Pharmacopoeia*; conversely, many kinds of *Artemisia* are valued for their healing properties.

Artemisia is named for the Greek goddess Artemis, who recognized its medicinal value and gave it, along with leeches, to the great healer Chiron the Centaur. Aboriginal peoples in Canada's boreal forest use *Artemisia* as a healing medicine, and here the Southern Tutchone people sometimes use *Artemisia* as an insect repellent, a smudge for ceremonial purposes or, one Elder remembers, to eliminate the human smell from traps—her mother packed sage in with the traps when she worked her trapline. Evidence of sage as an ingredient in Yukon First Nations cookery is harder to find—another Southern Tutchone woman said her dad cooked with sage, but he was European.

To my great satisfaction, I learned that Dall sheep do eat sage, typically from the early fall to the early spring; and the distribution of *Artemisia frigida* extends as far east as Faro, where the Fannin live (Fannin are a Dall-Stone sheep cross), so there's plenty of good solid evidence that Mary-El did taste sage in that wild sheep.

You can't buy wild sage in Whitehorse—Aroma Borealis on Main Street sells clary sage essential oil, but that's a

Salvia and not meant for internal use, and Yukon Indian Crafts Ltd., right next door, sells sage for smudging, but it's not Yukon sage. The clay cliffs loom just outside my back door, but I have never picked sage up there (crazy!) so when it came time to test these recipes, I was caught short.

Mary-El came to the rescue. She had a bunch of *Artemisia frigida* tucked away in a drawer—a friend of hers, concerned that Mary-El had no sage in the house for smudging, gathered some on the clay cliffs and bundled it up with Mary-El's best pink embroidery thread. Mary-El generously surrendered it for use in the *North of Ordinary* cooking experiments, as long as I left some to burn in her friend's honour. And so I did.

The results are here. Ideally, I would have had wild sheep for this shindig, but the hunters' larders were bare, so I used the last bit of domestic goat my household had purchased from Wild Blue Yonder farm in fall 2006—goat shank soup bones from the bottom of the freezer became a gourmand's adventure. Note that this ragout is not a light meal—it's best after a long springtime ski, when everyone's happy but tired, and sleep is next on the agenda. There's an apple-sage compote to accompany, flambéed with brandy, and finally, cheesy corn and sage muffins for a late spring brunch. If you intend to pick sage this year, go when it flowers in late June, and I'll see you on the clay cliffs.

Dall sheep in Kluane National Park, Yukon Territory.

LATE SEASON GOAT, SAGE AND APPLE RAGOUT

If you have wild sheep in the freezer (lucky you) use sheep shanks instead. Or substitute domestic lamb shanks. Remember not to go overboard on the *Artemesia* sage, especially if it's fresh. A friend told me a cautionary tale not long ago. He and his fellow biologists cooked up a moose stew on a field trip, and added handfuls of fresh sage from the hillside near their camp. The stew was too bitter to eat.

2 Tbsp (30 mL) olive oil

½ cup (125 mL) chopped onion

½ cup (125 mL) chopped carrot

peel from 2 BC Ambrosia apples (use the peeled apple in the ragout)

2 tsp (10 mL) crumbled indigenous sage (*Artemisia frigida*)

2 pieces goat shank

Splash of Calvados

2 bay leaves

8 cups (2 L) water

3 Tbsp (45 mL) olive oil

2 cups (475 mL) chopped onion

2 Ambrosia apples, peeled and chopped (Gala or Spartan are also good)

1 cup (250 mL) chopped carrot

2 Tbsp (30 mL) flour

4–5 cups (1–1.2 L) stock

6 pieces goat shank

1 Tbsp (15 mL) crumbled Artemisia sage

Salt and pepper to taste

¼ cup (60 mL) red wine

Stock

Heat oil in a stockpot or large saucepan over medium heat and brown vegetables and apple peel, adding sage when onion is translucent. Push vegetables aside and brown meat in same pot. Deglaze pan with Calvados; add water and bay leaves. Bring slowly to a simmer then cook over low heat for 2 hours. Strain, cool and skim. Reserve meat and extra stock for a nice goaty Scotch broth.

Makes about 8 cups (2 L) stock

Ragout

Brown vegetables and apple in 2 tablespoons (30 mL) of oil over medium heat in a large saucepan or oven-proof casserole, adding sage when onions are translucent. Add flour; let cook for 2 minutes before gradually adding stock, letting mixture thicken after each addition.

Meanwhile, dredge meat in salt, pepper and sage. Heat 1 tablespoon (15 mL) oil in a cast iron frying pan over medium heat and brown the meat (in two shifts if the pan is small). When vegetable and stock mix is thick, add meat. Deglaze the frying pan with red wine. Add wine to ragout. Stir well. Simmer over low heat or place in a 325F (160C) oven for at least 3 hours, until meat is falling off the bone. You might need to remove the lid for the last hour—if so, turn meat occasionally so it doesn't dry out. Serve with Apple-Sage Compote and the starch of your choice—**Baked Polenta** would be good (page 224).

Makes six servings

APPLE-SAGE COMPOTE

Brown onion slowly in butter over medium-low heat, adding apple after about 15 minutes. Let apple brown but not fall apart, another 10 to 15 minutes. Add sage and mix gently.

To finish, turn heat to high, douse pan with brandy and light. The flame should go out after a few seconds. (Keep a pot lid handy to smother if necessary.) Serve compote right away with the stew.

Makes about ¾ cup (180 mL) of compote—enough for six servings

2 Tbsp (30 mL) butter

1 medium onion, cut in half and sliced lengthwise

2 BC Ambrosia apples, sliced but not peeled

1 Tbsp (15 mL) crumbled sage

Splash of Calvados or brandy

CORNMEAL, CHEDDAR AND SAGE MUFFINS

Combine flour, baking powder, salt and sugar, stir in cornmeal, sage and 1 cup (250 mL) cheese. Make a well in the centre of the dry ingredients; add beaten egg, milk and melted cooled butter. Stir in a few quick strokes, just until dry ingredients are moistened. (Over-beating results in holey muffins.) Grease a 12-cup muffin tin and drop a teaspoonful of grated cheese in each cup. The cheese will melt and turn crispy on the bottom of each muffin. Add batter; bake at 400F (205C) for 20 to 25 minutes. Serve warm.

Makes 12 small muffins

¾ cup (180 mL) all-purpose flour

2½ tsp (12.5 mL) baking powder

¾ tsp (3 mL) salt

1 Tbsp (15 mL) sugar

½ cup (125 mL) yellow cornmeal

1 Tbsp (15 mL) crumbled sage

1 cup (250 mL) plus 2 Tbsp (30 mL) grated cheddar cheese

1 egg, beaten

¾ cup (180 mL) milk

2 Tbsp (30 mL) melted butter

Far left: Goat, Sage and Apple Ragout with Apple-Sage Compote.

Left: Apple-Sage Compote and Cornmeal, Cheddar and Sage Muffins.

Wild Mushrooms

M any edible mushroom species grow in the Yukon; I can only identify two of them with confidence, morels and shaggy manes. The famous maxim about mushroom picking always applies: there are old mushroom pickers and there are bold mushroom pickers, but there are no old, bold mushroom pickers. Even with those species you know and have eaten before, it's wise to tread carefully, especially when serving them to guests. Some people are sensitive to wild edible mushrooms, and may have an allergic reaction or gastro-intestinal upset; anecdotal evidence suggests that the reaction may be exacerbated when alcohol is consumed at the same time. This has never been my experience. However, when planning the menu, make sure your guests have tasted wild mushrooms before, or are game to try. Then wow them.

The Famous Morel

From the ashes of the Yukon's most severe forest fires in 2004 emerged the bumper crop of 2005: pounds and pounds of prized morel mushrooms. The professional pickers came out in force, their camps bristling with buyers— in a good year, a pound of morels sells for $100 US. All over Whitehorse, in backyards and on front porches, the amateurs dried morels on homemade screens and socked them away for the winter. As the 2006 season drew near serious pickers mulled over maps and marked last year's burn sites, getting ready for the next great foray into the soot, searching for the bonanza.

The morel is mysterious—though the connection between fires and morel growth is well known, not every burn site produces morels, and not in the same density. The first year after a burn is best, that's generally accepted. So is morels' preference for disturbed ground such as burn sites, clear-cuts and roadside gravel beds. The morel is not strictly a northern treat; it is as eagerly sought in southern Canada and in Kentucky, Michigan and Illinois as it is in the Yukon. The morel's unique nutty flavour inspires arcane and goofy websites like *The Great Morel* or *1 Morel Mushroom Lane*; numerous festivals are devoted solely to celebrating the emergence of its wrinkly head from the ground.

Dried morels have a long shelf life. I missed the 2005 bonanza, but recently found a cache of dried morels in the

There are two morel look-alikes that grow in the Pacific Northwest, both considered poisonous. According to "A Morsel After the Fire" published in the University of Alaska Fairbanks journal *Agroborealis*, a good rule of thumb for identifying the true morel is that the cap is fused to the stalk so that they are one unit, both cap and stalk are hollow, and the cap has a deeply pitted, sponge-like appearance. Should you want more information on identifying and harvesting morels, the article is available online; see Sources at the end of the book.

Dried shaggy mane and morel mushrooms; add them to your boreal pantry!

back of a cupboard, picked a few summers ago, and so had my own mini-festival with this sauce. The Calvados picks up on the mushrooms' earthy flavour, and the cream is divine. Try it on linguini—go easy on the Parmesan—or on rare sirloin moose steak.

MOREL, CALVADOS AND CREAM SAUCE

For pasta sauce, use the larger amount of cream; for sauce to be used over grilled or roasted meat, use the lesser amount.

Pour boiling water over the morels and soak until re-hydrated, about half an hour. Gently squeeze out the excess liquid. (Freeze the liquid for later use in soups or stews.) Slice the morels lengthwise, then crosswise in small pieces.

Melt the butter in a sauté pan over medium-low heat; add the garlic, but don't let it brown. Add morels soon after and sauté for about 10 minutes.

Turn up the heat to medium, add the Calvados, stir, and when the bubbling subsides, add the cream. Be careful not to let it boil over. Cook until the cream thickens, about 10 minutes.

Makes about 1½ cups (375 mL) sauce

8 small to medium dried morels

1½ cups (350 mL) boiling water

2 cloves garlic, chopped

2 Tbsp (30 mL) butter

¼ cup (60 mL) Calvados

1 Tbsp (15 mL) soya sauce

1–1½ cups (250–375 mL) 35 percent cream

Shaggy Manes

The typical enterprising Yukon old-timer, when he's out driving the highway, keeps a sharp eye on the ditches for possible windfall—a work glove, a roof strap, a wrench or a tire iron that has fallen off the back of someone's truck. The old-timer I live with is no exception. He says he equipped his first tool shed through these roadside gleanings, back in the day. Old habits die hard. A common occurrence on any given road trip is a sudden screeching of the brakes and a quick reverse to examine a promising shape on the shoulder. In the fall of 2009 when were cruising along the Skagway Road on the way home from berry picking the promising shape in the gravel was not industrial detritus but something that looked like—shaggy mane mushrooms! Now this was something I could get excited about.

We jumped out of the truck to have a closer look: they were pale, umbrella-shaped, had soft scales on the sides, and the gills on the older, taller ones were turning pink and even black from the base of the cap upwards. Excellent. Identification confirmed. We picked a whack of them, too eager to be discriminating, and brought them home for an instant feast. The thing about shaggy manes is they start to turn black and disintegrate (the term is "deliquesce") within hours of pushing up through the ground, and must be eaten or preserved right away. We realized that many of the mushrooms we'd picked were already too far gone, so sad, so we threw the pink or brown-gilled mushrooms into the compost and selected the smallest ones, whose gills were still white, sautéed them there and then in butter and garlic, added some white wine, swirled it around and served the shaggy manes as an accompaniment to pesto pasta and a green salad. Yum.

I dried the remainder of the good ones. I hadn't seen this advised for shaggy manes anywhere, but it worked. I tore them into strips and put them in the oven overnight at 170F (80C) (the lowest my digitally-controlled oven will go.) In the morning the house smelled beautifully of mushrooms and the shaggy mane pieces were dry and papery without being crisp or easily breakable. I peeled them off the parchment paper and stored them in a glass jar. Over the next few weeks I performed a number of experiments and I couldn't be more pleased with the results. Dried shaggy

Shaggy manes, whose flavour is the very essence of mushroom.

manes are easier to work with than fresh ones, which give off lots of liquid as they're cooking and tend to become flat and slimy, though the flavour is lovely. Never fear; flavour is not sacrificed in drying. My friend Priscilla, who sampled the following quiche, says the shaggy manes tasted like "the very essence of mushroom." I think she's right; I have come to prefer them to morels. You don't need very many to deepen the earthy, mysterious, mushroomy quality of a pasta sauce, a risotto (**Shaggy Mane and Wild Blueberry Risotto**, page 235) or this excellent quiche.

To Dry Shaggy Manes

Air-drying would not work for shaggy manes; they would disintegrate long before they dried. Steel yourself to use power. Clean mushrooms with an old toothbrush or your fingers, brushing off as much dirt as you can; avoid using water. Have ready a number of baking sheets lined with parchment paper. Tear the caps lengthwise in pieces about an inch wide, tear the bigger stems lengthwise in half, and leave the smaller stems whole. Preheat the oven to 170F (80C), lay the shaggy mane pieces on the baking sheets, and dry them eight hours or overnight. Store in glass jars in a dark place.

Keep an eye out for shaggy manes along the highway in the fall.

SHAGGY MANE AND LEEK QUICHE

Margo McKimm was a school friend of my mother's at the Gloucester Street Convent School in Ottawa in the 1930s and '40s. She wrote a wonderful cookbook for her friends and family, called *The Everyday Gourmet*, from which this pastry recipe is borrowed. Margo says, "There is much discussion in cookbooks about the merits of basic pastry (lard or shortening) and tart pastry (butter only) in the making of tarts in a pan with a removable bottom. Although tart pastry supposedly stands up better when baked, it is not as flaky as basic pastry. My solution has been to combine the two, by using half butter and half shortening or lard, and this seems to work perfectly for both tarts and pies."

It's very hard to bungle this recipe; it results in a light and flaky pastry for sweet or savoury fillings and produces enough dough for one shallow 9-inch (23-cm) pie and a few small tarts, or one deep 9-inch pie. Use a deep 9-inch pie plate here so you have room for enough egg-cream mix, essential to a thick, firm, creamy quiche.

Margo McKimm's Basic Pastry Recipe

1½ cups (350 mL) all-purpose flour

¼ tsp (1 mL) salt

¼ cup (60 mL) cold shortening or lard

¼ cup (60 mL) cold butter

3–4 Tbsp (45–60 mL) cold water

egg white, beaten

Blend the flour and salt and cut in the fat with a pastry blender or your fingertips until it resembles coarse crumbs. If you're using a food processor, pulse for a few seconds at a time, checking often to make sure you're not over-mixing. Sprinkle the water over the flour mixture a tablespoon at time, mixing or pulsing a few seconds, and stop adding water when the dough holds together.

Dump onto a piece of waxed paper, gather together into a disk, knead a couple of times, place another piece of waxed paper over top and roll out to a diameter of 11 to 12 inches (28 to 30 cm), for a deep 9-inch (23-cm) pie plate. Lay the dough out over top of the pie plate and press gently into bottom and sides. Trim off excess pastry, crimp the edges and chill in the refrigerator for 30 minutes. (Note: for quiche, don't prick the bottom with a fork as you normally would.)

Blind bake the shell, lined with weighted tinfoil, at 350F (175C) for 15 minutes, remove foil and bake for another 5 minutes. Cool. Before adding quiche filling, brush the base and sides with beaten egg white; this will help keep the crust from getting soggy.

Quiche Filling

2 cups (475 mL) fresh shaggy manes, torn lengthwise into strips *or* ½ oz (14 gr) dried shaggy manes

1 Tbsp (15 mL) each butter and olive oil

1 cup (250 mL) sliced leeks (white and pale green parts only)

2 cloves garlic

1 cup (250 mL) freshly grated gruyère cheese

A pinch each of ground nutmeg and cayenne

3 eggs, well beaten

1 cup (250 mL) each 35 percent cream and 10 percent cream

If using dried mushrooms, pour a cup of boiling water over the dried shaggy manes and let sit for 30 minutes. Drain, reserving the liquid for soup, and pat the mushrooms dry. If you're using fresh mushrooms, sauté them in a barely-oiled frying pan until the liquid has evaporated and the mushrooms just begin to stick to the pan, then remove them from the pan and set aside.

Melt the butter and oil over medium heat, add the leeks and garlic and sauté until the leeks are translucent, about 10 minutes. Add reserved shaggy manes and sauté another 3 or 4 minutes. Remove from heat and let cool slightly.

Spread the grated cheese over the pie crust, then the mushroom and leek mixture. Mix the nutmeg, salt, and cayenne into the beaten eggs. Add the cream. Slowly pour the custard mixture over the filling.

Bake the quiche in a preheated 350F (175C) oven for about 35 minutes or until the custard is set and the top is brown.

Makes six servings

Rosehips

The common refrain amongst Yukon berry pickers in the fall when rosehips are ripening is, "I *would* pick rosehips but I don't know what to do with them." Rosehips are familiar in jelly, syrup and tea, but those excellent items don't provide enough scope for the abundance of fruit on every hillside, trail, alley way and vacant lot in the Yukon. They are so common that we perhaps devalue them, even though we know rosehips are packed with vitamin C. According to Nancy J. Turner and Adam F. Szczawinski in their *Edible Wild Fruits and Nuts of Canada,* three rosehips from an Alberta patch were found to have as much vitamin C as an orange. During the Second World War, when German blockades cut off the supply of citrus fruits, rosehips became an important source of nutrients in England and Northern Europe—they're also packed with vitamin A, calcium, phosphorous and iron. (Turner and Szczawinski's book is an excellent source of information and recipes. See Sources.)

Rosehip soup is a common item in Denmark, Sweden, Germany and England, eaten sometimes as breakfast, sometimes as a sweet, and sometimes as a savoury beginning to a meal. Rosehips have the ability to move easily from sweet to savoury—when they are raw their taste is reminiscent of crabapples and when cooked they retain that flavour but also gain a tomatoey quality. The seeds are covered with tiny hairs that irritate the digestive tract and must be strained out. Some enthusiasts remove the seeds from the hips before processing them; I don't. Life is too short. Rosehips freeze well, with or without seeds. You can pick them in winter, too, when they're frozen on the bush, but avoid those with black marks, a sign of spoiling.

BASIC ROSEHIP PURÉE

Rosehip purée is a handy pantry item—it can be used as a thickener in savoury sauces, substituted for tomato paste in caribou or moose meatloaf or shepherd's pie, puréed with beets, or turned into jam or soup.

2 parts rosehips, fresh or frozen

1 part water

Bring rosehips and water to a boil, reduce to a simmer and cook until rosehips are soft, about 30 minutes. Cool the mixture and press through a strainer. Use right away or freeze in small batches.

Rosehips are packed with vitamin C.

SIMPLE ROSEHIP JAM

Bring rosehips and water to a boil, reduce to a simmer and cook until rosehips are soft, about 30 minutes. Press through a fine strainer into a pot, scraping off the outer sides of the strainer to get all the pulp. Measure the pulp and add sugar to taste—I use 2½ cups (600 mL) sugar to 5 cups (1.2 L) pulp. Cook the jam over medium heat until it thickens, about 30 to 40 minutes. Pour into sterilized jars, seal with two-piece metal lids and immerse in a boiling water bath for 5 minutes.

For a quick canapé, spread crackers with rosehip jam and put a slice of Manchego sheep's milk cheese, parmesan or Stilton on top. If you're feeling ambitious, make **Baked Polenta** (page 224) and when it has set, cut into diamond shapes, grill on a hot, well-oiled grill and use as a base instead of crackers.

Makes about five 1-cup (250-mL) jars

8 cups (2 L) rosehips, fresh or frozen

2 cups (475 mL) water, or enough to cover

2–4 cups (500 mL–1 L) sugar

SPICED ROSEHIP AND CRABAPPLE JAM

4 cups (1 L) each rosehips and crabapples (substitute Granny Smith or cooking apples, chopped, seeds and all, for the crabapples.)

Water to cover

2 inches (5 cm) lime peel

1 cinnamon stick

10 juniper berries

1 tsp (5 mL) mace

2 cups (475 mL) sugar (more or less according to taste)

Combine water, rosehips, apples, lime peel, cinnamon, juniper berries and mace, bring to the boil and simmer until the fruit is soft, about 30 minutes. Press through a strainer and return to the pot. Add sugar to taste and cook jam* for 30 minutes, pour into sterilized jars, seal with two-piece metal lids, and boil in a hot water bath for 5 minutes. Let cool to room temperature. Store in a cool, dark place.

Makes about six 1-cup (250-mL) jars

*After 20 minutes, you can divert 2 cups (475 mL) of this mixture to another pot and make the following ketchup recipe.

ROSEHIP AND CRABAPPLE KETCHUP

This ketchup is especially good with scrambled eggs or homemade French fries.

2 cups (475 mL) **Spiced Rosehip and Crabapple Jam** (previous recipe)

1 tsp (5 mL) sambal oelek or other chili sauce

1 tsp (5 mL) soya sauce

Pinch of salt

1 tsp (5 mL) raspberry or cider vinegar

Simmer until flavours are blended, 10 to 15 minutes, then bottle and seal as above.

Makes about 1½ cups (350 mL) ketchup

Yukon-picked crabapples.

ROSEHIP SOUP

This is adapted from a recipe that suggested adding Madeira; I tried this and found the Madeira added a bitter quality. Sherry might be more successful—experiment! Serve the soup with sour cream, yogurt or crème fraîche on the side, but taste it first on its own. It's really lovely, with echoes of tomato soup, and a texture like lobster bisque. Many recipes suggest adding grated almond as a garnish—I substituted chopped roasted almonds, but found they distracted from the essential flavour of the soup.

Bring the rosehips, water and shallot to the boil and simmer for 30 minutes or until the fruit is soft, strain and return the mixture to the pot. Add the lemon juice, syrup or honey, soya sauce and vinegar, and simmer until the flavours blend, about 15 to 20 minutes.

Makes six servings

4 cups (1 L) fresh or frozen rosehips, or ½ lb (225 gr) dried

4 cups (1 L) water

1 shallot, chopped

1 tsp (5 mL) lemon juice

3 Tbsp (45 mL) birch syrup or fireweed honey

1 Tbsp (15 mL) soya sauce

1 Tbsp (15 mL) balsamic vinegar

Salt and pepper to taste

BAKEWELL TART REINTERPRETED WITH ROSEHIP CRABAPPLE JAM

This English classic was invented in the town of Bakewell in Derbyshire in 1820 when, the story goes, the landlady at the White Horse Inn asked the new girl in the kitchen to make a strawberry jam tart. The new girl (she was probably nervous) got the recipe all wrong—instead of putting the almonds, eggs and sugar into the pastry she spread them on top of the jam and voila, a new dessert was born. Controversy reigns in the town of Bakewell; two bakeries claim to make the original recipe, and to confuse the issue, the dessert seems to be called either Bakewell Pudding or Bakewell Tart. (Though some feel very strongly that they are two different beasts.) In any case, the combination of almonds, rosehips and crabapples is divine, and this tart is even better the next day.

1 **Short-crust Tart Shell** (page 20)

½ cup (125 mL) **Spiced Rosehip and Crabapple Jam** (page 76)

1 cup (250 mL) ground raw, unpeeled almonds

½ cup (125 mL) butter, softened

½ cup (125 mL) sugar

3 eggs

Follow the directions to make a Short-crust Tart Shell, but omit the last 10 minutes of baking so pastry is cooked but not browned. Cool to room temperature, then spread the jam over the bottom in an even layer.

While the shell is cooling, make the filling: grind the almonds until they start to clump together in the bowl. Cream the butter and sugar together, add eggs one a time, beating after each addition, and then beat in the ground almonds. Pour the almond mixture over the jam, and bake at 350F (175C) until the top is a deep golden brown, about 40 minutes.

Serve with **Crème Fraîche** (page 150). Unbeatable!

Makes a 9-inch (23-cm) tart

Bakewell Tart Reinterpreted with Rosehip Crabapple Jam.

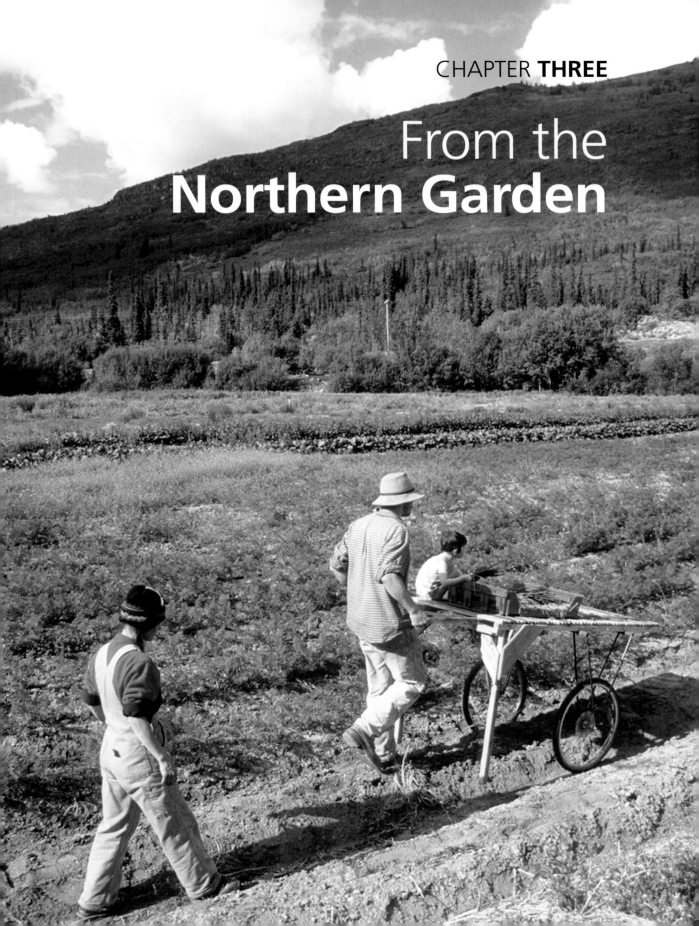

CHAPTER THREE

From the
Northern Garden

Yukon farmers hard at work, aided by World Wide Opportunities on Organic Farms volunteers, commonly known as WWOOFers.

In backyards, greenhouses, community gardens and on a growing number of farms throughout the Yukon the population does its best to coax produce from the soil for a brief liberation from that which comes up the highway in trucks: apples that started their life in New Zealand, broccoli from Southern California, oranges that come all the way from China, pears from Chile; all necessary to the continued survival of 34,000 people in a cold northern climate, but not local, not fresh, not satisfying in the way hauling something out of the dirt and preparing it for friends and family is satisfying.

Gardening is both a delicate and a fierce activity in the Yukon. The growing season is short and the yield comes quickly and with abundance. Then it's over. For a brief but exquisite moment in late August and early September the Fireweed Market in Shipyards Park in Whitehorse bristles with gorgeous bundles of kale, collections of pale and fragrant turnips, deep red beets, tiny carrots, potatoes, onions, bean and herbs. Earlier, in July, arugula and lettuce reign. In Dawson, where the sun shines longer each day, gardeners and farmers produce giant vegetables and flowers that belong in tall tales; Whitehorse envies Dawson its growing season, and Dawson revels in it.

The "eat local" movement is strong in the Yukon; especially since a few years ago when the number of producing farms, gardens and nurseries achieved if not a critical mass, then at least enough avoirdupois to provide a viable alternative to imported produce in summer for those who live close to market gardens, outlets and farmer's markets. Sometimes Yukon produce is even available in two of the big box grocery stores in Whitehorse. There are something like 55 producing farms, gardens and nurseries in the Yukon, two coffee roasters and numerous retail outlets for syrups, jams and jellies; there is a local Slow Food chapter, and since the 1970s, a cadre of growers with local expertise and home-grown plants who share seeds and contribute to the propagation of Yukon-hardy varietals. The Fireweed Community Market Society has published a cookbook with excellent seasonal recipes by its members, see References and Recommended Reading (page 249).

I have not yet grown a vegetable in the Yukon—I can't be held responsible for the tenacious rhubarb plant in the backyard that clings to life despite gross neglect bordering on the criminal. But I have enjoyed the bounty of other growers, at the market, at the community kitchen in Shipyards Park, at the grocery store, and in my friends' kitchens.

Organic root vegetables from a Yukon farm.

GREEN BEAN, NEW POTATO AND PANCETTA SALAD

This salad tastes best at room temperature.

6 medium new potatoes

1 lb (454 gr) green beans

4 oz (112 gr) double-smoked, thick-sliced bacon or pancetta, cut into 1-inch (2.5-cm) pieces and sautéed over medium heat until brown but still juicy, about 10 minutes

½ medium Bermuda onion, thinly sliced

Fresh Thyme Vinaigrette (below)

Salt and pepper to taste

Boil potatoes in water to cover until they're fork tender, drain, cool and cut into eighths or sixteenths. Cook bacon or pancetta and drain on paper towels. Steam the green beans or bring to the boil then simmer for 5 minutes, or until they are cooked but still crisp. Drain and plunge the beans into cold water to stop cooking. Combine all ingredients, toss gently, add enough dressing so that the vegetables are thoroughly covered but not oily and toss again. Before serving, taste for salt and pepper, and if necessary, add more dressing—the potatoes tend to absorb quite a bit.

Makes four servings

FRESH THYME VINAIGRETTE

1 tsp (5 mL) Dijon mustard

⅓ cup (80 mL) red wine or balsamic vinegar

⅔ cup (160 mL) olive oil

1 clove garlic, crushed

1 Tbsp (15 mL) fresh thyme leaves, or 1 tsp (5 mL) dried

Salt and pepper to taste

Whisk mustard and vinegar together, whisk in olive oil gradually, add garlic, thyme, salt and pepper, whisk again.

Makes 1 cup (250 mL) dressing

Tip: Let vinaigrettes sit at room temperature for a couple of hours before serving, to allow the flavours to blend.

FRESH TURNIP, RED PEPPER AND RASPBERRY SALAD

When I bought turnips in late August, the woman at the booth in Fireweed Market said, "They're so sweet, all you need is a bit of salt." She was right, but they were also delicious in this end-of-summer salad.

Toss all ingredients and serve immediately. This salad is a good accompaniment to **Chum Salmon, Chèvre and Lamb's Quarters wrapped in Phyllo Pastry** (page 96).

Makes four servings

1½ cups (350 mL) fresh turnip, peeled, halved and thinly sliced

½ large red pepper, cut lengthwise, then crosswise and thinly sliced

1 generous handful raspberries

a few fresh mint leaves, chopped

2 or 3 large fresh basil leaves, chopped

Dash of raspberry vinegar, sprinkled over top

Dash of basil olive oil, sprinkled over top

Salt and pepper to taste

Five Recipes Using Chard or Kale

Northern gardeners seem to have a super-abundance of kale and chard at the end of the summer. Happily it freezes well—in the case of kale, I've put a bunch right in the freezer without blanching, with good results. The freezing reduces the bitterness and tenderizes the stems so that they're useable in winter soups and stews. Most of these recipes work best with the super-fresh stuff though; the exception is the white bean, garlic and kale soup.

Swiss chard, stalwart of the northern garden.

STEAMED CHARD WITH MISO GINGER DRESSING

Place chopped stems in a steamer basket over boiling water, steam for 4 to 5 minutes, then add remaining chard and steam until tender but not wilted, about 5 minutes. Toss with miso ginger dressing and serve warm.

1 lb (454 gr) Swiss chard, washed and roughly chopped (keep stems separate and chop in 1-inch/2.5-cm pieces)

Makes two servings

MISO GINGER DRESSING

My friend and trusty sous-chef Priscilla Clarkin gave me this recipe; it is one of her staples. She doesn't remember where the dressing came from, but the original used 1 cup oil and ½ cup water. Priscilla reverses those proportions for a lighter version.

Mix miso and ginger, whisk in vinegar until smooth, whisk in oils and then add water, whisking constantly.

Makes about 2 cups (500 mL) dressing

3–4 Tbsp (45–60 mL) light miso

2 Tbsp (30 mL) fresh ginger, chopped

¼ cup (60 mL) cider vinegar or ⅓ cup (80 mL) fresh lemon juice

2 Tbsp (30 mL) dark sesame oil

½ cup (125 mL) canola or peanut oil

1 cup (250 mL) water

PASTA WITH KALE, FIGS, PINE NUTS AND TOASTED BUTTERED CRUMBS

The sweet-sharp-nutty combination of figs, vinegar and pine nuts works well with the pungent, almost bitter kale, and the Parmesan and crumbs get into all the nooks and crannies of both kale and pasta. Substitute Swiss chard for the kale, but if the plants are mature and the stems big, reserve the stems for another dish.

2 Tbsp (30 mL) olive oil

2 cloves garlic, chopped

3 Tbsp (45 mL) pine nuts

2 cups (475 mL) kale, removed from stems and torn into smallish pieces

3 dried black mission figs, chopped

Grated zest of one lemon

1 Tbsp (15 mL) fig balsamic vinegar

½ cup (125 mL) freshly grated Parmesan

2 Tbsp (30 mL) fresh bread crumbs, toasted then mixed with 1 Tbsp (15 mL) melted butter (melt the butter separately and mix in a bowl off the heat)

⅓ lb (150 gr) bow tie or penne pasta

Put the water on to boil for the pasta.

Heat the oil on medium-low in a heavy frying pan, add the pine nuts and sauté until they're lightly browned, add the garlic and sauté another few minutes, then add kale. Cook until the kale is just wilted, add the chopped figs and the lemon zest, toss, then add vinegar, cook another minute, remove from heat and cover to keep warm.

Cook the pasta for 8 to 10 minutes, drain and toss with the kale-fig mixture, Parmesan and bread crumbs. Serve at once.

Makes two servings

PESTO, SWISS CHARD, ROASTED GARLIC AND GORGONZOLA PIZZA

When Priscilla successfully grew chard in a pot on her balcony in downtown Whitehorse one summer we celebrated her green thumb with this pizza.

Sauté the onion and peppers over medium heat in 1 tablespoon (15 mL) oil until soft and slightly caramelized, about 10 minutes. Add a pinch of garlic, mix, sauté 2 more minutes, remove and reserve. Add 1 tablespoon (15 mL) oil to the same frying pan, add the chard and sauté until it's barely wilted, add the rest of the chopped garlic, a dash of wine and a pinch of salt, swirl around, cook another minute, remove the chard and reserve.

Drizzle the uncooked pizza crust with 1 to 2 tablespoons (15 to 30 mL) olive oil, then spread with pesto. Arrange pepper and onion mix evenly over top, then add chard. Squeeze garlic cloves from their papery husks directly on to the pizza, distributing evenly, then sprinkle with gorgonzola. Cook in a preheated 400F (205C) oven for 20 minutes and serve.

Makes three to four servings

Pizza Crust (page 186) or **Homemade Phyllo Pastry** (page 90)

Cilantro, Parsley or Basil Pesto (recipe follows)

½ each red and yellow pepper, sliced into strips

½ medium onion, sliced into strips

4-5 Tbsp (60–75 mL) olive oil

1 large clove of garlic, chopped

1 head of roasted garlic, broken apart

Six medium-sized leaves of fresh Swiss chard

Dash of red or white wine

Salt

6 oz (170 gr) gorgonzola cheese, crumbled

About ¼ cup (60 mL) pesto

Roasted Garlic Production

Roast several bulbs of garlic at once while you're baking something else in the oven. Cut off the top end of each bulb, drizzle liberally with olive oil, sprinkle with crushed thyme, and bake for 45 minutes to an hour in a 350F (175C) oven—the cloves should be soft as soft butter. Peel the cloves, place in a clean jar and cover with olive oil. Use in dips, spreads, soups, sauces, mashed potatoes and salad dressings.

CILANTRO, PARSLEY OR BASIL PESTO

2 cups (475 mL) fresh cilantro, parsley or basil, washed, dried and stems removed

2 cloves garlic, peeled

¼ cup (60 mL) almonds, walnuts or pine nuts

⅓ cup (80 mL) extra-virgin olive oil

½ cup (125 mL) freshly grated Parmesan

Salt and freshly ground pepper to taste

Put garlic and nuts in food processor, process until the nuts are still a bit chunky, add whatever herb you're using and process until it reaches the consistency you like. Add oil in a thin stream while machine is running, add Parmesan and pulse until everything is combined, add pepper, pulse, taste for saltiness, then add salt to your taste.

Makes about ½ cup (125 mL) pesto

The summer I first arrived on the Greek island of Alonissos, where I ended up living for three years, there were signs at every taverna along the waterfront advertising "Traditional Alonissos Cheese Pies!" But the signs appeared and disappeared according to some mysterious rhythm——eventually I learned that the physical labour required to make the pies in quantity was intense, and some days the local women in the restaurant kitchens flatly refused to do it. I never managed to eat a traditional Alonissos cheese pie that summer.

But that fall I learned how to make those traditional pies myself, taught by my boyfriend and his older sister Evanthea, who also taught me how to recognize and pick the wild greens considered appropriate for the local version of spanakopita, called "hortopita," a name derived from *horta*, the generic name for wild greens, and *pita*, or pie. There were many rules governing greens and how to serve them; the bitter ones took oil and vinegar, and never went into pies, the sweet ones required lemon and oil, and some of them were okay for pies, and the addition of dill (*maratho*) or fennel (*anitho*), both of which grew wild, was absolutely essential to the successful *hortopita*. A cheese pie was *tiropita*, and when you combined cheese and greens, it became a *hortotiropita*. Ditto spinach and cheese pie: *spanakotiropita*.

Greek women have a special, round wooden board about a metre in diameter for making these pies; in Alonissos they keep it hanging on the kitchen wall or tucked behind a piece of furniture until it's needed. They also have a special rolling pin— basically a dowel about one metre long and two centimetres in diameter, which allows them to roll out a tiny piece of dough into a circle that reaches practically to the edges of the board. The last time I was in Athens I was sorely tempted to buy a cheese pie board and bring it back with me but the challenge of getting it through all those airports was too daunting. I do have the rolling pin though, made from a length of $5/8$-inch dowelling bought at Home Hardware. But I can't, nor will I ever be able to, roll out homemade phyllo pasty to the diameter and thinness Evanthea can. For that I think you have to be born in Greece.

TRADITIONAL ALONISSOS CHEESE PIES WITH SWISS CHARD OR KALE

This recipe is really fun when you have a bunch of friends hanging around your kitchen and drinking wine (retsina!) while you cook. Each pie takes about 15 minutes to prepare, and another 10 to 15 minutes to cook in hot oil on the stove, so you serve them up as they're ready, like pancakes. Also like pancakes, the first pie is never the best pie, so persevere. By the fourth one you'll be a pro. It is easy to make these with a standard rolling pin, but if you're having fun and you really want to get into traditional Alonissos pie-making, invest the 98 cents in a piece of dowelling.

A word on shallow-frying: it's the only way. The whole point of these pies is the thin and crispy crust and the scant cooking time so the greens are just cooked and the cheese is just melted. I experimented with oven-baking to cut down on calories but it really didn't work: the pastry never crisped and the greens wilted and turned sour.

2 cups (475 mL) all purpose flour

1 tsp (5 mL) salt

1 Tbsp (15 mL) olive oil

½–¾ cup (125–180 mL) water

Top: Let homemade phyllo dough rest for 30 minutes before rolling out.

Bottom: Spread the greens with a restrained hand: liberal, but not excessive.

Olive oil for shallow-frying

Homemade Phyllo Pastry

Make the pastry first, and make the filling while the pastry is resting. The resting period is really important; without it, the dough is too springy and rolling out to the necessary thinness is both time-consuming and hard work.

Mix flour and salt together with a fork, make a well in the middle of the flour, add oil and half the water. Mix in a circular motion with a fork, adding water bit by bit until the dough begins to cohere. When you can form the dough into a rough ball, turn out onto a floured surface and knead until it's fairly smooth. Let rest for half an hour.

Cut the dough into quarters. Take the first quarter, knead it briefly on a floured surface and press it out with your fingers to form a flat patty 4 to 6 inches (10 to 15 cm) in diameter. Then roll out evenly from the centre to the edge, north, south, east and west and repeat over and over again, turning the dough occasionally, until the dough is about 16 to 18 inches (40 to 45 cm) in diameter and has become transparent enough that you can see the counter through it. Sprinkle with olive oil and then proceed to the filling and frying.

Preheat the Oil

Pour olive oil into a cast iron frying pan until it reaches a ¼ to ½ inch (0.6 to 1.25 cm) depth, and start heating slowly over medium heat. Have one of your friends keep an eye on it while you assemble the spanakopita.

Fold each long side twice towards the middle, with a light touch.

Curve the ends of the pie toward each other, almost like a croissant.

Slip the pie into the pan and shallow-fry; it's the only way to go.

Filling

Mix all ingredients together except the feta. Sprinkle the greens mixture over the rolled-out phyllo, sparsely covering the whole area to within an inch (2.5 cm) of the edges. Sprinkle a quarter of the feta evenly overtop. Starting from the right side, fold the dough over the filling, then fold it over again to the centre. Do the same from the left side, so that the two folds meet each other in the centre, see diagram. Pinch the ends closed, then bring the ends together in a loose coil, see diagram. Slide onto a lightly floured plate, then slide gently into the hot oil in the frying pan.

Cook for 5 to 7 minutes each side, until the pie is nicely browned. Repeat with the remaining three pieces of dough and the filling.

You may have to add olive oil to the frying pan from time to time; if so, give it a couple of minutes to heat up again before you slide in the next pie. As with pancakes, the later pies will cook more quickly than the first, so keep an eye on them. Encourage your pals to break the pies apart with their hands and gobble them down with retsina, and follow with your best tzatziki, a Greek salad and some grilled meat doused in oregano and lemon juice.

Makes 4 pies of about 9 inches (23 cm) in diameter

4 cups (1 L) of finely chopped, fresh Swiss chard or Russian kale

3 spring onions, greens and white, finely chopped

generous bunch of fresh dill, finely chopped

2 Tbsp (30 mL) olive oil

Salt and pepper to taste

1 cup (250 mL) feta cheese, crumbled

Pass the tzatziki and dig in.

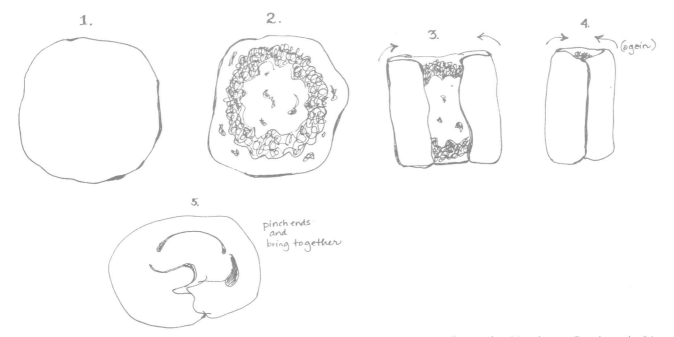

1.

2.

3.

4. (again)

5.

pinch ends and bring together

WHITE BEAN, ROSEMARY AND KALE SOUP

This is a mild, fragrant soup that highlights the taste of the beans, kale and fresh herbs. Use giant lima beans, ordinary lima beans or small white kidney, Great Northern or white navy beans. Soaking time will vary according to the type of bean, from 4 hours for lima beans to overnight for the small white varieties.

1 lb (454 gr) white beans, soaked for 4–8 hours

Water or stock

1 whole head of garlic, separated into cloves, each clove peeled and sliced lengthwise

1 large onion, chopped

4 Tbsp (60 mL) olive oil

6 cups (1.4 L) chopped fresh or frozen kale, tough ribs removed

1 Tbsp (15 mL) chopped fresh rosemary or 1 tsp (5 mL) dried

1 Tbsp (15 mL) fresh thyme leaves or 1 tsp (5 mL) dried

Pinch of nutmeg

2 Tbsp (30 mL) soya sauce

Salt and pepper to taste

Drain and rinse soaked beans, add cold water or stock to cover by 1 inch (2.5 cm) and heat to the boiling point. Turn down the heat to medium low, skim, and let simmer for 2 hours or until beans are soft. Remove from heat and let cool slightly, then purée. Lima beans tend to shed their skins, so it's best to purée the whole lot; other beans remain whole, in which case reserve two cups, purée the rest and then add the whole beans back into the mix. Return the beans to the burner turned to medium-low.

While the beans are heating up again, sauté onions and garlic in 1 tablespoon (15 mL) olive oil over medium heat in a cast iron frying pan, just until they begin to brown, about 10 minutes.

Add kale and increase temperature a couple of notches. Cook until the kale begins to wilt and brown slightly, about 5 minutes, then add rosemary and thyme, and cook 2 more minutes. Add the contents of the frying pan to the beans and bring to a slow boil.

Turn the heat down so the soup is just simmering and stir in 3 tablespoons (45 mL) olive oil, beating somewhat vigorously so oil and liquid emulsify. Add the nutmeg and soya sauce, stir, taste and add salt and pepper as needed.

Let simmer for 10 minutes or so, remove from heat, cool and refrigerate or serve right away with some croutons and a bit of grated old cheddar cheese, or a splash of hot sauce.

Makes about twelve 1-cup (250-mL) servings

GREEK POTATOES IN THE OVEN

In this dish, the potatoes half bake, half braise, so they're both crispy and soft. The lemon and oregano let you know you're in Greece. The secret to success is to pour the water in from the side of the pan, not over top.

Cut the potatoes in half lengthwise, then cut the halves lengthwise into thirds or quarters, depending upon the size, so that pieces are uniform. Place the potatoes in a 9-by-13-inch (23-by-33-cm) roasting pan, coat them with oil and lemon juice and sprinkle them with oregano, salt and pepper. Add garlic slices and toss together again.

The next part is key: pour the water in slowly at one side of the pan, not over top the potatoes, so that the water level slowly creeps up the potatoes from underneath. This ensures that the oil covers the exposed upper parts of the potato, helping it to stay moist as it roasts, and allows the lower part of the potato to braise. Tuck the bay leaf in amongst the potatoes, making sure it's covered with water.

Bake at 350F (175C) for about 40 minutes. If the water evaporates and the potatoes are still quite hard, add a bit more, as before, from the side of the pan. Don't stir until near the end of the cooking period. By the end there should be very little liquid and the potatoes should have a thin crust and a soft, moist interior.

Makes three to four servings, as accompaniment to grilled meat and salad

1 lb (454 gr) Yukon Gold potatoes, peeled

3 Tbsp (45 mL) olive oil

Juice of ½ lemon, about 2 Tbsp (30 mL)

3 cloves garlic, cut in half lengthwise and sliced

1 Tbsp (15 mL) oregano

Salt and pepper to taste

1 bay leaf

½ cup (125 mL) water

Yukon gold potatoes, harvest-time treasure.

POTATOES EN BRIOCHE, WITH YUKON GOLD POTATOES

This recipe comes from my friend Monika Broeckx, who got it from her first mother-in-law, Madeleine Vaillot of Autun, France. Monika is German, her husband is Flemish, they speak three languages each, though not all the same languages, and they are typical Yukoners, having moved here from far away, built their own house, become Canadian citizens and embraced northern life wholeheartedly.

2 cups (475 mL) all purpose flour

½ cup (125 mL) cold butter, diced

1 Tbsp (15 mL) olive oil

Pinch of salt

½ cup (125 mL) water

2.2 lb (1 kg) Yukon Gold potatoes, peeled, washed and cut into thin slices

1 bunch of parsley, washed, stems removed and chopped

1 small onion, chopped fine

1 clove garlic, minced

1 egg, beaten

Salt and pepper to taste

2 Tbsp (30 mL) butter

1 cup (250 mL) grated gruyère

1 Tbsp (15 mL) milk

¾ cup (180 mL) 35 percent cream

Pâte Brisée

Combine flour and salt, cut butter into flour by hand or in food processor, add olive oil, add water a bit at a time until the dough holds together, knead for 1 minute until the dough is firm and smooth, then let rest for 1 hour.

While the dough rests, make the filling:

Filling

Mix potatoes with the chopped onion, garlic and parsley, add the beaten egg and salt and pepper to taste.

Preheat oven to 350F (175C). Grease a 10-inch (23-cm) springform pan. Take two-thirds of the dough and roll it out to about 13 inches (33 cm) in diameter and ¼ inch (0.5 cm) thick. Lay it over the pan and gently press into the bottom and sides, allowing any excess to hang over the side. Fill with the potato mixture in layers, sprinkling cheese and small pieces of butter over each layer before adding the next. Now roll out the remaining third of dough and place it on top as a lid. Fold the excess dough from the bottom layer over the top and seal by pinching lightly with the fingertips. Brush the lid with milk, then cut one large vent in the middle of the lid and other smaller vents here and there. Bake for about an hour. Just after taking from the oven, pour the cream in the centre vent, let sit for 10 minutes, cut into slices and serve.

Makes 10 moderate or 8 healthy servings

Lamb's Quarters

Lamb's quarters are an invasive species in the Yukon, but apparently here to stay, and in the untrimmed yards and back alleys of Whitehorse they proliferate. One of my favourite cooks of all time, Lyn Fabio, picks bundles and bundles of lamb's quarters in July and early August, parboils them for 30 seconds and freezes them for use as the staple winter green in her household. She likes to cook them at high heat until they're browned and almost sticking to the pan. They have an excellent, pungent flavour when fresh and the tender leaves are great in salad or quickly steamed. Porsild and Cody, who wrote the botanist's bible, *Vascular Plants of Continental Northwest Territories, Canada*, say cooked young plants are "an acceptable substitute for garden spinach." That is truly a case of damning with faint praise—lamb's quarters have a flavour of their own that deserves to be explored and celebrated.

One afternoon in late August of 2009 photographer Cathie Archbould and I were in the kitchen fussing with plates for a photo shoot when my husband called us down to the basement. There, through the basement window, we had a wide-screen view of a tiny mouse straddling two lamb's quarter plants and chomping with ferocious concentration on a seed head. When he finished the seed head of one plant, he scrambled onto the other, and as he progressed up the stem toward the head the plant bent slowly down to the ground. As he ate, the weight of the seed head lessened and the plant swung slowly upwards again, taking him with it, still chomping away, until the plant was nearly upright and the seed head was eaten up. The mouse ran to the bottom of the plant and stopped there for a minute before scampering away.

Lamb's quarters, great in summer salads.
Or, blanch, freeze and eat all winter.

CHUM SALMON, CHÈVRE AND LAMB'S QUARTERS WRAPPED IN PHYLLO PASTRY

The key to this dish is its mildness: there's no added dill or other herb, just a hint of nutmeg, so you can really taste the delicate flavour of the fish, the cheese and the lamb's quarters. For a more robust flavour, substitute sockeye salmon and add some chopped fresh basil and dill. Defrost the phyllo sheets in the fridge for about 6 hours before you're ready to assemble the packages.

1 shallot, chopped

3 green onions, chopped

½ lb (225 gr), about 3 cups (700 mL) blanched lamb's quarters, either fresh or frozen

2 Tbsp (30 mL) olive oil

Pinch of nutmeg

1 egg, beaten

Salt and pepper to taste

2.5 oz (70 gr) chèvre

About ½ cup (125 mL) butter, melted

4 pieces (3 oz/85 gr) skinned chum or other salmon fillet, rinsed and patted dry

8 sheets of commercial phyllo pastry

Sauté the shallot and green onion in the oil until they're soft, about 5 to 7 minutes, add lamb's quarters, separating the leaves with two forks as they're sautéing to make sure the heat penetrates evenly, and cook for another 5 minutes or so. Add a pinch of nutmeg, preferably freshly grated, straight into the pan, and salt and pepper to taste. Remove from heat, let cool, and then mix with the egg.

Have the melted butter ready. Prepare the phyllo: open the package and lay the phyllo sheets on a clean towel. Cover with another clean tea towel, and replace the tea towel each time you remove a piece of phyllo from the pile. This will keep the sheets from drying out as you work.

Lay one sheet in front of you on the counter horizontally. Brush with butter. Lay a second sheet on top, brush with butter and repeat until you have four sheets. Cut them in half vertically.

Working with one half at a time, place a generous spoonful of lamb's quarter mixture about 2 inches (4 cm) in from the bottom edge of the pastry and spread it out slightly. Place a salmon fillet on top, crumble one quarter of the chèvre over the fillet, and then add another spoonful of lamb's quarter mixture on top of that. Fold the bottom edge of the pastry over top, fold again, then fold each vertical side of the pastry in (see diagram), brush with butter, and roll the package up away from you. Seal the seam by brushing with butter, brush the rest of the surface with butter, and place the package on a baking sheet lined with parchment paper while you finish the rest.

Repeat with the remaining buttered phyllo, and then repeat the whole process for the next two fillets. Refrigerate the phyllo packages for 15 minutes. Put the remaining phyllo back in its wrapping, seal tightly and freeze for another time.

Preheat the oven to 425F (220C). Remove packages from the fridge, and slice a small vent with a sharp knife in the top of each one. Bake for 14 to 16 minutes, until golden brown and slightly puffy. Serve hot or at room temperature.

Makes four servings

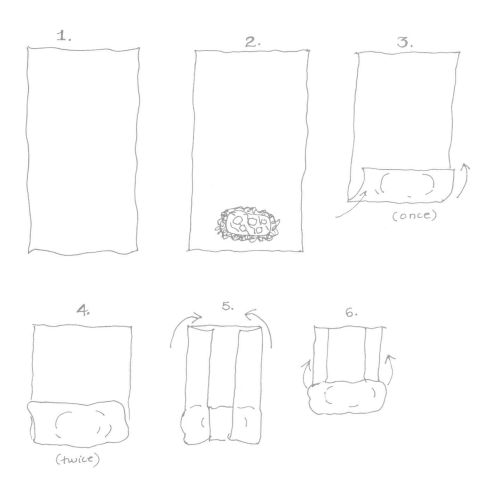

Rhubarb

Jack and the giant rhubarb.

When actors on stage need to fill in the muted rumble of a crowd, without distracting from the main action with recognizable words, they repeat "Rhubarb rhubarb rhubarb," in tones high and low, with shifting emphases, and that does the trick. Not only is rhubarb a highly useful nonsense word, it is automatically humorous—one summer on the Annie Lake Golf Course south of Whitehorse, a golf ball sailed into the bush after a stunning left hook, and the unlucky golfer said, "Ohhh, it's landed in the rhubarb." The plant, too, is intrinsically comic—those massive, outspreading leaves, those ungainly stalks.

Rhubarb is often relegated to the un-showy parts of the garden; it doesn't require any ingenuity on our part to grow, so we can't take credit for it, and it's huge, so it ends up in a kind of rhubarb ghetto behind the shed or at the side of the house, where members of the family are periodically sent by the cook to harvest the stalks with kitchen knives. Rhubarb is a great contributor to the northern table, in summer pies and jams, and then in winter, the season of potlucks, when we crave the new and the untried—it freezes well and goes with everything, transforming easily into relish, salsa, marinade, sauce, dessert filling, syrup, and, as we shall discover, highbrow cocktails.

Rhubarb, belonging to the genus *Rheum*, is a transplant to the North, not indigenous. Though we do have an indigenous plant, *Polygonum alaskanum*, whose common name is also rhubarb, and which grows in the Old Crow Flats and other Yukon locales (and for which there are recipes out there, for you who are curious—including a traditional Gwich'in recipe for pudding that uses whitefish eggs and stomach), it is not the rhubarb we are discussing here. The rhubarb in question came to the Yukon with the newcomers, and before that, to North America via a gardener in Maine sometime between 1790 and 1800. It moved from its native China, where its first recorded use (in 2900 BC, according to one website) was medicinal (it's a purgative), to Tibet, into Siberia and Mongolia, and from there to medieval Europe, developing new species all the while. There are currently some 28 edible varieties available, with enchanting names such as Egyptian Queen and Glaskin's Perpetual.

In the Yukon, various strains of *Rheum* thrive, growing sometimes four feet tall, with leaves two feet in diameter, and stalks as thick as a man's wrist. Wildlife biologist Bruce Bennett takes note of rhubarb in his wilderness explorations as a marker of former dwelling places, when little other evidence of human habitation remains. Bruce Bennett is a rhubarb enthusiast—he has a very large plant in his yard, and sent a photo of his three year old son carrying a stalk of rhubarb nearly twice his size. (Men in general tend to be pro-rhubarb. I came across my brother-in-law one summer afternoon chopping rhubarb stalks, a scale at his left elbow, freezer bags at his right. "Seventeen pounds!" he cried, "A banner year!")

Two recipes follow, one for a deluxe rhubarb crisp borrowed from the recipe box of Whitehorse resident Laurel Parry, and the other for a peculiarly northern cocktail, which uses ice wine, gin, rhubarb juice and crushed sage. Its name is Winter Summer Solstice, and it was invented by a chef at Splendido Restaurant in Toronto especially for the Niagara vineyard Henry Pelham Estate Winery, whose proprietors were being interviewed by food writer Margaret Webb for her book on sustainable farming, *From Apples to Oysters*, published by Penguin Canada in the spring of 2008. When Marg was in town in the summer of 2007 getting to know the folks in her Yukon chapter we recreated the classy cocktail from memory.

An etymological note: the word rhubarb derives from the medieval Latin *reubarbarum*, a variation of *rha barbarum*, which literally means barbarian rhubarb. The word barbarian derives from the ancient Greek *barbaros*, meaning foreigner, in turn derived from the Sanskrit *barbar*, meaning to stammer, or to make unintelligible sounds (the sounds that foreigners make). All this to say, be careful: the Winter Summer Solstice cocktail sneaks up on you. *Barbar* awaits the unwary.

Rhubarb is versatile, full of flavour and thrives despite neglect.

RUBY'S RHUBARB CRISP

Laurel Parry tells us, "My Scottish grandmother, Robina "Ruby" Ogilvy, used to make a wonderful rhubarb jam that was flavoured with ginger. The combination was divine, and warming on a cold day. She also used to make a simple brown sugar fudge for us when she came to visit. My neighbours grew the most marvelous rhubarb this summer, ruby red, rich and tender. Harvesting this rhubarb inspired me to remember my grandma and create this dessert. I couldn't resist adding a sauce as a nod to her delicious fudge."

Grease a 9-by-13-inch (23-by-33-cm) pan with butter. Preheat oven to 350F (175C).

In a large bowl, mix together:

> 1 cup (250 mL) white sugar
>
> ¼ cup (60 mL) flour
>
> 2 Tbsp (30 mL) finely grated fresh ginger
>
> 1 cup (250 mL) light cream
>
> Juice of one lemon
>
> Grated rind of one half lemon

Toss in:

> 8 cups (2 L) chopped rhubarb

In another bowl, mix together:

> ½ cup (125 mL) flour
>
> 1 cup (250 mL) quick cooking oatmeal
>
> 2 Tbsp (30 mL) finely grated fresh ginger
>
> Grated rind of one half of lemon

Rub in:

> ¾ cup (180 mL) cold butter until mixture is crumbly

Place rhubarb mixture in pan. Sprinkle crumbled mixture on top. Bake at 350F (175C) for 1 hour. Serve warm (not hot) with toffee sauce, next page.

Toffee Sauce

In a small sauce pan, mix together:

>   1 cup (250 mL) brown sugar
>
>   ½ cup (125 mL) butter
>
>   ½ cup (125 mL) light cream

Place on medium heat and bring to the boil, stirring frequently until somewhat thickened.

Makes eight servings

Ruby's Rhubarb Crisp with Toffee Sauce.

WINTER SUMMER SOLSTICE COCKTAIL

A caveat: Marg Webb and I concocted this cocktail from memory when she was far from home, visiting me in the Yukon, so it is not the same version you'll find in her book, *From Apples to Oysters*. I've left it as is, because it's a really good variation on the excellent original.

2 oz (30 mL) gin

2 oz (30 mL) ice wine or late harvest Chilean Sauvignon Blanc (the cheaper option)

2 oz (30 mL) rhubarb juice

2 crushed fresh sage leaves (indigenous Yukon sage leaves would probably not work in this case—too dry and crumbly)

Measure chilled ingredients into a martini shaker loaded with ice, shake and pour into short cocktail glasses with the crushed sage at the bottom.

Makes two cocktails

Rhubarb Juice

Thaw frozen rhubarb and juice it in a juicer—frozen actually works best—expect to get $^2/_3$ cup (160 mL) of juice from 2 cups (500 mL) of chopped rhubarb. If using a blender instead of a juicer, be sure to strain the pulp from the juice. Alternatively, place the thawed rhubarb in clean cheesecloth, gather up the edges, twist and squeeze hard to extract the juice.

RHUBARB AND SPRUCE TIP SALSA

In this northern version of the sunny southern classic, sour, juicy rhubarb stands in for cilantro, and the spruce tips add a citrus note, amplified by lemon juice. Use very young, thin stalks of rhubarb, no more than ¼ inch (.5 cm) in diameter.

Combine all ingredients except the avocado in a bowl, stir with a fork until blended, add the avocado, stir and serve immediately with your favourite tortilla chips.

Makes about 2½ cups (600 mL)

2 Tbsp (30 mL) spruce tips, chopped

1 tsp (5 mL) salt

Juice of ½ lemon

½ cup (125 mL) diced rhubarb

1 cup (250 mL) diced tomato

½ cup (125 mL) diced onion

1 ripe avocado, diced

RHUBARB AND LEMON MARMALADE

This marmalade, when it's done, won't look like Robertson's Silver Shred, all pale and elegant, but instead is kind of mushy and opaque. The elegance is all in the flavour.

2 lemons

2.2 lbs (1 kg) rhubarb

2 cups (475 mL) sugar

Quarter lemons, discard the seeds and slice each quarter thinly. Mix lemons, rhubarb and sugar together in a stainless steel or enamel saucepan and let sit for half an hour. Cook over medium-high heat for about 20 minutes, or until the mixture is thick and golden, and a cooled drop in a saucer doesn't run.

Bottle in hot, sterilized jars and process 5 minutes in a boiling water bath. Let cool to room temperature and store in a cool, dark place.

Makes about five 1-cup (250-mL) jars

CHAPTER FOUR

Home from **the Hunt**

Northern-Southern Fusion

In the North our cuisine comes from so many places, from countries and crossroads and kitchens unimagined until we start to explore. One of the places my cuisine comes from is my best-friend's mom's kitchen on Helendale Avenue in North Toronto, a kitchen with a crucifix over the door, a vegetable garden out back and the alien smell of garlic and oil spicing the air with difference, the difference between my friend and me.

Fil was an Italian whose parents moved to Toronto from a village in Italy, I was a mixture of French, Irish and Scottish. whose parents had moved to Toronto from Ottawa. We met in first grade and for the next 18 years, through the battles and truces of two girls growing up together, Fil's mom's kitchen was a place of refuge, friendly territory where her mom fed us the kind of food that would later become famous in noisy trattorias across North America and celebrated in cookbooks like Viana La Place's *Unplugged Kitchen*: simple ingredients prepared by hand, careful cooking, and not much herb or spice except parsley, garlic, oil and salt.

We ate platefuls of boiled bitter greens, served with olive

Keno Hill, Yukon Territory, a long way from everywhere.

oil and lemon; we ate pasta and stewed lamb and tomato sauce. In grade thirteen we'd come in ravenous from bars and tuck into fava beans and artichokes or anchovy and onion pie. We moved into apartments and cooked for each other: *spaghetti puttanasca, rapini* with currants and pine nuts, *tiramisu.*

Years passed, we went to university and college, patched together goofy careers, married and had kids (Fil) and moved to the Yukon (me). In the Yukon, I encountered a totally different kind of cuisine: moose stew, caribou sausage, elk heart, baked whole salmon, bannock. And berries: cranberries, blueberries, raspberries, cloudberries, saskatoon berries, soapberries, moss berries—everybody picked berries, everybody canned, everybody hunted. At potluck suppers, even the vegetarians scarfed down the caribou stew and gobbled up the salmon. I raved to Fil about this new cuisine: it was indigenous, it was delicious, it was exciting.

In November 2004, 40 years after we first met, Fil came to Whitehorse. She loved it here; she loved the sparkly snow, the cottagey houses, the clay cliffs and Gray Mountain and the Yukon River, she loved her first meal of Taku River salmon and little potatoes from the farm at Crag Lake. When she was all softened up and relaxed, I broke the news: I had to write a cooking story. The deadline was next week. Fil put down her fork. She rolled her eyes. (Fil used to live with a writer.) "No, it'll be fun," I said, "Really, you'll see. We're going to take a southern recipe and make it northern!"

"*Why*?" she asked, stuffed to the gills on northern salmon and potatoes. "Why would you *bother*?" Well, because you cannot live on grilled salmon and moose stew alone. First of all, it's not that easy to get, and when you do get it, you tend to get a lot (a whole moose, many pounds of salmon, a front quarter of caribou), so you must find different cooking methods, shake it up, cut loose, or you'll come to dread the sight of a salmon fillet. And, though you love the food of your adopted land and its people, sometimes you miss the food you grew up with. And so you must find ways to put the two together.

I told Fil about moose cooked with spinach, dried fruit, coriander and cinnamon. I described roasted spruce grouse with a sour cream and Madeira sauce (deglaze the roasting pan with Madeira, whisk in the sour cream), or caribou, ginger, Portobello mushrooms and red pepper sautéed in butter and finished with red wine, or salmon steaks marinated in soya sauce, maple syrup, garlic and sesame oil. She began to get the idea. So I hauled out a couple of frozen caribou sausages from the freezer and slapped them on the counter. "There's our challenge. We have to make that caribou taste like it came from Italy. And we have to do it with ingredients readily available in Whitehorse and Old Crow."

Next morning I went to my day job and Fil brooded. She read Viana La Place's *Verdura*, to get into the mood. She rummaged through the kitchen cupboards. She fretted. She stewed. She went to the supermarket, perused the shelves and tried to visualize Old Crow. When I got home from work, there was a pile of ingredients on the kitchen counter: canned plum tomatoes, fresh plum tomatoes, garlic, dried hot peppers, dried penne. And a couple of bunches of fresh cilantro. I raised an eyebrow. "Fresh cilantro? Do you know how much that will cost in Old Crow?" "It's an option!" she said. "We're doing penne arrabiata with caribou sausage with the option of cilantro pesto, as a garnish." Okay! We put on our aprons, rolled up our sleeves and went to work.

Here is the result: Penne arrabiata con salcicia caribou Filomena Di Ceglie, with optional pesto cilantro.

Tomatoes in Winter

For those who can't find decent fresh tomatoes in the dead of winter, or even canned plum tomatoes, Fil has a caveat: you can substitute other canned tomatoes but they must be whole. This comes from her brother, who since her mom's death, has taken over as the family's kitchen maestro. "Dominic says he would never use chopped tomatoes because they've lost all their flavour." We used canned plum tomatoes one night and chopped fresh plum tomatoes the next; there was no noticeable difference in the end result. And the addition of the caribou? "It's amazing," said Fil. "The gaminess of the meat is perfect, with the tomato and the garlic and the heat." She went home with a package of caribou smokies from the Yukon Deli; not quite home-cured but pretty darn close.

PENNE ARRABIATA CON SALCICIA CARIBOU FILOMENA DI CEGLIE

On the Friday after our experiments, Fil and I drove to Haines, Alaska, for the Bald Eagle Festival. When we came home on Sunday night and opened the front door, the kitchen smelled just like Fil's mom's, spiced with something northern.

Bake the caribou sausage in a 350F (175C) oven for 30 minutes, cool, reserving fat, and cut into medallions.

In the meantime, make the sauce: sauté the garlic in the oil over slow heat, being careful not to let it brown. Add the red pepper flakes. Stir in the tomatoes; if you're using canned, break them up with a fork in the frying pan. Turn the heat up to medium; let the sauce bubble and get thick. Start the pasta water boiling. Add the caribou medallions and the reserved fat to the sauce.

Cook the pasta until it's al dente. Drain, toss with oil, and transfer to a platter or a bowl.

Here, you have a choice: to mix the arrabiata sauce in, or to spoon it over the top of the pasta. We tried it both ways; Fil thought it was best mixed in. "The flavours blend that way." Also, the penne absorbs some of the heat from the chili flakes, and that's good because this sauce is hot. Fil said the sauce lives up to its name: *arrabiata* means angry. If you're going for the cilantro pesto option, use it sparingly—just a dollop on each serving of penne. (Have the leftover cilantro pesto on its own the next night, thinned out with a bit of pasta cooking water. Toss it with bow tie pasta, pitted black olives, chopped anchovies and grated Parmesan.)

Makes four servings

2–3 homemade **Coriander, Lemon and Rosemary Sausages** (page 112)

5–7 cloves of garlic, chopped

2 Tbsp (30 mL) olive oil

1 tsp (5 mL) red pepper flakes (or chili paste, or Tabasco, or ½ tsp (2.5 mL) cayenne pepper)

25 oz (750 mL) can plum tomatoes, or 8 medium fresh plum tomatoes, chopped

1 lb (454 gr) penne

Optional:

Cilantro Pesto (page 88)

Homemade Caribou Sausage

Making sausages at home, before I actually did it, seemed a daunting and even formidable task—the hog gut, the special machinery, tying off the links, pricking the air bubbles—there were so many places to go wrong. I had heard numerous tales of frustration and failure from other cooks. But when I finally took the plunge, with the help of a trusty sous-chef, sausage making turned out to be really easy, though time consuming.

For the experimental cook the best investment is a good teaching cookbook—I found a real friend in Bruce Aidells's *Complete Sausage Book,* written with Denis Kelly. His sausage-making instructions are clear and easy to follow, his recipes for sausages are excellent, and much of the book is devoted to creating dishes with the sausages you've made or the ones you've purchased. If you're going to invest in the sausage-making equipment to add on to your stand mixer and really get into sausage making on a regular basis, I recommend acquiring this book. I don't think you'll be sorry.

I'm ashamed to say my fear of sausage making was so great that I let some pork fatback go bad in the fridge while I procrastinated, and made fennel and orange meatloaf with the ground caribou that was supposed to be turned into sausage. But there was a silver lining—I learned you have to be careful with the amount of grated orange peel you use, it so easily dominates all the other flavours.

These recipes were made with lean ground caribou that did contain some pork fat already, I didn't know how much. With that unknown fat starting point, I still followed Bruce Aidells's suggestion to keep the added fat to 15 to 25 percent of total volume. The result was great—not fatty at all. Though I didn't grind my own caribou meat, if you do, you'll have more control over the proportion of fat to meat. My hunter friends say it's best to cut and grind the meat when it's still partially frozen. They also say, make small batches at a time; that way if you make a mistake you don't have to live with 20 pounds of it. I say, err on the side of too little seasoning and add more after the taste test.

Special Ingredients

Hog casings come packed in salt or liquid; ours were packed in salt and came from the Yukon Deli in Whitehorse; try a specialty butcher shop in your area for both hog casings and pork fatback. Our fatback came from a pig raised about 15 km south of Whitehorse, a "farm gate" purchase.

ORANGE AND FENNEL SAUSAGE

This method uses a KitchenAid stand mixer with food grinder and sausage stuffer attachments (horn) but it can be easily adapted to a hand-operated grinder and stuffer. Or if you're not yet ready to commit to the entire sausage-making enterprise, simple sausage patties are as delicious as sausage in casings.

Wash the hog casing in a bowl of warm water. Flush out the interior by attaching one end to the faucet and running water gently through—the casing will puff up like a skinny balloon. Change the water, and keep the casings soaking until you're ready to use them.

Grind the fatback using the meat grinding attachment on a stand mixer with a bowl containing the ground meat underneath. Unplug the mixer, remove the blade, clear the remaining fat from behind the blade and drop it into the bowl. Wash the equipment in warm water, and set aside for the stuffing phase.

Add all remaining ingredients to the meat except the wine and mix together with your hands. Add the wine at the end and knead briefly with your hands once more. Make a small tester patty and cook it in a dry frying pan over medium heat. Taste for seasoning and adjust.

Attach the sausage-making horn to the mixer. Bring the bowl of water and hog casing over to the mixer, and feed the whole length of casing carefully onto the horn, leaving about five inches dangling off the end. You'll be tempted to tie a knot in the bottom now, but don't; if you do the casing will fill up with air before the sausage meat starts coming out of the horn.

When the first bit of meat emerges from the horn, wait until it reaches a length of three inches, turn off the machine and tie off the bottom of the casing. Turn the machine back on and fill the entire casing; you can help by gently stroking the meat downwards in the casing as it fills. Your trusty sous-chef's extra pair of hands is a great addition to the project. Prick any air bubbles with a skewer or a toothpick.

1 lb (454 gr) ground caribou

4 oz (115 gr) fatback, skin removed, chopped into pieces small enough to grind

1 tsp (5 mL) grated orange peel

1 tsp (5 mL) anise seed

1 Tbsp (15 mL) fennel seed

3 cloves garlic, minced

½ tsp (2.5 mL) ground chili

½ tsp (2.5 mL) each salt and pepper

1 Tbsp (15 mL) red wine

About 2½ feet (75 cm) hog casing; Bruce Aidells suggests 2 feet per pound of meat (60 cm per 454 gr)

Why Not Cassoulet?

When I was finally ready to embark on the sausage-making adventure, I searched through the freezer for ground caribou and came across all kinds of treasures, including a whole goose. So I decided to tackle cassoulet, that slow-cooked, three-day French classic, for Christmas dinner, with goose confit and homemade sausage. Why not? For the cassoulet recipe, see page 238 in the feasts chapter. You'll need a pound of Orange and Fennel Sausage.

Two Further Variations

Follow the mixing and stuffing instructions for Orange and Fennel Sausage.

Sun-dried Tomato, Chili and Cumin Sausage

1 lb (454 gr) ground caribou

4 oz (115 gr) pork fatback, skin removed

¼ cup (60 mL) sun-dried tomatoes, soaked and chopped

3 cloves garlic, minced

1 Tbsp (15 mL) roasted cumin seeds, coarsely ground

½ tsp (5 mL) ground chilies

1 tsp (5 mL) smoked paprika

½ tsp (5 mL) each salt and pepper

1 Tbsp (15 mL) red wine

Coriander, Lemon and Rosemary Sausage

1 lb (454 gr) ground caribou

4 oz (115 gr) pork fatback, skin removed

3 cloves garlic, minced

1 Tbsp (15 mL) coriander seeds, crushed slightly in a mortar and pestle

1½ tsp (7.5 mL) rosemary

1 Tbsp (15 mL) grated lemon rind

½ tsp (5 mL) each salt and pepper

1 Tbsp (15 mL) white wine

1 Tbsp (15 mL) lemon juice

Near the end the sausage meat will emerge more and more slowly and then stop all together, but there will still be quite a bit of meat that hasn't come through. Unplug the mixer, detach the horn from the mixer while keeping the hog casing still attached to the horn's end, and have your sous-chef press the remaining meat through the horn with the end of a wooden spoon while you hold the horn. Be gentle with the wooden spoon: we managed to rip the casing at this stage. This was no big deal, we just pushed out the sausage meat until we had enough casing to tie a knot at the top end, and ate the extra sausage meat for dinner.

Pinch the casing between your fingers at sausage-length intervals—usually five to eight inches (13 to 20 cm). The pressure will push meat away from either side of your fingers. With your hand on either side of the pinch, twist the sausage in opposite directions, gently. Repeat down the whole length of the sausage. Cut each link in the middle of the twisted bit of casing; the cut seals the casing closed.

Dry the sausages on a rack overnight in the refrigerator; the skin will become tight and somewhat shiny. Pack in butcher's paper or waxed paper and plastic. The sausages will keep for three days in the fridge or two months in the freezer.

Makes about five 6-inch (15-cm) sausages

SPETZOFAI, OR HOMEMADE SAUSAGE WITH MIXED PEPPERS

This recipe starting showing up on restaurant menus in Alonissos the second summer I was there; it is a specialty from the Mount Pilion region outside of Volos on the mainland, where one of the taverna owners lived in the winter. Greeks would use *loukanika*, which aren't that different from the fennel and orange sausages on the previous page. *Spetzofai* is a homey dish, quick and easy to make, and it really highlights the flavour of the sausage. It's important to use a mix of red, green and yellow peppers; the first time I made this I used red peppers exclusively, and the tasters were so unimpressed they thought this recipe shouldn't be included in this book. So I went back to the drawing board. The additions of anise seed, vinegar and wine may make this dish less authentic, but they add needed flavour when you don't have access to the super-fresh peppers, onions and tomatoes of sunny Greek (or southern Canadian!) summers.

Sauté the onion in the oil over medium low heat until translucent, add the garlic and the peppers and cook until the peppers have softened and lost their raw smell, about 15 minutes. Stir in the vinegar and red wine and cook until the liquid is syrupy. Add the sausage and cook for 3 to 4 minutes, until the sausage pieces have shrunk a bit, then add the tomatoes. Turn the heat to medium and cook until the peppers have softened entirely and the liquid is no more than a coating—think of ratatouille—about 30 minutes. Serve with mashed potatoes on the side for a delicious mid-winter family meal.

Makes four servings

1 medium onion, chopped

2 Tbsp (30 mL) olive oil

3 cloves garlic, minced

1 red, 1 green and 1 yellow pepper, cleaned and roughly chopped into 1-inch (2.5-cm) pieces

½ tsp (2.5 mL) anise seed

1 tsp (5 mL) dried tarragon

1 tsp (5 mL) balsamic vinegar

2 Tbsp (30 mL) red wine

1½ cups (350 mL) chopped fresh tomatoes or canned plum tomatoes, without the juice

1 lb (454 gr) homemade fennel and orange sausages sliced into ½-inch (1.25-cm) pieces

Wrapped Caribou Roast with Rowan Jelly

I love the different ways wild meat comes into the Yukon household—it can be a gift, a barter, a favour returned…. One winter a friend appeared at our house with a front quarter of caribou that he'd brought with him on the flight from Old Crow, packed into a knapsack: an unexpected exchange for some wild sockeye we'd passed on to him in the fall. A hunter had given our pal the caribou in return for looking after the hunter's dogs while he was away.

I love the way recipes come into the house too, and how they evolve from the original. I owe this dish to Ann MacKenzie, a long-time Yukoner who was born and raised in Scotland. She helped us eat the first roast from the Old Crow caribou. I had braised the meat slowly in a tomato and red wine sauce but was disappointed with the result—beautifully flavoured meat but a texture that was dry, dry, dry. Ann told me in Scotland they sometimes seal a venison roast in a flour and water crust before cooking it, to lock the juices in the meat.

The next day she turned up with the Scottish Women's Rural Institute cookbook, one of those old-fashioned treasures that is as much social history as cookbook. The authors advised to "make a paste of flour and water and seal the roast within." I inferred that "paste" meant "dough," and adapted the Greek recipe for homemade phyllo pastry, which I knew from experience would be pliable and up to the task.

Ann also introduced me to rowan or mountain ash berry jelly—another Scottish classic often served with venison. In Scotland rowan trees, or *Sorbus aucuparia*, are planted in churchyards to ward off the evil eye—a Scot who gave me a ride many years ago from Ballachulish to a hiker's inn in Glencoe told me so. When I asked him if he believed the old stories, he said, "I may not believe, but I pay attention."

In the Yukon, the distribution of the mountain ash is mostly in the southern regions, and is more often than not the *Sorbus scopulina*, or western mountain ash, though *S. aucuparia* is sometimes brought in by nurseries for planting in domestic gardens. Those who wish to harvest the berries might have to race the bohemian waxwings; they are infamous mountain ash berry lovers. In Whitehorse we are visited every December by migrating flocks of

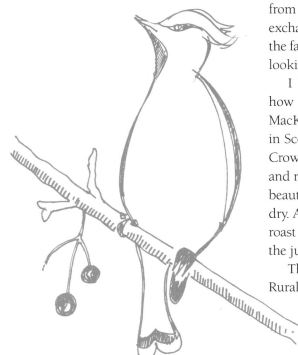

Bohemian waxwing on a mountain ash branch.

waxwings, which land like a fluttering gray cloud and strip a tree of berries in minutes—an awesome sight.

Be forewarned that mountain ash jelly is more bitter than the usual jellies that accompany meat—the effect on the palate is similar to the soapberry's: a sudden cessation of sweetness, followed by an astringent, almost grainy aftertaste, slightly reminiscent of whisky. Thinking to enhance this aftertaste I made a first version of the jelly with the addition of a half-cup of Laphroaig whisky, one of the more iodine-y whiskies from the Islay region, which seemed to exacerbate the bitterness without complementing the taste. A milder, less peaty whisky like Bowmore or Scapa or even a blend like Grant's or Johnny Walker is a better choice. I do advise adding a couple of apples, too. I found that the recipe below, made with milder whisky and three apples, resulted in a more flavourful jelly than my first effort. But Ann and the Scottish Women's Rural Institute stick to the basics: berries and sugar in equal parts—also worth a try.

Cooks, take note: this meal in its totality is a project that requires commitment, but will reward your dedication with a caribou roast that is tender and strongly flavoured, a sauce that illuminates the intense, gamy flavour of the meat, and a jelly whose combination of sweet beginning and bitter aftertaste turns out to be completely right for caribou.

WRAPPED, ROASTED CARIBOU WITH DEMI-GLACE

2 cups (475 mL) flour

½ to ¾ cup (125 to 180 mL) water

1 Tbsp (15 mL) olive oil

The roast

¼ lb (120 gr) double-smoked bacon, cut into 1 inch by ¼ inch (2.5 cm by .6 cm) strips and chilled (optional)

1 head **roasted garlic** (page 87)

2 Tbsp (30 mL) butter, room temperature

4 pound (1.6 kg) caribou shoulder roast, bone in

1 tsp (5 mL) each crushed thyme, rosemary and sage

½ tsp (2.5 mL) ground black pepper

The Crust

Make a well in the middle of the flour, add water and oil, and mix until the dough holds together in a ball, adding more water if necessary. Knead briefly until the dough is smooth, then let rest for half an hour. Roll out until the dough is an eighth of an inch (3 mm) thick and big enough to encase the roast in a package. (You may not need to use all the dough—refrigerate the rest and use for a thin pizza crust.)

If you wish, lard the roast with bacon by making slits with a sharp, thin-bladed knife at two-inch intervals and inserting a piece of chilled bacon into each slit. The chilling makes the bacon easier to handle.

Preheat oven to 425 F (220C). Slip the cloves of garlic out of their skins into a bowl and mash with a fork. Add the butter, herbs and pepper to make a paste, and cover the roast with the paste. Place the roast on the rolled-out pastry, wrap as you would a birthday present, and set in a roasting pan seam side down.

Place in the oven and cook for 20 minutes, then turn the heat down to 350F (175C) for another 40 minutes. (As a general rule, roast for 15 minutes per pound for medium rare, or until the internal temperature reads 145F (60C) on a meat thermometer.) Take the roast out of the oven and let it sit in its crust for 10 minutes while you finish the Caribou Demi-glace (recipe follows).

Break the crust and discard. Place the roast on a warmed serving platter, carve and serve on warmed plates with a pool of sauce poured onto the plate, and more sauce drizzled over top. Accompany with **Rowan Jelly** (page 118).

Makes six servings

The Demi-glace

Ahead of time, make a strong **caribou stock**:

Roast caribou bones in the oven at 400F (205C) until they're brown, from 30 to 45 minutes. In the meantime, heat the oil or butter in a stockpot or large saucepan over medium heat and brown the vegetables. Add the bones, the roasting juices deglazed with red wine, and enough water to come three-quarters of the way to the top of the ingredients. Bring to a slow simmer, without letting the sauce boil. For the first hour, be attentive and skim the top to remove scum every 10 minutes or so. Simmer for 3 to 4 hours altogether; strain, chill and skim off the fat, which should solidify in a layer on top.

On the day you prepare the roast, make the sauce:

Combine the reduced wine and stock and reduce them further to one cup of liquid. While the roast is sitting in its crust, take the sauce off the heat and beat in the butter, one tablespoon at a time. Important: the butter must be cold, or the emulsion won't work. The texture will be smooth and almost syrupy, but not thick like a roux-based gravy. Remember not to put the sauce back on the burner, or it will separate. Serve warm or at room temperature.

Makes 1 cup (250 mL) of sauce

2 lb (about 1 kg) caribou bones

2 Tbsp (30 mL) oil or butter

1 onion

1 celery stalk

½ carrot

1 fennel bulb, including stalks and fronds

½ cup (125 mL) red wine

Water

4 cups (1 L) stock reduced over high heat to 1 cup (250 mL)

2 cups (475 mL) red wine reduced to 1 cup (250 mL)

2 Tbsp (30 mL) cold butter

Rolling out the crust for Wrapped, Roasted Caribou.

The roast is wrapped and set in a roasting pan.

Wrapped, Roasted Caribou and Demi-glace.

ROWAN JELLY

Pick rowan berries (mountain ash berries) after a couple of frosts, or better still, store for a few weeks in the freezer. This helps to reduce the bitterness. For this recipe I used a candy thermometer to judge when the jelly was ready, which reduced the usual anxiety considerably, and resulted in the lovely slippery jelly that our mothers and grandmothers used to make.

8 cups (2 L) rowan berries

3 cups (700 mL) chopped apple, skin and seeds included (use crabapples if you can find them)

Water to cover

Sugar

½ cup (125 mL) Scapa or other mild whisky

Rowan Jelly with a touch of Laphroaig whisky—lovely with meat.

Bring the berries, apples and water to a boil, reduce, skim the top and simmer for about an hour.

Strain through a jelly bag suspended over a bowl. When the liquid has thoroughly drained (after 4 to 6 hours) measure juice into a pot. For each cup of juice add 1 cup of sugar. Boil over high heat, removing scum, until the juice reaches the jelly stage (220F / 104C), about an hour. Add the whisky about halfway through the process.

Pour into sterilized jars, seal and immerse in a boiling water bath for 5 minutes.

Makes about five 1-cup (250-mL) jars

MARINATED CARIBOU BLADE STEAK WITH BLUEBERRY REDUCTION

To be consumed with close friends or family—the blueberry reduction turns teeth a scary dark blue. Don't go out into the streets without brushing, lest you be mistaken for a zombie.

Whisk together the mustard, oil, wine and garlic. Place steaks in a flat dish and pour the marinade over them. Turn the steaks so both sides are coated. Marinate for 4 to 8 hours.

Make the blueberry reduction just before you're ready to grill the steak.

1 Tbsp (15 mL) Dijon mustard

3 Tbsp (45 mL) olive oil

3 Tbsp (45 mL) red wine

2 cloves garlic, chopped

2 caribou blade steaks, about 10 oz (280 gr) each

Blueberry Reduction

Cook the blueberries and chopped onion or shallots in a small saucepan for 5 minutes on medium heat. Add red wine, cook for 90 seconds, add cream and cook for 90 seconds more. Remove from heat and beat in the cold butter. Important: the butter must be cold or the emulsion won't work. Remember not to place the sauce back on the burner, or it will separate.

Remove the caribou steaks from the marinade and pat dry. Sprinkle with salt and pepper. Grill on a smoking hot grill for 3 minutes each side. Divide into four portions, drizzle a bit of reduction over top and serve the remainder on the side.

Makes four servings

¾ cup (180 mL) wild blueberries, fresh or frozen

2 Tbsp (30 mL) chopped shallot or onion

2 Tbsp (30 mL) red wine

2 Tbsp (30 mL) 35 percent cream

1 Tbsp (15 mL) cold butter

Moose

Several years ago, I went on my first and only moose hunt, with my boyfriend at the time, on a lake about an hour south of Teslin. In the summer of 2008, by a total fluke, I ended up on the shores of that same lake with my husband, who doesn't hunt—he says he can't take himself seriously, moose-calling in his Scottish accent—so I took him on a tour of all the landmarks of that distant and mind-altering experience. As I relived the hunt—the moose's slow collapse into the water after he was shot, the dragging of the moose by the antlers to a small island, the horrific six-hour grind of field dressing, with a grizzly staring from one shore and a black bear pacing on another—I remembered why I haven't hunted again. Semi-comatose with bear-induced terror and in shock from witnessing the death of a large animal, I was barely able to keep it together. Not a great asset on a hunt.

But in the year of abundance that followed, as we fed our friends and family from a freezerful of moose meat, I realized my contribution to a hunt is not the shooting or the field dressing, it's the cooking afterwards. I have a recipe book stuffed full of experiments from that year, and if I never find the nerve to hunt again, at least I can do my bit to banish insipid stews, leathery steaks and roasts that taste like sawdust. Now to hunters I say, Bring me moose meat! You will not be sorry.

Photographer Cathie Archbould is one such hunter. When she goes into the wilderness in the fall there's a good chance she'll emerge with a fine moose or caribou, which she shares with her friends and acquaintances (hunters are famously generous). This fall she appeared at my house with two packages of ribs and issued a challenge that was almost a plea: make these ribs succulent, flavourful and fall-off-the-bone tender. For as Cathie knows, as everyone who's ever tackled moose ribs knows, meat that is fall-off-the-bone tender and still retains its flavour is the hardest thing in the world to achieve.

Cathie sent me a recipe for beef short ribs that called for chipotle peppers and coffee, which she said resulted in moose ribs meat that were tasty but not f.o.t.b. tender, try as she might. This recipe was a good starting point for a virtual hunt on the Internet, where I tracked down recipes with similar ingredients, but most importantly, a promising methodology.

I found the right method in a recipe for braised beef short ribs from *Globe and Mail* food columnist Lucy Waverman:

Ingredients for Braised Moose Ribs with Espresso Stout and Chocolate.

start the oven high and turn it down just before the dish goes in, make sure the liquid almost covers the meat, and remove the meat from the pot while you finish the sauce. From the excellent Ms. Waverman I also pilfered the idea of serving the finished ribs with braised Swiss chard. I poached ingredients from two further recipes; taking tomatoes, chilies and unsweetened chocolate from one, and from the other, coffee porter.

I substituted Yukon Brewing Company's Midnight Sun Espresso Stout for the coffee porter, kept the chocolate, called in Yukon-made Uncle Berwyn's Birch Syrup for the sweetener and practiced with beef short ribs to get the recipe moose-ready. I cooked the ribs in two stages over two days— the overnight resting did wonders for flavour development— and I recruited the usual suspects for a taste testing. Success! The beef had kept its flavour, was fork-tender and slid off the bone. And the combination of espresso stout, tomatoes, chilies and chocolate had transformed the sauce into something rich, dark and mysterious, like a Mexican mole, but more complex. The tasters were ecstatic and so was I; together we demolished a kilo and a half of beef ribs.

Braised moose ribs on a bed of greens.

A week later I tackled the moose. The only thing I did differently was to add a bit of salt pork to the pot—beef short ribs are fatty enough on their own, but moose is lean and needs the extra help. Again, I cooked the ribs in two stages over two days. And then the fateful moment came: Cathie Archbould and her partner, at my dining room table, knife and fork raised expectantly. Cathie took a bite. She took another. "Oh my god. It's fantastic." Yes, but is it—? Another bite. "You've done it. This is truly fall-off-the-bone tender." Ahh, the cook's finest reward: words of praise from the hunter. I did an internal dance of triumph and we all set to in a frenzy of ooh-ahing, lip-smacking moose rib appreciation.

A final note—the chocolate, lime and cilantro are crucial to the success of the dish. The chocolate tones down the bite and provides a long, smooth finish. And, as one of the tasters said, the lime and cilantro "add a higher note, lifting the darkness of the sauce." Trust me, your hunter friends will not stint on the wild meat offerings after they've tasted this dish.

BRAISED MOOSE RIBS WITH ESPRESSO STOUT AND CHOCOLATE

2 ounces (60 gr) salt pork, blanched for 10 minutes in simmering water, cooled and diced

2 Tbsp (30 mL) olive oil

5 lbs (2.25 kg) moose ribs

1 large carrot, chopped

1 large onion, chopped

2 large stalks celery, chopped

4 cloves garlic, minced

2 dried ancho chilies, crushed

1 Tbsp (15 mL) smoked paprika (if not available substitute regular paprika)

1 Tbsp (15 mL) cumin seed, crushed and dry roasted in an iron frying pan until aromatic

1 Tbsp (15 mL) oregano

1 Tbsp (15 mL) tomato paste

25 fl oz (750 mL) can plum tomatoes, coarsely chopped

2 bottles (341 mL each) Yukon Brewing Company Midnight Sun Espresso Stout

2 Tbsp (30 mL) birch syrup

2 Tbsp (30 mL) soya sauce

1 tsp (5 mL) salt

3 bay leaves

3 squares (3 oz / 85 gr) unsweetened chocolate

Juice of 1 lime

½ bunch of cilantro

Brown salt pork in olive oil for 10 minutes in a heavy casserole or Dutch oven over medium heat. Remove salt pork and brown ribs in batches over medium-high heat, reserving ribs on a platter.

Turn heat to medium and sauté vegetables for about 5 minutes, or until they've softened. Preheat oven to 425F (220C). Add garlic and spices to vegetables and cook for a further 2 minutes. Add tomato paste, work in thoroughly, then add tomatoes, espresso stout, birch syrup and soya sauce, salt and bay leaves.

Stir, bring to simmer and add the moose ribs, making sure the liquid almost covers the ribs—use another ½ bottle of stout, if necessary.

Put the casserole into the oven and reduce heat to 320F (160C). Cook for 3 to 3½ hours. Remove from oven, cool, and store in fridge overnight.

The next day, take out the casserole about 4 hours before you're ready to serve. Two hours before, heat the mixture to a slow simmer in a 320F (160C) oven.

Finish the sauce on the stove top on low heat—first take out the ribs and reserve them on a platter, covered. Add the chocolate and stir until melted. Add the lime and cilantro, return the meat to the sauce briefly to warm up, and serve. Pour extra sauce into a gravy boat for the table. Rice, quinoa or polenta are all good accompaniments, and so is Swiss chard braised in a sauté pan with garlic and balsamic vinegar.

Makes six servings

Possibly the most useful equivalent you will ever learn

1 square of unsweetened chocolate = 1 oz = 28 grams = 3 Tbsp (45 mL) cocoa and 1 Tbsp (15 mL) butter

MIDDLE EASTERN MOOSE WITH SPINACH AND DRIED FRUIT

This recipe is adapted from *Joy of Cooking*'s simple "Casseroled Beef with Fruit." The adapted version, with beef, became a signature dish at the Chocolate Claim in the late '90s, when we expanded it to the power of ten and served it to visiting and local musicians at a Frostbite Music Festival banquet one cold February night. Those musical types gobbled it up. I like it even better with moose; the fruit and spices work in counterpoint with the mild gaminess of the meat, and the spinach adds a strong, earthy note. In the absence of moose, beef or bison are more than adequate, venison would be great and so would lamb or goat. This version is my adaptation, reduced to family size.

The Marinade

Combine spices and rub into the meat. Whisk wine and oil, add garlic and stir into meat, mixing well. Cover and marinate overnight in the fridge.

Next day, take the moose out an hour before you're ready to cook and let warm to room temperature. Just before adding meat to the casserole to brown, drain the meat, pat dry and discard the marinade.

While the moose is coming to room temperature, prepare the dried fruit:

1 tsp (5 mL) turmeric

1 tsp (5 mL) ground cumin

½ tsp (2.5 mL) cinnamon

1 tsp (5 mL) ground coriander

3 lbs (1.4 kg) moose stew meat, cut into bite-sized pieces

½ cup (125 mL) red wine

½ cup (125 mL) olive oil

1 clove garlic, chopped

The Dried Fruit

Chop the dried fruit into pieces the size of a nickel, then combine with the stock and lemon and soak until soft, about an hour.

3 cups (700 mL) dried fruit, a mix of prunes, apricots, and apples or pears

2 cups (475 mL) beef stock

Juice and zest of one lemon

2 Tbsp (30 mL) olive oil

2 Tbsp (30 mL) butter

1 medium onion, chopped

1 clove garlic, chopped

1 tsp (5 mL) turmeric

1 tsp (5 mL) ground cumin

½ tsp (2.5 mL) cinnamon

1 tsp (5 mL) ground coriander

2 lbs (900 gr) spinach, washed
(chopped if the leaves are big)

Saffron Butter

For each cup (250 mL) rice use 1 Tbsp (15 mL) butter and 2 or 3 threads of saffron.

Melt butter in a small saucepan over medium heat, add saffron, cook for a couple of minutes, pour over rice and mix well, fluffing with a fork.

Assemble the Stew

Heat the oil and butter in a heavy-bottomed, oven-proof casserole over medium-low heat, add the moose meat in batches and sauté briefly until browned. Remove each batch as it is done and reserve on the side. When the meat is all browned, add onion to the casserole, adding more oil if necessary, and sauté until softened. Add garlic, sauté another couple of minutes, then add spices and stir so that onion and garlic are thoroughly coated.

Preheat the oven to 300F (150C). Add the meat back to the casserole along with the fruit and stock mixture. Bring to a simmer, cover and place in the oven. Cook, covered, for 2½ hours. Every now and then check to make sure the liquid has not evaporated, and if necessary, add a bit more stock or a splash of red wine, just enough to produce a small amount of broth but not so much that the meat and fruit start to swim. (The spinach will add more liquid.)

Add spinach and cook for another half hour and remove from oven. There should be just enough sauce to hold the stew loosely together, but if not, add another splash of red wine, stir and let cook over medium-low for a couple of minutes.

Serve with quinoa, bulghur or couscous (beware the packaged kind! Sniff to make sure it's not rancid) flavoured with saffron butter (recipe at left).

Makes six to eight servings

GRILLED MOOSE STEAKS

This isn't really a recipe, but a plea. Even if you don't like rare meat, please try your moose steaks that way, just once. When moose is cut into steaks it's so sensitive to dry heat that it shrivels up and turns to leather the minute your back is turned. Even at medium rare the outer edges become chewy. The texture and flavour of a rare moose steak is beyond compare, and needs no more seasoning than salt and pepper.

My father, master of the barbecue, used to serve rare beef steak cut into very thin slices. I can still picture him bent over the platter, holding a thin-bladed knife in his bearish paw, sawing gently with great concentration, scarfing a slice when he thought no one was looking. Thin slices are a great way to go with moose too, arranged on heated plates with some garlicky roast potatoes and roasted fennel with red pepper: it doesn't get much better.

Heat the barbecue grill to smoking hot. Season meat with salt and pepper. Grill steaks for a scant minute each side, then an additional 30 seconds each side. Remove from heat, let sit for a few minutes then slice thinly and serve on warm plates.

Makes two to four servings

Two 8–10 oz (225–280 gr) moose rib steaks

Salt and pepper to taste

Gilding the Lily

If you really want to serve a sauce with your grilled moose, make a quick reduction: combine 1 cup (250 mL) each of red wine and rich stock (such as **caribou stock**, page 117) and reduce over high heat to ½ cup (125 mL), beat in 1 Tbsp (15 mL) cold butter off the heat, and serve the sauce on the side. While you're at it, sauté some portobello mushrooms in butter and garlic and serve those on the side too.

ROASTED FENNEL AND RED PEPPER

Great with grilled moose steaks.

1 fennel bulb

2 red peppers

Juice of 1 lime

1 in (2 cm) piece fresh ginger, chopped

¼ cup (60 mL) olive oil

1 tsp (5 mL) sesame oil

1 Tbsp (15 mL) tamari or soya sauce

Salt and pepper to taste

Preheat oven to 350F (175C). Trim leaves from fennel bulb, leaving only the bulb part, trim bottom. (Save the stalks and fronds for flavouring stock.) Cut in half lengthwise, and slice into pieces a third of an inch (8 mm) thick. Core and clean white pith from red peppers and slice lengthwise into half-inch (1-cm) pieces. Put vegetables in a shallow baking dish. Mix together remaining ingredients, pour over vegetables and toss so that vegetables are fully coated. Roast for 60 minutes or until red pepper and fennel are soft.

Makes four servings, as an accompaniment

MOOSE MOUSSAKA

The first summer I lived in Greece I got a job in a taverna on the waterfront for a couple of weeks at the end of August, when the tourist season was winding down. The kitchen wasn't under as much pressure then and there was room for a foreign rookie. Work started at eight in the morning with the proprietor filling up the fuel tank for the massive iron cooker, which ran on kerosene gravity-fed through a thin copper pipe. He filled the tank, which sat on a shelf up near the ceiling, by standing on a milk crate balanced on a wooden chair and pouring kerosene from a 10-kilo container held high over his head. Thus was death or serious injury courted and defied every morning. When he was safely down off the chair his wife lit the pilot, the stove roared into life and the day's cooking began: *moussaka*, stuffed peppers, stuffed aubergines (eggplants to us North Americans), goat *yiouvetsi*, *pastichhio*, all of which had to be ready, dished and displayed in the glass case by noon, when the tables out front started to fill. My job was to scrub out the round *tapsis* and the heavy, long-handled aluminum pots, clean the knives, dig out the gunk from the strainers, wash the spoons and the plastic bowls, and try to keep my head as the kitchen wreckage piled higher and higher in the tiny dank room at the back where the sink was. Sometimes I'd get a break around 10:30 or so, and sometimes on those breaks I'd take a spoon and scrape out the remnants in the béchamel pot. The combination of milk, flour and cloves tasted warm and comforting, and reminded me of home.

Now when I make béchamel sauce for moose moussaka in my kitchen in Whitehorse, I'm reminded of home again, but of course it's Greece that I miss this time.

Start the eggplant first, do the meat filling while the eggplant is salting, and the béchamel while the eggplant is cooking. The prep takes about 1 hour 30 minutes.

Eggplant

2 large eggplants, about 1½ lb (680 gr) each

Salt

¼–½ cup (60 to 125 mL) olive oil

Slice the eggplant into rounds about a quarter of an inch (6 mm) thick. Lay them out in a big bowl and salt the slices on each side. Let sit for 30 minutes. Preheat oven to 350F (175C). Rinse eggplant slices with cold water, drain, lay them out between two tea towels and pat dry, then lay out on baking sheets lined with parchment paper. Brush the tops with olive oil. Bake for 20 minutes, remove from oven, flip the slices over and brush the other side with oil. Bake for another 20 minutes, but check for doneness after 10 minutes. The eggplant slices should be soft but not falling apart or sticking to the paper. When they're ready, remove from the oven and let cool.

Meat Filling

2 Tbsp (30 mL) olive oil

1 medium onion, chopped

2 cloves garlic, minced

2 lbs (900 gr) minced moose meat

1 tsp (5 mL) oregano (Greek if you have it.)

1 tsp (5 mL) cinnamon

½ cup (125 mL) red or white wine

1½ lbs (680 gr) ripe tomatoes, coarsely chopped or 25 fl oz (750 mL) can whole plum tomatoes, broken up with a fork

Salt and pepper to taste

Sauté the onion over medium heat until translucent, add the garlic, oregano and cinnamon, sauté 2 minutes, and add the meat. Brown the meat, breaking up any chunks that form with a fork.

Add wine, cook for 2 minutes, then add the tomatoes. Turn the heat down to medium-low and cook until much of the liquid has evaporated but the mixture is still good and moist, about 30 minutes. Add salt and pepper to taste, remove from heat and reserve.

Béchamel Sauce

Melt butter over low heat. Add the flour and cook for 5 minutes, stirring often. Don't let the flour brown. Heat the milk, and add slowly to the roux, stirring constantly until all the milk is added and the sauce is thick and smooth. Cook over low heat for a further 20 minutes, stirring frequently, strain and let cool. To stop a skin from forming on the cooling sauce, place a piece of waxed paper directly onto the sauce.

3 Tbsp (45 mL) butter

3 Tbsp (45 mL) all-purpose flour

1½ cups (370 mL) milk

1 shallot or small onion studded with 3 whole cloves

1 small bay leaf

Salt and pepper to taste

Assemble the Moussaka

Preheat oven to 350F (175C). Lay one-third of the eggplant slices in a row on the bottom of an oiled 9-by-13-inch (23-by-33-cm) baking dish. Spread half the meat mixture over top, then sprinkle one-third of the grated cheese over the meat. Lay the next third of eggplant slices over top, follow with the rest of the meat, sprinkle with one-third of the cheese, and finish with a layer of eggplant.

2 cups (480 mL) grated cheese, a mix of Parmesan and old white cheddar

Pour the béchamel sauce over the eggplant, sprinkle the remaining cheese over top, and bake for 30 to 40 minutes until sauce bubbles at the edges and the top is golden brown.

Let sit for 10 to 15 minutes before serving. Serve with salad, **Two-day Sourdough Bread** (page 193) and a crisp white wine.

Makes six servings

Elk

One Saturday morning in the fall of 2009 my friend Sophia Marnik called me up. "Help. I have five pounds of fresh elk liver and I have no idea what to do with it." This is the kind of problem that I like.

Historically, small numbers of elk have strayed northward into the Yukon in years when herds in northern BC expanded. In the late '40s, the Yukon Fish and Game Association convinced the commissioner of the Yukon to release captured elk into the southwestern Yukon, where they were to roam freely and increase the stock of big game for recreational hunting; the herd was supplemented in the late '80s and early '90s. The introduced elk have tended to roam within a triangle roughly bounded by Whitehorse, Carmacks, and Haines Junction in two separate herds, the Braeburn herd and the Takhini herd. Both herds were off limits to hunters, and continue to be listed as specially protected wildlife under the Yukon Wildlife Act. But in the fall of 2009 a limited hunt was introduced in order to bring down the size of the herds to a target population. Sophia's husband accompanied a friend on his hunt, and the elk liver was his reward. A friend who was an outfitter in northern BC in the mid '80s happened to call while I was contemplating what to do with this gift. He was jealous. "Female elk liver is one of the great wilderness delicacies," he said.

Nonetheless, five pounds of liver was overwhelming, so I asked Sophia to give me half, and keep the other half for her own household. (I believe her half is still in her freezer.) Her husband dropped it off that afternoon, and I made this pâté, adapted from a recipe I found on eatingelk.com—a great website for elk recipes. This pâté is unbelievably rich, subtle and satisfying; I've never tasted better, even in France. Sophia concurred, and so did my gourmand mother, visiting from Toronto at the time, high praise from that discerning palate.

Elks browsing in winter.

ELK LIVER PÂTÉ

Put water in a large saucepan and add all the ingredients except the liver. Bring to the boil, reduce the heat, cover and simmer for 10 minutes. Add liver and bring to a boil again. Cover, reduce the heat to low and simmer for 15 minutes. Remove pot from heat and let stand covered for 20 minutes.

Use a slotted spoon to remove meat and discard everything else. Allow to cool, then remove the thin, shiny membrane from the liver by peeling it away with the fingers. The membrane looks like very thin, tight plastic. A small, pointed knife helps to lift up one corner, after that the peeling is fairly easy. Cut the liver into 1-inch (2.5-cm) pieces, and remove any bits of gristle you come across, for the smoothest pâté possible.

Put the liver into a food processor and pulse until the liver resembles coarse meal.

4 cups (1 L) water

¼ tsp salt

1 celery stalk, split lengthwise and halved

3 whole cloves

1 bay leaf

6 juniper berries

4 sprigs parsley

12 peppercorns

½ tsp (2.5 mL) dry chili flakes

One 2-in (4-cm) piece of cinnamon stick

Pinch of salt

1 lb (454 gr) elk liver, cut into 6 pieces

Continued next page

To the ground liver add:

> ½ lb (225 gr) softened unsalted butter
>
> ½ tsp (2.5 mL) mace or grated nutmeg
>
> 2 tsp (10 mL) dry mustard
>
> ½ tsp (2.5 mL) ground allspice
>
> Pinch of ground cloves
>
> 3 green onions, finely chopped
>
> ½ tsp (2.5 mL) minced garlic
>
> ¼ cup (60 mL) cognac
>
> 2 Tbsp (30 mL) finely chopped parsley

Process until the pâté is well blended and completely smooth, then add:

> ⅓ cup (80 mL) 35 percent cream

Put into ramekins or bowls from which you can serve directly—I used a few different sizes and gave some away as gifts.

Let the pâté sit overnight in the refrigerator for the flavours to develop, and allow to warm up to room temperature before serving—both the flavour and spreadability are vastly improved. The pâté will keep for up to a week, tightly wrapped in the refrigerator.

Makes 2½ cups (600 mL)

GRILLED ELK LIVER WITH BACON, ONION AND MUSHROOMS

The cooking method was suggested by eatingelk.com, the bacon and mushroom accompaniment was adapted from *Cooking Fish and Game French Canadian Style* by Quebec journalist Francine Dufresne, published in 1975. Dufresne is an eccentric and racy companion who calls herself "Leopoldine" and sprinkles references to hunting and sex equally liberally throughout the book.

I accompanied this dish with **Rowan Jelly** (page 118), which was fabulous. Hector said, "This is the best liver I have ever eaten."

Fry bacon in an iron pan over medium heat. Don't let it get too crunchy. Remove from pan and drain on paper towels. Pour off most of the bacon fat (retaining it in case it is needed), add the mushrooms to the pan and sauté for 3 to 4 minutes. Remove from pan. Sauté spring onions and garlic in the pan—add a bit more bacon fat if necessary.

Chop bacon and mushrooms together, but not so the mixture is mushy, and add to the onions and garlic. Add a splash of red wine and turn heat to high. When wine has reduced, add 2 tablespoons of cream and cook until the mixture just holds together. Remove from heat, add pepper to taste, and reserve, covered, off the heat.

Cut the liver into pieces ¾ of an inch (2 cm) thick, coat with olive oil, salt and pepper. Heat grill so it's smoking hot. Grill the liver for 2 minutes on each side. Time it. No more than 2 minutes, seriously.

Serve the grilled liver with the bacon-mushroom mixture on the side or on the top.

I first tried this recipe using fresh organic shiitake mushrooms, but any mushroom will do, including the lowly field mushroom commonly available in supermarkets.

3 strips double-smoked bacon, diced

½ cup (125 mL) dried morel mushrooms*, reconstituted in 1 cup hot water

3 spring onions, chopped

1 clove garlic, chopped

Splash of red wine

2 Tbsp (30 mL) 35 percent cream

1 lb (454 gr) elk liver

Olive oil

Salt and pepper to taste

DELIRIOUS GOAT—YUKON-RAISED GOAT BRAISED IN BEER WITH SPRUCE TIPS AND PRESERVED LEMON

The goat was domestic, not wild, but it was born and raised on Brian Lendrum and Susan Ross's farm at Lake Laberge just north of Whitehorse. Every fall Brian and Susan provide humanely treated organic young goat to a limited number of customers; the waiting list is long. Brian and Susan's cuts of meat are basic: a butcher-paper package given to me by my sister Anne Louise was labeled simply "front leg of goat" in black felt pen. I pulled it out for a dinner party in the fall, but it didn't look like enough for four people, so I pulled out a leg of lamb, too, and planned to cook them both in a pomegranate-tomato marinade from Paula Wolfert's *The Slow Mediterranean Kitchen*. But when I opened up both packages and put the two cuts of meat side by side in the pan, there was an overabundance of meat, so on the spur of the moment I decided to make something up for the goat. What freedom: no expectations, no pre-conceptions and nothing to lose. For a couple of hours I was lost in what writer Claudia Dey has called "the delirium of risk," improvising with abandon.

Here is the result: easy, unusual, and vaguely Thai—the spruce tips, coriander and preserved lemon combine to create flavours reminiscent of lime leaves, lemon grass and coconut. It's quite magic.

1 front leg of goat, shank and shoulder separated (substitute 6 domestic lamb shanks)

Salt and pepper

2 Tbsp (30 mL) olive oil

1 medium onion, chopped

1 stalk celery, chopped

1 carrot, chopped

Preheat the oven to 250F (120C) Season the goat pieces with salt and pepper and brown them in oil over medium heat in a heavy casserole or Dutch oven.

Remove the goat, set aside and sauté the onion in the same pan until translucent, then add the garlic, celery, carrots and sauté another 5 minutes.

Add the red wine, scraping any bits from the bottom of the casserole, and cook until the liquid becomes syrupy. Add the coriander, spruce tips, chili and cinnamon, stir and cook another 2 minutes, then return the goat pieces to the casserole.

Tuck the lemon in four corners of the casserole, and pour the beer over top. It may not quite cover the meat, that's okay. Cook in the oven for 4 hours, until the meat is falling off the bone.

Remove casserole from the oven, take the goat pieces out and keep them warm on a platter—not in the oven. Place the casserole on a burner set at medium. Thicken the sauce by combining the butter and flour in a small bowl to make a paste, and slowly adding hot liquid from the casserole to the bowl, whisking constantly.

When you have about a cup of flour, butter and sauce, add it back to the casserole, still whisking, until the sauce is a uniform colour and starts to thicken. (Start with one tablespoon each of flour and butter, and then if the sauce doesn't thicken sufficiently, repeat the step.) Reduce the heat to low, and cook for 10 to 20 minutes.

Return the goat to the casserole for about 10 minutes until it's heated through. Serve over rice, polenta or Thai noodles with green beans on the side.

Another option

After removing goat, reduce the cooking liquid over medium-high heat to about half its original volume, add 1 can of good coconut milk, reduce heat to medium low and simmer for 10 minutes, then add 1 teaspoon (5 mL) of cornstarch dissolved in 1 tablespoon (15 mL) of water and cook until sauce has thickened, about 2 minutes, before returning goat to heat through.

Makes six servings

2 cloves garlic, minced

2 Tbsp (30 mL) coriander seed, slightly crushed with a mortar and pestle

¼ cup (60 mL) **spruce tips** (see page 51)

1 Tbsp (15 mL) birch syrup

2 small dried chilies, crushed

½-in (1-cm) piece of cinnamon stick

1 whole **Preserved Lemon**, separated into quarters and seeds removed (recipe follows)

2 bottles (341 mL each) honey brown lager

1–2 Tbsp (15–30 mL) each butter and flour

Top: Delirious Goat seasonings.

Bottom: Delirious Goat, the lamb shanks version.

PRESERVED LEMONS

Adapted from Paula Wolfert's *The Slow Mediterranean Kitchen*.

Quick Method

2 organic lemons, washed and well-dried

⅓ cup (80 mL) coarse or kosher salt

½ cup (125 mL) fresh lemon juice

Cut each lemon into eight wedges and toss with the salt. Place wedges in a 1-cup (250-mL) jar and pour in fresh lemon juice, pressing with a wooden spoon to make sure the juice penetrates to the bottom. It's best to seal the jar with a plastic lid, but if using a metal lid, place a piece of waxed paper over the jar first.

Leave the lemons at room temperature, shaking the jar every day to distribute the juice and salt. The lemons will be ready to use after seven days, and can be stored in the fridge for another week. Rinse before using and pat dry.

Long-term Planner Method

10 organic lemons, washed and well-dried

½ cup (125 mL) coarse or kosher salt

Cut six lemons into quarters, cutting from the top down to within ½-inch (1 cm) of the bottom. Sprinkle the flesh of each lemon with salt, close it up and place in a bowl, adding each lemon as it's done. Toss the lemons gently with the remaining salt and pack them into a dry, sterile 4-cup (1-L) jar. Squeeze the juice of the remaining four lemons over top, pressing down on the lemons with a wooden spoon so the juice penetrates to the bottom. The lemons will not be completely covered with juice: don't worry. After a few days the salt will have drawn enough liquid out from the lemons to cover them. Leave at room temperature for one month, then store in the refrigerator. They will keep for up to a year, if covered with a layer of olive oil. Rinse briefly before using and pat dry. Don't forget to remove seeds before adding to a dish.

Opposite: Preserved Lemons.

Sheep

The Royal Treatment

Queen Elizabeth II
Whitehorse
Visit 1959.

Queen Elizabeth II visited the Yukon on July 16, 1959, and ever since, her family has been hopping in and around the North like whisky-jacks around a campsite, though, it must be said, with considerably more decorum. They have come singly and in groups, their Royal Highnesses, to celebrate a centennial here, walk the Millenium Trail there, visit schools, greet Brownies and Boy Scouts, give out awards and medals, open legislatures, honeymoon on northern rivers, and generally whoop it up with the locals. And each time they've come they have chowed down, as the Department of Canadian Heritage's website tells us they like to do, on the food of the region. Recently, I went on a sleuthing mission to ferret out the northern recipes considered by chefs and royal protocol people to be worthy of the royal table.

Back in July, 1959 the *Whitehorse Star* welcomed Queen Elizabeth with the headline, "Queen, You are Okay by Us." Publisher Harry Boyle's editorial assured Her Majesty that citizens would toast this happy event "in spirited assemblies throughout the Yukon," that hangovers would be forgotten, "in the honour that lingers with us."

The Queen herself was not joining in the revelry, at that time, being newly pregnant with the future Duke of York. (Indeed, one chef informs us that the Royal Family drinks nothing but Coca-Cola, though this report is unsubstantiated.) Nor, apparently, was she eating much, despite the best efforts of RCAF Cpt. Frederick Johnstone of Moose Jaw, charged with cooking for the Royal Household.

Poor Cpt. Johnstone. Not only did he have a queasy queen on his hands, one night the electricity at the VIP house foiled him with a power outage at the crucial moment. A feast of fresh grayling had to be scrapped, and the Royal Household fed on cold meat and ice cream and peaches instead. But the *Whitehorse Star*'s Stroller White tells us the chef came back with a bang the next night, presenting roast mountain sheep to the assembled company. Sadly, the captain's recipe is lost in the mists of time, but I surveyed a number of northern chefs to learn how they would roast sheep in a manner fit for a Queen.

"I put mine in a slow cooker, add salt and pepper, and

cover it with bacon," said Diane Strand of the Champagne and Aishihik First Nations, who grew up in Kluane, Dall sheep country. Chef Mary-El Kerr wouldn't roast a sheep at all. Rather, she cuts a sheep roast into steaks about half an inch thick and grills them 30 seconds per side on a hot barbecue, with nothing but pepper for seasoning. Mary-El reports that with this method you can taste the wild sage the sheep has grazed on, right in the meat.

But what would Cpt. Johnstone have done, in the kitchen of the VIP house, just off the runway at the Whitehorse Airport? Chances are he got his sheep from an outfitter, and probably had some experience cooking on the land himself, having been stationed in Whitehorse. So I unearthed an old recipe, from *Wilderness Cooking* by Berndt Berglund and Clare E. Bolsby. This husband and wife team, who were chefs and wilderness survival experts, spent a lot of time hunting in the MacKenzie Mountains in NWT in the fifties and sixties. Guide Ernie Roseen "just as spry at seventy as the Dall Sheep he hunts," taught them this method.

ROAST STUFFED SHOULDER OF DALL LAMB

Preheat oven to 300F (150C). Remove the bone from the shoulder by cutting all around it with a long, narrow filleting knife, cutting as close to the bone as possible. Rub the inside and the outside with all but ½ teaspoon (2.5 mL) salt and ¼ teaspoon (1 mL) pepper. In a large mixing bowl, make the stuffing by mixing the crumbs, onions, spicebush powder, salt and pepper. Add just enough water to moisten the mixture so it will hold together. If there are small pieces of meat stuck to the bone, remove them and add to the stuffing. Stuff the hole in the meat loosely with the stuffing and sew the edges of the hole together. Place the meat with fat side up on a rack in a deep roasting pan. Cook for 4 hours. Serve steaming hot with potatoes and mint jelly.

5–6 lb (2–3 kg) shoulder of lamb

1½ Tbsp (22.5 mL) salt

1½ Tbsp (22.5 mL) pepper

2 cups (475 mL) sourdough bread or bannock crumbs

4 Tbsp (60 mL) onions, grated

1 tsp (5 mL) spicebush powder (allspice will do)

BASIC BANNOCK

This is the classic bannock recipe, a beloved northern staple. For a basic bush bannock recipe, see page 214.

2 cups (475 mL) all purpose flour

1 tsp (5 mL) baking powder

1 tsp (5 mL) salt

1 tsp (5 mL) sugar

1–1½ cups (250–350 mL) water

½ cup (125 mL) canola oil for frying

Mix dry ingredients together, make a well in the centre and add one cup water, stirring dry ingredients in with a fork in a circular motion. If mixture looks dry and clumpy, add the remaining water a bit at a time. Heat a cast iron frying pan on medium heat, add oil and heat until the surface shimmers. Drop the bannock mixture a tablespoon at a time into the hot oil, and fry until golden brown on the underside, 5 to 6 minutes, flip over and fry the other side. Serve hot with cranberry preserves and butter. For a variation, add a handful of your favourite berries. For stuffing, tear cooled bannock into small pieces and follow directions in recipe on page 139.

Poor Queen Elizabeth was so ill she had to cancel the rest of her trip to Dawson City, Mayo and the NWT. She's never been back to the Yukon, but has since popped into Rankin Inlet once and Yellowknife and Iqaluit twice each. In 2002, she flew straight from Heathrow to Iqaluit, arrived at 11 a.m., and ate nothing there, though she observed students at Inukshuk High School preparing caribou meat in a demonstration of traditional knowledge, flew on to Victoria, and was finally off the hook for official duties at 5:30 in the afternoon. You can imagine the sigh of relief as she slipped off her pumps in the Royal Suite.

Princess Anne dropped by Whitehorse in 1982, and chef Mary-El Kerr was part of the cooking team. She and her cohorts designed a menu that included avocado stuffed with shrimp salad, then the hottest number going in chic cuisine. They fired the menu off to Rideau Hall for approval. A fax came back: NO SEAFOOD! Out with the shrimp, in with the chicken salad, not quite so hip but at least the Princess would eat it. At that luncheon a local dignitary, in the spirit of Harry Boyle, toasted the Princess with the whole assembly and then continued toasting her quietly on his own until he fell off his chair.

Chef Lisa Williams of the Westmark Whitehorse Hotel was on board for Prince Charles' visit in 2001, not only for the official banquet but for his breakfasts and lunches too. This involved many telephone tête à têtes with the Prince of Wales' personal chef, who advised Williams on the royal likes and dislikes. For breakfast, the Prince preferred fresh-squeezed orange juice, a 12-minute egg, and a slice of fruity pound cake with apricot marmalade. Williams was not at liberty to share the recipes for pound cake and marmalade, since they were given to her in confidence by her colleague at the castle, but she did divulge the secrets of her Fireweed Vinaigrette. This she served on a salad of baby greens, which introduced a meal of Arctic char with lemon-caper butter compound and duxelles-stuffed chicken breast in a Chardonnay cream sauce, for 225 hungry souls, including Prince Charles, who was served on fireweed pottery to distinguish his plates from the others. As she cooked, Williams was observed by a security officer, who kept a close eye on the Prince's plates. But the best part of the whole experience, she said, was that she got to hang out with Nigel, the Prince's personal aide, who tasted everything and gave it the thumbs-up. "Nothing happened without wonderful Nigel!"

LISA WILLIAMS'S FIREWEED VINAIGRETTE

Lisa used a scant teaspoon of dressing per serving of baby greens for the royal banquet in Whitehorse. She advises that if you're serving leaf and especially tougher romaine lettuce, add a bit more honey and olive oil to the dressing to loosen it up.

Combine the fireweed jelly, white wine and honey in a pot and stir over low heat for about five minutes, or until jelly dissolves. Let cool, add olive oil and salt and pepper. Whisk well, until slightly thickened and creamy.

Makes a scant ½ cup (125 mL) dressing

¼ cup (60 mL) fireweed jelly

1 Tbsp (15 mL) white wine

1 Tbsp (15 mL) honey

2 Tbsp (30 mL) virgin olive oil

Salt and pepper to taste

fireweed

Somebody out there in NWT knows what Fergie and Andrew ate on their honeymoon trip on the Hanbury-Thelon river in 1987. And Rankin Inlet in 1994—who cooked for the Queen in Rankin? And was anybody actually there at the apocryphal moment, claimed by communities across the country to have occurred at a banquet in their home town, when the Duke of Edinburgh's server told him *sotto voce* as she whisked away his dinner plate, "Keep your fork, Dukie. There's pie coming."

Spruce Grouse

Spruce grouse nearly ended my relationship, on that same fateful moose hunting trip described earlier in this chapter. What I didn't say was that the day after we caught and field dressed our moose, a lone hunter in a canoe on the same lake caught his moose at about three o'clock in the afternoon, an hour before dusk. We felt compelled to help him. So on my first hunt I helped to field dress not one but two moose. Next day, as we drove back toward home along a dirt road, just before we turned onto the highway my partner spied a spruce grouse in the branches of a spruce tree. He stopped the truck, shot the grouse, stepped on its feet and pulled its skin and feathers over its head like a sweater in one deft move that hunters know, and I burst into tears.

But many years have passed since that difficult day, and when Cathie Archbould told me recently she had some spruce grouse for me I said bring it on. She left four whole breasts in the secret cache we've arranged for such occasions at my house, and I got to work, aided and abetted by suggestions from friends.

STUFFED, MARINATED SPRUCE GROUSE WITH CRANBERRY REDUCTION

Rinse and pat dry the grouse breasts and place in a deep bowl. Whisk the oil, lemon and lime juice and wine together, add the remaining ingredients and pour over the grouse breasts, turning to make sure all surfaces are covered. Marinate in the refrigerator for 4 hours, turning occasionally.

4 whole spruce grouse breasts, skinned but not deboned (in other words, both sides of the breast, attached)

1 cup (250 mL) red wine, boiled over high heat for 10 minutes

Juice of 2 lemons and 2 limes

¼ cup (60 mL) olive oil

4 cloves garlic, minced

14 juniper berries, crushed

1 Tbsp (15 mL) **spruce tips**, chopped (see page 51)

¼ cup (60 mL) wild blueberries, mashed

Stuffing

Sauté the onion in the butter in a cast iron pan over medium heat until the onion is translucent; add the sage, savoury, salt and pepper, cook for two more minutes and scrape into a bowl with the bread. Mix lightly with a spatula, add the cognac and mix again. Cover and reserve.

½ medium onion, chopped

2 Tbsp (30 mL) butter

1½ tsp (7.5 mL) wild sage

½ tsp (2.5 mL) summer savoury

4 slices stale bread, pulled into small cubes

1 Tbsp (15 mL) cognac

Salt and pepper to taste

8 thick slices of bacon

12 toothpicks and 4 lengths of string about 12 inches (24 cm) long

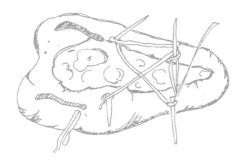

1 cup (250 mL) lowbush cranberries

1 Tbsp (15 mL) maple syrup

¼ cup (60 mL) chopped onion

¼ cup (60 mL) rich meat stock (such as **caribou stock**, page 117)

¼ cup (60 mL) red wine

¼ cup (60 mL) 35 percent cream

2 Tbsp (30 mL) cold butter

Stuff the Breasts

Remove the breasts from the marinade and pat dry. Discard the marinade.

Stuff the cavity between the breasts of each bird with as much stuffing as it will hold. Run three or four toothpicks through the flesh on either side of the cavity, closing the gap as best as you can. Take a piece of string, anchor it with a knot around one toothpick and then thread it around all the others in a criss-cross pattern, making a loop around each toothpick, pulling tightly to close the gap. Tie the string off with a couple of half-hitches. When you're finished, wrap each breast in two slices of bacon and place in a small roasting pan stuffing side up. Cook in a 400F (205C) oven for 30 minutes.

Remove from oven and let sit for 5 minutes. Then, remove the string and toothpicks and serve the grouse breasts on a small pool of Cranberry Reduction (recipe follows), with more reduction in a gravy boat on the side.

Makes four servings

Cranberry Reduction

Cook the cranberries, maple syrup and onion over medium heat for 10 minutes, until cranberries start to pop. Add the stock and red wine, cook for a further 5 minutes until the liquid is syrupy. Stir in the cream, cook for another 2 to 3 minutes, remove from heat and beat in the butter one tablespoon (15 mL) at a time. Remove from heat and reserve, keeping warm until you're ready to serve.

Makes 1½ cups (350 mL) sauce

CHAPTER FIVE

Rivers, Lakes and **Ocean**

There are around twenty fish species in Yukon waters suitable for catching and eating, including five kinds of salmon, four whitefish, three trout, Dolly Varden, northern pike, Arctic char, Arctic grayling and the elusive and mysterious inconnu. In this chapter we barely penetrate the surface of the cold lakes and rivers of the Yukon; here you will find no grayling (eat it the same day you catch it), no whitefish, no inconnu (though many will remember with fondness the band of that same name who played on northern stages in the mid '90s). Instead this chapter concentrates on the fish I have so far encountered—salmon, pike, trout, char—but the great hope is that these recipes will stimulate readers, cooks and fishers to venture out, bring in the fish, experiment in the kitchen and report back.

A happy fisherman with his catch.

Northern Pike

The northern pike is a favourite of Yukon anglers; it's plentiful, a good fighter and the flesh is firm and delicious. My sister, who used to go fishing with our father in Southern Ontario, has recently taken up the habit again, and caught a whack of pike in the weedy section of Marsh Lake last summer. She made a fabulous pike chowder with some of the meat, largely because the filleting was so challenging that the pieces she ended up with were best suited to soups or stir-fries.

Dennis Zimmerman, an enthusiast for all things piscine who writes a fishing column in the bi-weekly newspaper *What's Up Yukon,* says he watches an instructional video before he fillets a pike, just to remind himself where all the bones are. I asked Dennis what his favourite pike recipe was, one that really highlighted the flavour of the fish, and his immediate response was, "I am enthralled with pickled pike, for its texture, taste and overall yumminess. Next time I have a chance to get into a mess of pike, which isn't that hard around here, that's where I'm going with it!"

Dennis is the kind of cook who researches, puts together a bit of this and a bit of that and improvises, and he was kind enough to go back and recreate his recipe for inclusion here.

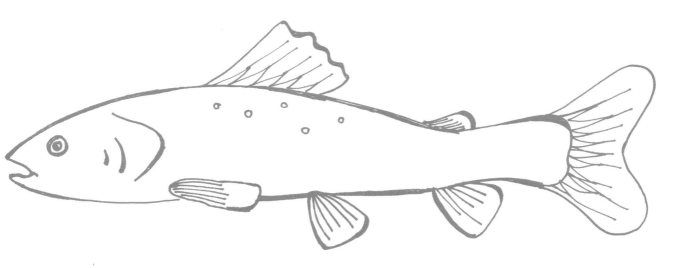

DENNIS ZIMMERMAN'S PICKLED PIKE

Dennis says, "I think the key to taste and texture is our Yukon-cold water. Even in the middle of the summer most lakes stay relatively cold and the pike meat firm. I like to catch pike in the spring, fall or through the winter."

4½–5 lbs (2–2.24 kg) pike fillets, deboned

14–16 cups (3.5–4 L) water

2 cups (475 mL) coarse salt (Dennis uses pickling salt)

Enough white vinegar to cover

1 white onion, sliced

Dissolve the salt in the water in a large non-metallic bowl. Cut fish into 1.5- to 2-inch (4- to 5-cm) bite-sized strips—something you can sink your teeth into, like you would a cocktail shrimp. Add the fish to the salt water. Leave for 24 to 48 hours in the fridge. Remove fish and rinse well under cold water. Cover the fish with white vinegar for 24 hours and refrigerate.

Take the fish out of the vinegar and stack in sterilized 4-cup (1-L) jars with some pieces of sliced onion. Cover with pickling solution:

Pickling Solution

4 cups (1 L) white vinegar

4–5 cups (1–1.25 L) sugar

1 onion

4 teaspoons (20 mL) pickling spice

1 cup (250 mL) dry white wine

Boil all ingredients together except the wine. Remove from heat and let cool, add the white wine, mix briefly and pour over the fish in the jars. Scald the lids and seal the jars. Refrigerate for at least a week before eating to let the pickling solution work its magic.

The pike will keep for a month in the refrigerator. Dennis says, "Great just to pick at out of the jar or on crackers, dark firm breads or salad."

Makes three 4-cup (1-L) jars

Old Trout

My mother, who calls herself an old trout (as in, "not bad for an old trout" when she triumphs over adversity and bags a parking spot, say, right in front of the dry cleaners in downtown Toronto) is a great cook, in the classic French style. Her signature items on the kitchen counter when I was young were a bottle of Mommesin red table wine and a pound of butter. When I reached the age of 35, she gave me a copy of *Traditional French Cooking* by Curnonsky, the writer and gourmand who chronicled and celebrated French cooking with such commitment in the first half of the twentieth century that near the end of his life his culinary friends, a passel of two- and three-star chefs, agreed he should never have to pay for another meal again, and affixed a brass plaque with his name on it to the best chair in each of their restaurants, so that he could come in any time and enjoy a fabulous meal, free of charge. Not bad for an old trout.

This year I cracked open Curnonsky's tome for the first time, in search of a suitable recipe for a lake trout, caught the summer of 2009 (and donated for the cause) by my friend Matt Willis, in Lewes Lake, 40 minutes south of Whitehorse on the Carcross Road.

All the trout in Lewes Lake are probably old trout, according to Yukon fish biologist Susan Thompson. I sent her a picture of Matt's trout for identification. Yup, she said, looks like a *Salvelinus namaycush* from Lewes Lake: old and skinny. How old? About 20 years old. Matt said he had to work hard for that trout, but it was worth it, because the trout from Lewes Lake always taste so clean.

The first recipe I read in Curnonsky said, "Gut the trout through their heads, without cutting open the stomachs." The second one I read said poach the fish in Champagne. I said, Why not? Then it asked for a fish velouté made from court bouillon and fish fumet, which I was to pour over 4 egg yolks, add 14 tablespoons of butter and some crème fraîche. I called my mother in Toronto in a panic: fumet, court boullion, crème fraîche? She walked me through the crème fraîche (the French version of sour cream) old hand that she is. I said, but the eggs, the butter, the excess! She said, "Your point is?" We compromised: 2 egg yolks and 7 tablespoons of butter might do the trick.

I made many mistakes in putting together this dish: the trout was ready long before I'd finished the sauce, I shirked on the fish velouté and used salmon stock instead, I poured hot poaching liquid over the trout, which made the skin tighten and the stomach butterfly open before *M. Truite* was even in the oven. In the oven, the trout's head exploded. (I think the initial temperature was too high.)

But after 20 minutes at 350F (175C), the flesh of the trout was beautiful: pink, delicate, tender and clean-tasting. And the sauce? Now I understand why Julia Child found her calling in Paris in the early 1950s, and I understand why she and her husband Paul developed liver trouble after a few months and had to go on a cleansing diet. This sauce, despite its rich ingredients, is delicate, complex and subtle; you could chase its flavours around your tongue every day, trying to find the right descriptor for the alchemy of sauce and fish together, until finally you'd have to shrug, smile, raise your glass to Curnonsky, your mother and Lewes Lake and say, pretty darn stellar, for an old trout.

CRÈME FRAÎCHE

2 cups (475 mL) 35 percent cream

½ cup (125 mL) buttermilk

Pour half the cream into a ceramic bowl, then the buttermilk, then the remaining cream. Don't stir. Cover bowl tightly with plastic wrap, wrap in a towel and set in a warm place. Let sit for 24 to 36 hours, until set. Pour off any liquid that has accumulated with a plate over top of the bowl, beat the mixture vigorously and refrigerate for 24 hours. The crème fraîche will finish thickening in the fridge. Use leftover crème fraîche instead of whipped cream in summer desserts—simply sweeten with a bit of icing sugar.

Makes about 2½ cups (600 mL)

OLD TROUT POACHED IN WINE

For those who, like me, need the security of a roux-based sauce, one is provided here, with the addition of saffron and kumquat for interest. In both versions, the method is the same: Start the sauce well beforehand, keep it warm, poach the fish, finish the sauce. Note that homemade crème fraîche takes 24 to 36 hours to be ready, so do factor that in to your plans.

The Exacting Method
(A Variation on Curnonsky)

Combine the fish stock, shallot and 2 tablespoons (30 mL) of lemon juice in a saucepan, reduce over high heat to ½ cup (125 mL); strain. Reduce the wine to ½ cup (125 mL) in another pot. Combine the reductions while still hot; pour slowly over the egg yolks, whisking constantly. Pour mixture into the top half of a double boiler over barely simmering water. Heat until the sauce begins to thicken slightly, whisking constantly. Don't let the sauce boil. After about 5 minutes, remove from heat and add the butter, a tablespoon at a time, still whisking.

Keep the sauce warm in the double boiler over minimal heat, whisking now and then, or better still, take the double boiler off the heat entirely while you deal with the trout. If you like, you can refrigerate overnight at this point.

When you're ready for the final step, make sure the sauce is warm; if you're reheating cold sauce, do it slowly in a double boiler. To finish, reduce 1 cup (250 mL) poaching liquid to a ½ cup (125 mL) over high heat and add to the warm sauce in the double boiler. Finally, whisk in the crème fraîche. Test the seasoning, add lemon juice to taste and keep warm until you're ready to serve.

Makes about 1½ cups (350 mL) sauce

1½ cups (350 mL) fish stock (such as **Simple but Excellent Salmon Stock,** page 171), clam liquor or, in a pinch, chicken stock

1 small shallot, chopped fine

3–4 Tbsp (45–60 mL) lemon juice

1½ cups (350 mL) white wine (Prosecco or Sandhill Pinot Gris)

2 egg yolks

7 Tbsp (105 mL) cold butter

1 cup (250 mL) reserved poaching liquid

½ cup (125 mL) **Crème Fraîche** (page 150)

The Curnonsky variation—note the double boiler.

The Forgiving, Roux-based Version

Reduce stock, shallots and wine, as above. Omit the lemon. Make a roux with 2 tablespoons (30 mL) each of butter and flour, cook for 2 minutes, add reductions, a few threads of good saffron, the rind of two kumquats, sliced thin, or 1½ teaspoons (7.5 mL) grated lemon, lime or orange rind. Cook over low heat for half an hour, add reduced poaching liquid and whisk in crème fraîche.

Makes about 1½ cups (350 mL) sauce

Poaching the Trout

1 large trout or 4 fillets

3¼ cups (750 mL) white wine (Prosecco or Sandhill Pinot Gris)

Enough fish stock (such as **Simple but Excellent Salmon Stock,** page 171) or clam liquor to cover the fish

Choose your cooking vessel and heat source according to the size and number of your trout: a frying pan on top of the stove or a baking dish in the oven. If you're cooking the trout whole, rub the skin with a small amount of olive oil or butter—this will help with removing the skin later. Pour the cold cooking liquid over the fish. If your dish doesn't have a lid, improvise with a layer of parchment paper, then a layer of tin foil—don't use tinfoil alone because it will react with the poaching liquid. Cut a small hole for the steam.

Heat the fish and liquid over low heat on top of the stove, or at 350F (175C) in the oven. Once the poaching liquid starts steaming, calculate the time: 7 to 10 minutes for whole small fish or fillets, 13 to 18 for larger, whole fish. When the trout is almost cooked, remove to a warm platter. (The fish will continue cooking.) Reserve 1 cup (250 mL) poaching liquid for the sauce and freeze the rest of the poaching liquid for a future soup or chowder.

Finish the sauce (see above) and keep it warm while you or your trusty side-kick remove the skin from the whole trout and lift nice serving pieces off the bone. Pour a bit of sauce on each plate, place a serving of fish on top, pour more sauce over and garnish with greenery and a bright tomato or carrot. Serve with a summer salad and the same wine you used for poaching.

Makes four servings

Top: Readying M. Truite for the oven.

Bottom: M. Truite, plated and sauced.

The Joy of Home-Smoked Salmon

In the summer of 2004 Hector and I bought 150 pounds of wild Taku River sockeye and king salmon from a fishing family in Atlin, BC. Then we bought a freezer. Does this sound familiar? This mad leap into bulk living was our next-door neighbours' doing—they had introduced us to the pleasures of home-smoked salmon that spring. Their usual practice every May or June was to clear the remainder of the previous year's salmon from the freezer in order to make way for the new salmon that would start to trickle in, mid- to late June, from fishers on the Taku River.

Each spring they smoked the last three or four fish and held large and generous dinner parties, at which lucky guests feasted on home-smoked salmon and then took the leftovers home. Freshly home-smoked fish, new to me in 2004, was a revelation, completely different from canned or candied. The prospect of eating relatively inexpensive wild salmon all winter, and then a glorious smoke-fest in spring was too much. We succumbed: bought the fish, bought the freezer, ate salmon all winter and in June 2005, embarked on the much-anticipated smoke-fest.

I enrolled in the ad hoc school of home smoking, hastily set up by our neighbours Rob and Tina at the behest of their one pupil: me. The first order of business was a lesson in filleting. Let us draw a veil over the results of that first attempt, and commend the instructors for their kindness in saying, "Never mind, you can make a beautiful chowder with the meat left on that bone." The salmon yielded six good-sized pieces, despite my inexpert handling, and Rob demonstrated how to make slices in the thicker pieces, leaving the skin intact, to let the brine, smoke and heat penetrate faster. (If you too are less accomplished with a fillet knife, see page 172 for a **fresh salmon chowder** to use up the leftover meat on the bone.)

Tina had already made a huge batch of brine, which they shared with me, giving me strict instructions about how to place the fish in the brine (flesh side down) and the kind of pan to use (glass, enamel or plastic).

A word here about brine, straight from the *Joy of Cooking*: its purpose is to "draw the natural sugars and moistures from foods and form lactic acids, which protect them against spoilage bacteria." Brining is key to food safety in home-smoking, and a 10 percent solution, or six tablespoons (90 mL) of salt to a quart of water, is recommended. As Rob and Tina instructed, the brine should completely cover the fish, fish should be placed in one layer in a non-metal container, refrigerated and left for eight to twelve hours. There is different advice out there on brining times per weight and for different types of fish; we stuck to the safest. The brine not only protects, it infuses flavour into the fish before smoking. As long as you follow the basic proportion of salt to water, you can experiment with flavourings and ingredients as much as you like. Tina adapted her brine recipe from the useful little recipe book that came with her True North smoker.

After brining comes the drying stage. The morning of smoking day we patted the fish dry with paper towel and then laid it skin side down on a rack—Tina advised balancing the rack over the sink to catch the drips. The key here is good air circulation; some people set up a small fan to keep the air moving over the fish. During this stage the fish forms a "pellicle" or hard, slightly tacky surface. The pellicle keeps contaminants out and moisture in, and can take anywhere from one to three hours to form. Ours took about two. But don't rush it.

Next comes the smoking, which is both exciting and slow. Exciting because you can't believe you're actually doing this, slow because smoking and then finishing the salmon in a slow oven (depending on how dry you like it) can take all day. Plan to hang out at home so you can keep an eye on the smoker, or if you can't, finagle a pal (Tina!) with promises of treats to watch the smoker while you're away.

The True North smoker we used was basically a tall metal box with a lid, wire racks, a drip pan underneath, a pan to hold wood chips under that and an electric element in the bottom. For the wood chips we went to Canadian Tire and selected alder and hickory chips from the array of bagged hardwood chips on the shelves, which included cherry, maple or apple. The chips are of a size somewhere between sawdust and the bits of wood that collect around the wood-cutting block, and a panful of chips takes about 45 minutes to burn. Note that while the smoke imparts flavour, it has no bacteria-reducing effect. That comes from the heat. The wonderful flavour-imparting smoke seeped out of the cracks around the door, and while I was at work

Tina sat with her detective novel and imported beer in my backyard, waiting for the salmon to smell ready. I came home from lunch in time to see Tina remove the salmon after three pans of chips, or 2 hours and 15 minutes. She took her portion of salmon home to dry in a 150F (65C) oven for a few hours—Tina likes a drier smoked salmon, but I prefer a wetter texture. So I wrapped my six portions and put some in the fridge and some in the freezer, and over the next few days and weeks experimented with some of the recipes you'll find in the rest of this chapter.

After we finished that first batch of salmon I tackled the process on my own. I pulled another sockeye fillet from the freezer, went to our local fish store (out of business now, so sad) and selected some Alaskan halibut, some Arctic char caught in a lake near Lake Laberge, and some Atlantic cod. I followed the basic brine recipes from Tina's smoker cookbook and divided it into four portions, once for each type of fish, and added a different kind of booze to each portion: grappa for the salmon, vermouth for the halibut, rye whisky for the cod and saki for the char.

Next day, Hector and I ran a garage sale in the backyard while we smoked the fish for the several hours it required. The smell brought the neighbours over (and their cats and dogs), and many discussions ensued about methodology, and smoking times, and brines and will there be samples? Of course there were samples, and I believe they had a positive effect on the sale of unwanted household items that day.

But the definitive taste testing was to take place later that night and in preparation I assembled some accompaniment: asparagus, new potatoes (cooked, then chilled, no added butter or oil), cream cheese, pumpernickel (the dark, dense, square kind), dill, tomato and lemon. I purchased three white wines: an American Viognier, a New Zealand Sauvignon Blanc, and an Italian Pinot Grigio.

The tasters assembled at 11 p.m., after a series of social mishaps (a play that went on longer than expected, an empty house, an unanswered phone…). The results of the experiments were fascinating. First of all, none of the booze added to the brine made a single bit of difference to the final product—you couldn't even taste it. And the fish took the brine and the smoke in completely different ways. Neither the cod nor the halibut absorbed the smoke all the way through, it just stayed on the surface; even the colour of the flesh didn't really change. By contrast, the char and the salmon were saturated through and through, the char too much so—the flavour, oddly, reminded us of salami. The tasters agreed that char is so delicate the simplest of brines is probably best, possibly even plain salt and water.

One taster thought halibut was far better smoked than not, and said if he ever caught a halibut, he'd be tempted to smoke the whole thing. The halibut's texture was buttery smooth, while the cod was chewy ("bouncy" said one) and the salmon, because of the structure of the meat, was immediately melt-in-your-mouth. Because of its high fat content, salmon can take strong flavours, so it stood up well to the chilies and soya sauce in the basic brine recipe. The tasters returned to the salmon most often; at this particular session it was hands-down the most popular. As for accompaniment, the asparagus (steamed, buttered) though delicious, was a distraction, and the potatoes a non-starter. (I had envisioned hunks of cod on potato, combining two Maritime staples, but nope, it didn't work.) Good old pumpernickel and cream cheese was best of all, with tomato or lemon as palate cleanser between bites of different fish. As for the wine, the California Viognier was the popular choice.

Remember to observe the rules of safety first and last— be sure to refrigerate smoked fish and eat it within two weeks; if you freeze it, consume it in two months. This was not something we had to worry about, that summer night in 2005: by one in the morning it was all gone.

SMOKED SALMON

Mix all brine ingredients together. Slice salmon fillets into four or five pieces each and place in a non-metallic dish, flesh side down. Pour brine over the salmon pieces, making sure they are entirely submerged and not touching each other. Cover and refrigerate eight hours or overnight.

Remove from the brine and dry on a rack over the sink until a hard, tacky surface forms, up to three hours.

Once the pellicle is formed, the salmon is ready to smoke. Arrange the pieces in the smoker with the thickest on the lower racks and the thinner tail pieces on the upper racks. For a drier result, smoke the salmon for two hours, and then finish it in the oven at 150F (65C) for three hours. For "wet" smoked salmon, which I prefer, two hours of smoking is enough.

Brine ingredients:

- 1½ cups (360 mL) soya sauce
- 1 cup (250 mL) water
- 1 cup (250 mL) white wine
- ⅓ cup (80 mL) brown sugar or maple syrup
- ¼ cup (60 mL) kosher salt (non-iodized)
- 2 Tbsp (30 mL) sambal oelek or other hot sauce
- 2 cloves garlic, chopped
- Juice and rind of 3 lemons
- Juice and rind of 2 limes
- 2 fillets of salmon, about 1 lb (454 gr) each

A smoked Taku River sockeye fillet emerges from the smoker, ready for drying in the oven or immediate sampling.

Smoked Arctic Char Revisited

In the summer of 2009 I tried a new recipe for smoked char. Older and wiser after the '05 experiments, I eliminated everything in the brine but the grappa and the maple syrup, and increased the grappa to two cups. I will be honest: I needed to get rid of the grappa. It was not top-quality. But the char did not suffer from the quality of the grappa as we had—this smoked fish was a smash hit at a birthday potluck on the banks of the Watson River in late June, and when I took the remainder with me on a visit to my mom's place in Southern Ontario near the Pretty River valley, those Pretty River trout-eaters were blown away.

SMOKED ARCTIC CHAR WITH GRAPPA

Brine ingredients:

2 cups (475 mL) water

6 Tbsp (90 mL) salt

2 cups (475 mL) Grappa

3 Tbsp (45 mL) maple syrup

1 whole Arctic char, filleted, with the skin left on

Follow the directions in the previous recipe for mixing the brine, slicing, placing and refrigerating the fish. In the morning, dry the char on racks until the pellicle forms, and then smoke for two hours over alder chips. The flesh will be almost translucent. Even if you normally like a drier, chewier smoked fish, try a bite first before smoking it any longer, or finishing it in the oven. You might discover you're a convert to this version. Serve on plain crackers spread with just a scrape of soft chèvre.

Taku River Sockeye Revisited, December 2009

Looking back from December 2009 it's hard to believe the happy nonchalance with which Hector and I once stocked our freezer with wild Taku River sockeye. In the spring of 2008 two food-related stories dominated the news. The first was riots over food shortages around the world, and the loss of arable land to crops raised for biofuel. The second was dismal reports of diminishing salmon stocks in the rivers of the Pacific Northwest, including chinook salmon in the Yukon River. Then, in the summer of 2009, the big story was the complete and utter crash of the Fraser River salmon run.

In the midst of the alarming news from around the world and from the rivers close to us, Taku River sockeye became even more precious. In 2008, we weren't able to purchase any Taku River salmon at all, but this was more because our usual supplier had gone out of business for personal reasons than because the salmon had crashed. But the red flag was raised, and I did some research. I learned that Taku River sockeye are in relatively good shape, compared to other species and compared to sockeye in rivers down south. Monitoring by the Canadian and American governments and the Taku River Tlingit, who work together to implement the Pacific Salmon Treaty, and sustainable harvesting by local fishing outfits, have helped to maintain a fairly healthy stock.

The annual Taku sockeye stock is about 240,000 fish. Alaskan fishermen divert about 110,000. Of the 130,000 fish that run up the Taku River in Canada about 25,000 are caught. The fish that get away (the escapement) go on to reproduce, to be eaten by eagles and bears, to rot and to contribute their nutrients to the soil and the trees. This is reassuring.

But now I pay close attention to the fish news from BC, the Yukon and Alaska; my Internet bookmarks file is filling up with links to websites for the Pacific Salmon Commission, Fisheries and Oceans Canada, Rivers Without Borders and salmon activist and fish biologist Alexandra Morton.

At home the first imperative now is to use every part of the fish in the freezer. The scraps go into stock: tails, fins, bones, all of it. The other imperative is to serve fresh

Best Salmon Purchase Ever

In July of 2009, in the midst of the search for salmon, photographer Cathie Archbould sent me an email: her supplier from Atlin was taking orders for sockeye. I called him up right away and a few days later a white cube van with a Taku River Tlingit crest stenciled onto the side pulled into the driveway: the salmon had arrived. John Williams and his assistant opened up the back of the cube van, which housed a vast container of crushed ice in which many sockeye and coho were buried. John sat in a chair in the van beside the old-fashioned scale with his notebook and calculator while his assistant lifted each gleaming salmon from the ice and slipped it into a plastic bag with such skill that the fish didn't touch the outside edges of the bag. He made a game of guessing how much each fish weighed, and nailed it within a couple of ounces each time. Then he helped me carry the fish down to the basement.

or smoked salmon so that every morsel is appreciated. For example, in the tour de force featured here: smoked salmon cheesecake, a recipe kindly provided by Joyce Moore of Calgary, Alberta, whose daughter Carolyn Moore serves this killer appetizer at her annual Christmas party to roomfuls of eager guests in Porter Creek, Whitehorse.

SALMON CHEESECAKE

Mrs. Moore notes: "In winter, I garnish with a slice of smoked salmon that I have saved to make a rosette in the middle of the top of the cake. I use bits of spruce to make a pin wheel out from that."

3½ packages (2 lb / 875 g) cream cheese, room temperature

4 eggs, room temperature

⅓ cup (80 mL) 35 percent cream

3 Tbsp (45 mL) butter

½ cup (125 mL) onion, chopped

½ cup (125 mL) green or red pepper, chopped

⅓ lb (145 g) smoked salmon, diced

¼ cup (60 mL) Parmesan, grated

½ cup (125 mL) gruyère cheese, grated

Pepper to taste

Heat oven to 300F (150C). Mix cream cheese, eggs and cream with electric mixer or food processor until ingredients are smooth and blended. Set aside.

Melt butter in frying pan over medium heat and sauté onion and pepper. Fold the salmon, grated cheese, onion mixture and ground pepper into cream cheese mixture. Pour batter into a 9-inch (23-cm) springform pan and shake gently to level the mixture. Wrap the bottom of the pan in a single sheet of aluminum foil and set in a pan of water. Bake 1 hour and 40 minutes, turn oven off and leave cheesecake in oven 1 more hour. Lift pan out of the water bath and place on rack to cool for 2 hours. Unmold. Serve with crackers or thinly sliced baguette.

Makes a 9-inch (23-cm) cheesecake

Joyce Moore's Salmon Cheesecake served with Scottish Oatcakes (page 229).

SMOKED FISH MOUSSE

This is a delicious shortcut for when you don't have time to go the whole cheesecake route. This mousse can be made with home-smoked salmon or indeed any smoked fish; the combination of sour cream and cream cheese lends stiffness and substance, while the whipped cream folded in at the end lifts it into the realm of the heavenly.

Grind the smoked fish in a food processor for one minute. Reserve a quarter cup (60 mL). Add the cream cheese and onion to food processor, blend thoroughly, then add the lemon juice and sour cream. Process until uniform in colour. In another bowl, whip the cream until stiff. Add the reserved ground salmon and the salmon cream cheese mixture to the whipped cream, folding them together with a spatula. When the mousse is thoroughly blended, spoon into a pretty bowl and refrigerate for an hour. Serve with light, thin crackers like rice crackers or Kavli bread.

Makes about 2 cups (480 mL), and keeps for two days, refrigerated

4 oz (115 gr) of smoked sockeye salmon, Arctic char or trout

½ package (¼ lb / 125 gr) cream cheese, softened

2 Tbsp (30 mL) purple onion, chopped

2 Tbsp (30 mL) lemon juice

¼ cup (60 mL) sour cream

½ cup (125 mL) 35 percent cream

POTATO-APPLE LATKES WITH SMOKED SALMON AND WASABI CRÈME FRAÎCHE

These gorgeous little numbers are a dynamite appetizer to serve at a party: they look great on a platter, and if you make the latkes small enough, can be eaten in one bite, thereby reducing your guests' cocktail party anxiety. The secret is to bake, not fry!

1 lb (454 gr) Yukon Gold potatoes, peeled and quartered

1 medium onion, peeled and quartered

½ small celery root (celeriac) peeled and cut into slices

1 medium Granny Smith apple (unpeeled), cored and quartered

1 large egg

1 green onion, finely chopped

¾ tsp (4 mL) salt

½ tsp (2.5 mL) black pepper

¼ cup (60 mL) all purpose flour

1 tsp (5 mL) wasabi powder

½ cup (125 mL) **Crème Fraîche** (page 150)

6 oz (170 gr) thinly sliced **Smoked Salmon** (page 157)

Capers or thinly sliced green onion

Latkes, Smoked Salmon and Wasabi Crème Fraîche.

Preheat oven to 400F (205C). Line a colander with a tea towel or cheesecloth and place the colander in a bowl. Using a processor fitted with the grating blade, coarsely grate potatoes, onion, celery root and apple at the same time. Dump the mixture into the tea towel in the colander. (Alternatively, grate the vegetables and apple with a hand grater directly into the cloth-lined colander.) Gather towel tightly around potato mixture and squeeze out as much liquid as you can. Discard the liquid and put the vegetables into the same bowl. Add the egg, green onion, salt and pepper, mix well, then add the flour and toss to blend.

Line baking sheets with parchment paper. Drop spoonfuls of the latke mixture onto baking sheets, aiming for a bite-sized piece, about half a tablespoon. Flatten each mound slightly with the spoon. Bake for about 8 minutes, remove from oven, turn over, and bake another 8 minutes. If you like, brush the top side with melted butter, flip, and brush the other side; this will lend a bit of that traditional, fried latke sensation that some can't live without.

While latkes are cooking, mix the wasabi powder with a small amount of crème fraîche until blended, then add the rest of the crème fraîche and mix lightly. Taste and add more wasabi, if you like a hotter version.

Cool latkes briefly, then top each one with a small pile of smoked salmon, a dab of wasabi crème fraîche and a caper or a couple of slices of green onion. Turn, face the ravening hordes, and present.

Makes 65–75 pieces

RICE NOODLES, SMOKED SALMON AND GINGER-SCALLION SAUCE

This dish is best served cold, as a salad. I tried both soba noodles and thick rice noodles or rice sticks, the kind used for pad thai, and the rice noodles were by far the best choice for both taste and texture. The rice noodles are light and slippery with an almost neutral flavour, the vegetables are mild and yet provide excellent crunch, and the two work together to showcase the sprightly ginger-scallion sauce, and of course the salmon. Smoked salmon and gravlax work equally well in this recipe.

Place noodles in a large bowl and pour boiling water over to cover. Soak noodles until al dente, from 10 to 13 minutes, then drain noodles in sieve. Fill the bowl with cold water and place the noodles, in the sieve, back in the bowl. Once noodles have cooled, drain thoroughly, return to the bowl and reserve. Don't forget to dry the bowl first.

Stir-fry the mushroom in a cast-iron frying pan at medium high heat in one tablespoon oil. Add one teaspoon of soya sauce once the mushrooms have wilted, toss, and continue cooking until the mushrooms stick to the pan. Remove from heat, let cool in the pan and reserve.

Blanche the snap peas for one minute in rapidly boiling water, remove from heat and plunge immediately into a bowl of cold water to stop the cooking process and retain colour. Repeat with the sliced carrots and reserve.

While noodles are soaking, make the sauce. Combine ginger, scallions, the remaining sunflower or grape seed oil and soya sauce, sesame oil, vinegar and fresh lime juice. Stir with a fork to combine.

8 oz (225 gr) package thick rice sticks

¼ cup (60 mL) sunflower or grape seed oil

1 large portobello mushroom, cut in quarters and then sliced

2 tsp (10 mL) soya sauce

1 cup (250 mL) whole mange toutes or sugar snap peas, strings removed

1 medium carrot, sliced in half lengthwise and then diagonally

½ cup (125 mL) peeled and finely minced fresh ginger

2 cups (475 mL) finely sliced scallions, both white and green parts

1 tsp (5 mL) sesame oil

2 Tbsp (30 mL) seasoned rice vinegar

2 Tbsp (30 mL) fresh lime juice

1 tsp (5 mL) chili flakes or sambal oelek hot sauce

Salt and pepper to taste

4 oz (115 gr) **Smoked Salmon** (page 157) or **Gravlax** (page 228) sliced or broken into bite-sized pieces

A quartered lime, sesame seeds and a few slices of scallion for garnish

Toss the noodles with the ginger-scallion sauce, add the reserved vegetables, toss again until well mixed and divide between four bowls. The vegetables tend to sift to the bottom; make sure everyone gets some. Arrange one ounce of smoked salmon or gravlax on top of each serving, sprinkle with sesame seeds and sliced scallions, and serve with quarters of lime on the side. A nice, light miso soup would be a good starter, and some **home made ice cream** (pages 39–42) an excellent finisher for a great summer lunch during one of those unexpected early August heat waves.

Makes four servings

Smoked Salmon and Rice Noodle
mise-en-place.

STELLAR SMOKED SALMON LASAGNA

Cheese lovers, rejoice. There are four different kinds in this lasagna. It also requires four pots and a frying pan; enlist a helper!

Cheese Sauce

Warm the milk in a saucepan over low heat. In another saucepan, sauté the onions in butter over medium-low heat for 5 minutes, then whisk in the flour. Cook for 3 to 4 minutes, then gradually add the warmed milk, whisking constantly. Cook over low heat for 20 minutes, then gradually add the cheese, whisking well after each addition. Add the sherry or port and the nutmeg, taste, add salt and pepper, remove from heat and reserve.

Note: I have had cheese sauces curdle on me before when I've added the cheese too fast. If this happens, rescue the sauce by making a new roux with one tablespoon (15 mL) each of butter and flour, cooking it for 2 minutes, and then gradually stirring in the curdled sauce, bit by bit, whisking the whole time.

- 4 cups (1 L) 2 percent milk
- 1/3 cup (80 mL) butter
- 4 spring onions, chopped
- 1/3 cup (80 mL) all purpose flour
- 1/2 cup (125 mL) grated Parmesan
- 1 cup (250 mL) grated old cheddar cheese
- 2 Tbsp (30 mL) sherry or port
- Pinch of nutmeg
- Salt and pepper to taste

To Assemble

Sauté the mushrooms in the butter or oil over medium heat until they've softened, then add garlic and sauté for another 2 minutes. Add the soya sauce, then turn the heat up to medium-high and cook until the mushrooms are dry and start to stick to the pan and caramelize. Remove from heat and reserve.

Steam the spinach until it's barely cooked and squeeze out any excess water. If the spinach is mature and has stems, chop it roughly when it has cooled. Reserve.

Preheat the oven to 375F (190C). Butter a 3-quart (3-L) baking pan or casserole dish. Spread a layer of cheese sauce on the bottom with a rubber spatula, sprinkle about 1/2 cup (125 mL) cheese over top and then lay down the first 3 lasagna noodles. Spread a thin layer of sauce on top, then scatter half the smoked salmon over top, followed by 1 cup (250 mL) of cheese. Layer the next set of lasagna noodles,

- 1 Tbsp (15 mL) butter or oil
- 8 oz (225 gr) field, portobello or cremini mushrooms
- 2 cloves garlic, minced
- 1 Tbsp (15 mL) soya sauce
- 1 cup (250 mL) each of grated gruyère, provolone, old cheddar and Parmesan, tossed together
- 1 lb (454 gr) spinach
- 12 oz (340 gr) **Smoked Salmon** (page 157), separated into flakes, pin bones removed

Continued next page

12 lasagna noodles, cooked to al dente. Drain, and cover in cold water until you're ready to start assembling, then drain again in a colander and shake off the excess water. (I never use the no-boil kind, but go ahead if you know and trust them.)

spread with sauce, and scatter the mushrooms and spinach over top followed by 1 cup (250 mL) of cheese. Repeat with a layer of noodles, sauce, salmon and cheese, then lay down the last three lasagna noodles, cover with the remaining sauce and the remaining cheese.

Bake uncovered for an hour, or until the top is browned and the sides are bubbling, and a knife inserted in the middle comes out hot to the touch. Let stand for 15 minutes before cutting.

Makes 8 to 12 servings

Snake River, Yukon.

Chum Salmon

David Curtis loves chum salmon. The former arts administrator, fine art teacher, film festival founder and visual artist from Dawson City has now transmogrified into an enthusiastic commercial salmon fisher, with a small fish camp on an island on the Yukon River south of Dawson. David is convinced that chum, long considered the least interesting salmon in the pantheon of sockeye, coho, chinook and pink, gets a bad rap, and it is undeserved. He and his partner Chris Clarke are in the first stages of building a small company, testing recipes and developing frozen and fresh chum and chinook dishes and products that will eventually be available in retail outlets and by mail order.

We've been talking about doing a chum hand over for a couple of years so I could experiment and report back, and in the fall of 2009 we finally got the chance. At first it didn't look like there would be a chum season at all on the Yukon River, the numbers were so low, but early in October a short chum opening was finally announced and David and Chris rushed out to their camp, travelling through a blizzard in their open boat. Two weeks later he showed up at my house with two nice-sized chum, about four pounds each, and gave me a lesson in chum preparation, including filleting, and I actually got the hang of it. (David had just bought a brand-new filleting knife from the local kitchen supply store, and he was quite excited about it.) One of the things about chum that turns people off, he said, is the thick slime that covers the outside of the fish. He held a fish firmly under the gills over the sink and scraped downwards, and a coating of slime rippled in waves down the fish and off the tail into the sink. He scraped and rinsed and scraped and rinsed and finally the fish was relatively free of slime, enough so that it wouldn't slide on the cutting board while he filleted. (A splash of white vinegar applied directly to the counter then wiped off with a sponge, followed by hot water, is an effective cleaner.) We skinned two fillets, left the skin on the other two because I intended to smoke them, and I tucked them away in the freezer.

David separated the fins and tail from the bones, and with the bones I made a beautiful delicate stock and turned it into chowder the next day, with some left over baked sockeye. He and Chris are going to turn their scraps into commercial dog biscuits.

A few days later, I tried a method I'd read about in Paula Wolfert's *The Slow Mediterranean Kitchen* and which seems to be making the rounds of the cooking shows these days: salmon poached in olive oil. It worked beautifully with the skinned fillet, and allowed the mild, sweet flavour of the chum to shine, unadorned. Chum is more delicate than the other salmons in both colour and flavour, and to my palate tastes closer to trout than salmon. The trick is to keep a close eye on the temperature of the oil, and never let it get above 155F (68C). This way the fish really is poached, not deep fried.

The second chum recipe included here I owe to my friend Janet Moore, a former Yukoner who has now re-located to the wilds of the Madawaska Valley in Ontario, and with whom I shared many a culinary adventure in the good old days when she lived just up the hill in Hillcrest on the ridge that overlooks Whitehorse. Janet left a message on my voicemail that was basically a list of ingredients and a shorthand methodology: halibut wrapped in prosciutto, seared then cooked in a hot oven with black olives, cherry tomatoes, capers, onions and basil or cilantro. This sounded tailor-made for David's chum, and it was.

CHUM POACHED IN OLIVE OIL

Rinse the pieces of fillet and dry thoroughly. Pour the oil into a deep-sided saucepan and heat slowly to about 130F (55C). Slide the pieces of fish gently into the oil—you'll find that the temperature of the oil suddenly increases by 30 to 40 degrees and then subsides to about 155F (65C).*

Poach the salmon for 10 to 12 minutes, and then remove the saucepan from the heat and let the fish continue cooking for 2 to 3 minutes. Remove the fish from the oil and let sit for a couple of minutes on a paper bag before serving.

This is counter intuitive, you'd expect the temperature to decrease. But the moisture in the fish causes the oil to bubble up rapidly, and the intense activity raises the temperature of the oil.

Makes four servings

1½ lb (680 gr) skinned chum fillet, cut into 4 pieces

2½ cups (600 mL) good quality olive oil

Paula Wolfert suggests cooking a branch of thyme and three cloves of garlic in the oil for 10 minutes, removing them before adding the fish. I did this, but didn't discern any noticeable fragrance or taste in the fish, and so I've left out that step. But a good quality olive oil is essential here. (Oil can be strained through a coffee filter, stored in the fridge and used again to poach another fish, but takes on a fishy odour after a couple of weeks, whether it's used for more poaching or not. Taste before using a second time.)

CHUM WRAPPED IN PROSCIUTTO AND BRAISED IN TOMATOES, OLIVES AND CAPERS

1 lb (454 gr) chum fillet, cut into 4 pieces

8 slices of thinly-sliced prosciutto or Westphalia ham

2 Tbsp (30 mL) olive oil

4 spring onions, chopped

2 cloves garlic, minced

2 cups (475 mL) cherry tomatoes, halved

½ cup (125 mL) Kalamata olives, pitted and roughly chopped

2 Tbsp (30 mL) capers

Pepper to taste

½ cup (125 mL) chopped fresh basil or cilantro

½ cup (125 mL) white wine

Preheat oven to 400F (205C). Wrap each piece of chum in two pieces of prosciutto, one slice lengthwise and one crosswise, pulling tightly, and press the meat onto itself so it seals. Sear the packages of prosciutto and fish in olive oil in an oven-proof frying pan or casserole over medium heat for 2 minutes each side, remove from heat and reserve. In the same oil (add another splash, if necessary) over medium-low heat, sauté the spring onions for 2 minutes then add the cherry tomatoes and cook for another 5 minutes.

Add the olives and capers, pepper, wine and the basil or cilantro. Cook for 2 minutes more, then slide the prosciutto and fish packages in with a spatula. Spoon some sauce over each piece of fish, place the dish in the oven uncovered and cook for 15 minutes. Remove from the oven and let sit for a further 5 minutes in the sauce to finish cooking—this way you avoid over cooking.

Serve with pasta tossed with oil and garlic and a green salad.

Makes four servings

SIMPLE BUT EXCELLENT
SALMON STOCK

Heat the butter and oil in a pot over medium-low heat; add vegetables all at once, stir and cook without browning until soft, 10 to 12 minutes. Add white wine or lemon juice, stir, and cook for another 2 minutes. Add salmon scraps, bay leaf and enough water to barely cover. Bring to a boil and cook over medium heat for about 30 minutes. Remove from heat, strain, cool and refrigerate.

Makes about 8 cups (2 L) stock

2 lbs (900 gr) salmon scraps, meat, bones, head and fins (if your salmon is chum, just use the bones and flesh, not the skin; it's slimy and doesn't taste great)

1 medium onion, diced

1 medium carrot, diced

1 stalk celery, diced

2 Tbsp (30 mL) olive oil or half oil, half butter

1 bay leaf

Optional:

Splash of white wine or juice of ½ lemon

A Yukon fisherman sets his nets.

FRESH SALMON CHOWDER WITH COCONUT MILK AND CILANTRO

There are two ways to go when you're chopping vegetables for a soup—either small enough so they'll fit nicely on a soup spoon, or large enough that each vegetable retains its distinct flavour. I go back and forth. In this recipe I chop the sweet potato into ½-inch (125-mm) square chunks; they tend to get soft and disintegrate if the pieces are any smaller.

4 cups (1 L) **Simple but Excellent Salmon Stock** (page 171)

1 medium onion, chopped

2 Tbsp (30 mL) butter or canola oil

2 celery stalks, chopped

2 carrots, chopped

2 cloves garlic, minced

2 Tbsp (30 mL) flour

2 cups (475 mL) coconut milk

2 large sweet potatoes or yams, peeled and chopped

8 oz (225 gr) cooked salmon, bones removed and flaked

2 Tbsp (30 mL) fresh lime juice

2 tsp (10 mL) crushed chilies or hot sauce

A handful of fresh cilantro

Salt and pepper to taste

Heat the salmon stock over medium heat. Meanwhile, sauté the onion in the butter or oil over medium-low heat until soft and translucent, add garlic, celery and carrots and sauté another 5 minutes. Add flour, stir and cook for a further 2 minutes, then gradually add the first cup of heated salmon stock, stirring until the liquid has thickened, then add the remainder in a steady stream, stirring the whole time.

Add the coconut milk, bring to a slow simmer over medium heat, reduce the heat to low and add the sweet potato.

Simmer until the sweet potato is cooked, 15 to 20 minutes, then add salmon, crushed chilies or hot sauce and lime juice. Simmer until salmon is heated through, add salt and pepper to taste and the chopped cilantro, and serve.

Like all soups, this one is even better the next day. Reserve some fresh cilantro for the second day to chop and add to each bowl before serving.

Make eight servings

CHAPTER SIX

Sourdough

**The Tradition, the Care and Feeding,
the New Artisanal Approach**

Time for Sourdough
Boot Camp.

Cooks! It's minus forty, you're housebound, you've colour-coded your wardrobe and reread your old journals to the point of terminal boredom...you need a project. You need Sourdough Boot Camp. It's time you got to know that stalwart, faithful, life-saving ingredient the gold-fevered Klondike stampeders brought with them over the Chilkoot Pass, rolled into a tight ball and buried in a sack of flour or tucked into the bedroll at night; time to test yourself against that combination of wild yeast, water and flour on which Yukoners have fed for a hundred years, and by which newcomers who survive the winter still define themselves; time to tame the ancient leaven that creates bread with a lovely, elusive tang and is easy on the stomach, too.

I first tackled sourdough in the spring of 2009, and am now a total sourdough convert. Once you've gotten through the starter-building phase (which you *can* avoid by getting some from a friend, or ordering dry starter over the Internet and bringing it to life—see supplier on page 249) your sourdough will become your lifelong pal, producing loaf after loaf of exquisite artisanal bread, melt-in-the-mouth pancakes, light and tender scones, and endless, delicious variations on the classic cinnamon roll.

A Yukoner cannot discuss sourdough without calling on Ione Christensen, formerly mayor of Whitehorse, Commissioner of the Yukon, senator, Member of the Order of Canada since 1994 and always, keeper of the starter her great-grandfather Wesley Ballantine carried over the Chilkoot Pass. Ione thinks her ancestor and his four sons probably acquired their sourdough at Dyea in 1898: "They were all men," she says. "I can't see them thinking, 'We're going to need sourdough starter,' when they set out from New Brunswick."

The lump of sourdough the Ballantine clan and other gold seekers kept in their flour sacks was technically a "levain"—a piece of dough pinched from their last batch of bread or bannock. At night they'd add water to the levain for the next day's baking, and keep the mixture warm by the fire in the tent if they had one, or in the blankets with their own body heat if they didn't. In the morning they'd add enough flour to make a dough, some bacon grease, maybe throw in some currants, and whip up a batch of bannock for the day's journey.

From those early days the sourdough starter evolved in its own way in each Yukon household. Though Ione's sourdough was brought over the Pass by the men in the family, it was kept alive and handed down through the decades by the women, from mother to daughter to granddaughter. Ione's grandmother kept a sourdough starter going all the time, and refreshed it with the leftover breakfast porridge. (Ione says, "Starter seems to love oatmeal.") Ione's mom stored her starter in a blue-speckled pearl enamel pail hung from a ceiling rafter in their kitchen at Fort Selkirk on the Yukon River.

Ione is now the last remaining source for her starter; her kids have some but they still come back to her for replenishment. So do the rest of us—Ione's starter is a sourdough celebrity, the subject of numerous articles, radio programs, interviews and a Martha Stewart television special. After Martha Stewart, Ione received so many requests for her starter, and her recipes, that she composed a two-page handout that includes a short history, feeding instructions, and recipes for hot cakes, waffles and bread. (See page 189 for **Ione's Sourdough Hot Cakes**.)

Ione is generous with her sourdough starter, and with her time. When we chatted early in the fall of 2009, I realized how much one needs a sourdough buddy when embarking on the great adventure, to compare methods, discuss results and share triumphs and failures. Note to sourdough rookies: enlist a friend!

During the summer of 1998, to commemorate the 100th anniversary of the Klondike Gold Rush, Ione, her friends Pat McKenna and Judy Dabbs and folks from the Yukon Outdoors Club set up camp in a wall tent at Bennett Lake on the site of an old bakery, where over the course of the summer they served sourdough hot cakes to 2,400 hungry hikers fresh off the Chilkoot Trail. Ione remembers that summer as one of her best ever—cooking in the morning, hiking and kayaking in the afternoon, hard-earned rest at night.

When she was Senator Christensen, from 1999 to 2006, Ione took some starter with her to Ottawa. "I could never get it working properly in Ottawa. I just didn't like the taste." And this is one of the most interesting (and sometimes vexing) things about sourdough: it takes on the characteristics of its environment, whether that be

When Sourdough Goes Bad

"Before refrigeration, you had to use starter fairly regularly or else it would go bad," says Ione Christensen. "My mother used to keep the pot of starter hanging from a nail on the beam in our kitchen in Selkirk. She forgot it up there once. Totally forgot it. There was this godawful smell in the house, and mother liked to keep her house smelling nice and really clean. So she started housecleaning, and she went from head to toe and she could not find what the smell was. She had my dad taking things out and shaking them and it was a week of this housecleaning, you know. Finally my dad happened to look up and he said, 'Martha, what's that pail up there?' That was what the smell was. Oh it was awful. So it got thrown out, and she got some more from my grandmother."

Dyea, Dawson, Ottawa or your own kitchen. As Ione says, "Sourdough is very environmentally sensitive." So if you get some starter from a friend, feed it in the unique environment of your private ecosystem and bake with it regularly, it will incorporate the wild yeasts in your kitchen and become entirely yours; it's no longer the starter you got from your friend. How cool is that?

On to the new artisanal approach: in recent years the interest in wild yeast has exploded in the baking world. Many commercial bakers incorporate sourdough starter into their breads, rolls, pretzels and cakes, augmented with commercial yeast, because they like the sourdough taste. Others, including many home-baker-bloggers, are total purists and won't allow commercial yeasts anywhere near their starter. The community of bakers is as diverse as the breads they produce. But both purists and the more easygoing types are producing great breads and other baked items and publishing their recipes on the Internet. (One of the best sites I've discovered is wildyeastblog.com; an excellent source for tips, ideas and advice. See Sources, at the end of the book, for a few others.) A two-week stint in Sourdough Boot Camp is designed just to get you started on the long sourdough road; it's really only the beginning. I hope you enjoy the adventure.

Sourdough—what is it?

Sometimes I wonder if the character of the djinn or genie, like the one in Aladdin's lamp, was modelled on sourdough—dormant when contained, expanding to many times its size when woken up, powerful, unpredictable, able to grant wishes and liable to go bad if not treated with the correct protocol.

For the chemically inclined amongst us, here's a basic explanation of the science: flour and water act as a medium to which wild yeasts and bacteria are attracted and in which they live, multiply and grow in a mutually beneficial arrangement. The wild yeasts present in the ordinary kitchen thrive in the air and on the surface of grains, fruits and vegetables; they digest sugars and produce ethanol and carbon dioxide, or gas, which helps the bread to rise. The "friendly" bacteria of the lactobacillus family convert simple sugars into lactic and other acids; this creates an acidic atmosphere that wild yeasts like, but other bacteria do not.

(The wild yeast and bacteria in the famous San Francisco sourdough starter have both been isolated, and are peculiar to that neck of the woods.) When sourdough goes bad, it usually means that the balance between the yeast and the bacteria has somehow gone off; the best way to keep this from happening is to keep all your utensils squeaky clean, and to feed the starter regularly.

Sourdough Boot Camp

There are lots of different ways to build a starter, and plenty of advice available on how to do it. I found Nancy Silverton's book, *Bread from La Brea Bakery,* really helpful in breaking the process down into steps. Silverton uses grapes and some fairly intense science when she builds her starter; I wanted a simpler approach, using only unbleached white flour and tap water.

I thought I found it on an online video by a guy called The Kilted Chef, whose formula started with a tablespoon each of water and unbleached flour. But the Kilted Chef suggested that the starter would be ready in only four days. Oops. My first attempt at cinnamon rolls, using a four-day-old starter as the only leavening, turned out like lead. The lesson: you need to put in the time to build a strong starter.

So the method here is a combination of the Kilted Chef's simple formula of unbleached flour and water, and Nancy Silverton's slow two-week-build approach. If you follow this method you will end up with a fairly liquid starter, made with equal parts flour and water, commonly described as a "100 percent hydration" starter, a term you will come across if you explore sourdough territory more thoroughly. In that territory you will also find whole wheat and rye starters, where I have not yet ventured.

A note on Sourdough Boot Camp: I was an unwitting camper, and it was only in retrospect I realized I'd been through a process that might work for others. After the cinnamon bun fiasco, I retreated to recipes that used sourdough starter for flavour and an additional leavening agent like commercial yeast, baking soda or baking powder for a guaranteed rise. I gained confidence with each project, and between projects I kept feeding the starter on an ad hoc basis, dumping in equal parts flour and water every time I removed starter. It seemed to work.

Sourdough Boot Camp Recipes
A Note on Measurements

Most professional bakers measure by weight, not volume. I've tended to stick with volume, because I find it easier, and that's the way I developed and tested the recipes, with the exception of the cinnamon rolls. There, I've included weight measurements. The drawback is that volume is less accurate than weight, so these measurements are approximate. You may need more or less flour than the recipe indicates—I reserve the last cup of flour and add it slowly, rather than adding liquid if the dough gets too stiff. Gradually you get to know what the dough should look and feel like. If the dough is unusually sticky (cinnamon buns!) the recipe will say so.

When is dough ready?

After kneading, the dough:

- Holds together in a ball, is soft and smooth, but not dry;
- Is elastic—it springs back when lightly pressed with a finger;
- Stops sticking to your hands and the work surface. **Exception**: Doughs that contain eggs and butter tend to stay sticky even after kneading. This is normal.

After proofing:

- When you press the dough with a finger, it doesn't spring back, but keeps the indentation mark.

But I didn't attempt to make bread using starter as the sole leavening agent until Doug Fesler, an Alaskan friend, sent me his recipe for a sourdough bread that only rises once, in the pan. His breezy instructions didn't include measurements, but gave the cook total permission to experiment with flavours, and to add flour and water according to the look and feel of the dough. After a few trials I developed a formula that worked, with measurements (because I still need them), based on Doug's excellent template, and that's what you'll find here (**Two-day Sourdough Bread, A Basic Recipe with Variations**, page 193). With this recipe I've successfully "raised" many delicious sourdough loaves, with hard, tasty crusts and moist interiors with small to medium holes and a nutty-textured crumb. This is a great basic recipe for both the beginner and the experienced baker; it's sturdy, adaptable, forgiving and it just keeps on churning out excellent bread.

It's a good way, too, to end Sourdough Boot Camp, which is simply an attempt to formalize the hazardous, anxiety-provoking but eventually successful route I took.

Celebrate the end of Sourdough Boot Camp with this crusty loaf.

SOURDOUGH BOOT CAMP

While you're building the starter, every time you add flour and water to the starter, use a ratio of 1:1:1, starter, flour, water, until the 11th day, when you switch to a ratio of 1:2:2.

Once the starter is built you feed it using an approximate ratio of 1:2:2, starter, flour, water.

As you build your starter, follow two rules: Keep the starter at room temperature, or around 68F (20C), for the whole 14 days, and use lukewarm water.

If you start boot camp on a Wednesday, you'll bake **Sourdough Buttermilk Cranberry Scones** (page 184) on Sunday morning, **Pizza Crust** (page 186) on Monday night, **Fig, Anise, Hazelnut and Gorgonzola Sourdough Bread** (page 187) the next Saturday morning, **Ione Christensen's Sourdough Hot Cakes** (page 189) on Sunday and **Two-day Sourdough Bread** (page 193) the next Wednesday. You can opt out of the extra baking any time you like, but do keep your starter growing. You can also opt in at any time to projects that use the starter you'll be discarding, see days 11 to 14 below.

Day 1
Mix ½ cup (125 mL) unbleached flour with ½ cup (125 mL) warm water in a glass, pottery or plastic bowl. (I use a glass bowl with a plastic lid.) Cover loosely: either rest the lid on the bowl without closing, or arrange plastic wrap loosely over top and let sit at room temperature. It will look like papier mâché paste. A few lumps are not a problem.

Day 2
Bubbles may start to form.

Day 3
Bubbles continue to form and you might notice a yeasty smell—sometimes quite strong and almost unpleasant. Don't worry. Also don't worry if the culture is active and bubbly and then subsides.

Day 4, afternoon or evening

Time to mix in more flour and warm water—1 cup (250 mL) of each. Again, a few lumps are fine. If a browny-purpley liquid has formed, just stir it back in to the mix. You'll now have about 3 cups of starter.

Day 5, morning

Option: Remove 1 cup (250 mL) of starter and make scones. Replace what you have removed with ½ cup (125 mL) flour and ½ cup (125 mL) warm water. If you don't make scones, do nothing to the starter; neither remove starter nor add flour and water.

Day 6, morning

If you're planning to make pizza in the evening, feed the starter with 1 cup (250 mL) flour and 1 cup (250 mL) warm water.

Day 6, afternoon or evening

Remove 1½ cups (375 mL) of starter and make **Pizza Crust** (page 186). Replace what you've removed with ¾ cup (180 mL) flour and ¾ cup (180 mL) warm water.

Day 7 to 9

Do nothing except check on your starter from time to time, giving it a stir. The mixture should not get mouldy, but if it does, remove the mould, transfer the mix to a clean bowl and add 1 cup (250 mL) flour and 1 cup (250 mL) water.

Day 10, morning

For the next 4 days, you will be using a lot of flour, as you feed the starter twice a day. Stock up. Feed the starter with 1 cup (250 mL) flour and 1 cup (250 mL) warm water.

Day 10, evening

Remove all but 1 cup (250 mL) of starter from your main mix. (It will hurt to do it, but discard what you remove—in the compost, not down the sink—unless you want to make scones, hamburger buns, English muffins or pizza dough tonight. If you have the time and the energy, you can do it—the starter is active from the morning feeding.)

To the main mix, add 1 cup (250 mL) flour and 1 cup (250 mL) warm water, cover loosely and leave as usual. Tomorrow, you will make Fig, Anise, Hazelnut and Gorgonzola Bread.

A nice, active sourdough starter.

Day 11, morning

Remove 1 cup (250 mL) of the main mix, and use it to make **Fig, Anise, Hazelnut and Gorgonzola Bread** (page 187). Discard all but 1 cup (250 mL) of the remaining mix, add 2 cups (475 mL) of flour and 2 cups (475 mL) of water, stir, cover and leave in a warm place as usual. (Note that you've switched now to a ratio of 1:2:2 for feeding the starter.) By this time the starter will almost be doubling in size. You might need to move it to a larger bowl.

Day 11, evening

Remove all but 1 cup (250 mL) of the starter and add 2 cups (475 mL) of flour and warm water. Discard the rest, or make pizza dough and refrigerate it for tomorrow night. If you're feeding the starter at 6 p.m. or so, you have active sourdough starter and could make scones, English muffins or hamburger buns tonight. In any case, psych yourself up to make sourdough pancakes in the morning.

Day 12, morning

Today you'll make **Ione Christensen's Sourdough Hot Cakes** (page 189) with the extra starter from the main mix. From the main mix, measure out 4 cups (1 L) of starter for pancakes. Follow Ione's recipe from the point, "Add to starter…"

Reduce the main mix to 1 cup (250 mL), add 2 cups (475 mL) of flour and 2 cups (475 mL) of warm water, stir and leave as usual.

Day 12, evening

Remove all but 1 cup (250 mL) of the main mix, add 2 cups (475 mL) of flour and 2 cups (475 mL) of warm water. It's really hard to keep throwing away the starter that you've removed; see day 11 for ideas. Your starter is active from the morning feeding if you have time to make some boot camp items.

Day 13, morning

As usual, remove all but 1 cup (250 mL) of the main mix, add 2 cups (475 mL) flour and 2 cups (475 mL) of water, stir, cover and leave out. As on days 11 and 12, if your schedule permits, you could make something with the extra starter.

Day 13, evening

Reduce the starter to 1 cup (250 mL), add 2 cups (475 mL) of flour and 2 cups (475 mL) of water, cover and leave overnight.

Day 14, morning

Your starter is ready! You probably have 9 or 10 cups of bubbly, active, yeasty-smelling starter. This is great; it's also a lot. Decide how much you want to keep—I usually store a cup or so in the fridge. If you are ready to start **Two-day Sourdough Bread** (page 193) today, measure out 6 cups (1.4 L) of starter before discarding any. Skip steps 1 and 2 in the recipe and proceed with step 3, using your 6 cups of brand-new starter as the sponge.

This is also a good time to dry some starter to have on hand in case the starter goes bad, and to bring on hikes or canoe trips. Spread a cup of starter on a baking sheet lined with parchment paper and dry at room temperature for 2 to 3 days, peel off the flakes and store in a plastic container or zip-lock bag. For those of you in damp climates, simply freeze your extra starter. When you're ready to use it again, thaw and bring to room temperature before feeding. To reconstitute dried starter, stir the starter into warm water and dissolve. Measure what you have and add flour and warm water in the usual 1:2:2 ratio. It should be ready to go in about 12 hours, but might not be up to full strength until you've used and fed it a few more times.

Then, for the last time, discard all the starter you can't dry or work with right away, stir the remainder and put it in the fridge, loosely covered until you're ready to use it. If you're using a jar with a screw top lip, don't screw the lid down tightly. Starters have exploded in the fridge when still fresh and active, before they calm down into the dormant phase.

Care and Feeding of the Starter

As you now know, starter must be fed before it can be used; starter is at its strongest 8 to 12 hours after feeding (though mine seems to be ready at 6 to 8 hours.). Though every baker has a slightly different formula, the basic method is to measure the amount you have and add twice that amount each of flour and warm water, for a ratio of 1:2:2.

After a few hours or days in the fridge, the starter goes dormant. Ione says, "In the dormant stage, there will be a cream-coloured paste on the bottom with a clear liquid on top." Sometimes the liquid turns blackish-brown. This liquid is "hooch" in the vernacular, contains alcohol as its name suggests, and can be poured off or stirred back in for extra sourness.

At least 8 to 12 hours before you plan to start a recipe, feed the starter and leave the mixture out in a warm place, in a glass or pottery bowl, loosely covered. In the morning return what you don't need for the recipe to the fridge for the next time. This is cardinal rule number one. Cardinal rule number two is, try to feed the starter once a week to keep it alive and happy, but if you can't, don't sweat it too much. When life or holidays intervene, extend the feeding period to 24 hours before you start a recipe to bring the starter back to life.

You'll find that every baker has different instructions on how often to feed the starter and what to do after it has been dormant for a while. Ione likes her starter to have a few days to come back to life. Nancy Silverton suggests that for up to a week of dormancy, you bring your starter to room temperature and then feed it three times the day before using it; if more than a week, feed it three times a day for three days before baking. You will find the method that works best for you.

SOURDOUGH BUTTERMILK CRANBERRY SCONES

Boot campers, proceed directly to "Mix."

The night before, to ½ cup (125 mL) of starter add 1 cup (250 mL) flour and 1 cup (250 mL) warm water. In the morning, return all but the one cup of starter you use in the recipe to the fridge.

Preheat oven to 375F (190C).

Mix:

> 1 cup (250 mL) sourdough starter
>
> 1 cup (250 mL) buttermilk
>
> 1 cup (250 mL) all purpose flour

Add:

> 1 egg
>
> 3 Tbsp (45 mL) melted butter, cooled

Stir together and add:

> 3 Tbsp (45 mL) sugar
>
> 1 tsp (5 mL) salt
>
> 2 tsp (10 mL) baking powder
>
> 1 tsp (5 mL) baking soda

Fold in :

> 2 cups (475 mL) additional flour
>
> 1 cup (250 mL) lowbush cranberries or blueberries

The dough will be sticky and gloopy. Drop from a dessert spoon onto two baking sheets lined with parchment paper. Bake for 20 to 25 minutes. These are great fresh and really good the next day, toasted and buttered.

I make 12 scones, but if you like them smaller this recipe will stretch to 18

VARIATIONS ON THE SCONE THEME

The inventive Laurel Parry eliminates the berries and in their place adds a cup (250 mL) of grated cheese (half old cheddar, half Parmesan) to the basic scone recipe, along with a teaspoon or so of mixed dried herbs, and makes a delicious sourdough quickbread and bakes it in a Dutch oven.

Pre-heat the Dutch oven in a 475F (245C) oven for 15 minutes. Then simply follow the directions above, drop the entire dough onto a heavily floured board, turn the dough over with a spatula so it's covered with a layer of flour so you can pick it up without it sticking to your hands and drop it into the Dutch oven. Bake for 30 minutes covered and then another 15 minutes uncovered.

Another option is to make individual cheese and herb scones, equally delicious.

Windy Arm of Tagish Lake, just south of Carcross in early winter.

PIZZA CRUST

1½ cups (375 mL) recently fed
   sourdough starter

1 Tbsp (15 mL) olive oil

1 tsp (5 mL) salt

1½ cups (375 mL) all-purpose flour

Tip: If you have a pizza stone, place it in the oven before preheating.

Mix olive oil and salt into the starter, then add flour until you have a soft dough. You may not need all the flour. Knead the dough briefly, oil the surface lightly, cover with a tea towel and leave to rest for half an hour. Note that this dough won't rise, you're just letting it rest so it will be easier to work with. The point is to enjoy the taste of sourdough and to get used to working with starter.

Preheat oven to 450F (230C). Have your toppings ready to go. (See pizza recipe, page 87.)

When the dough has rested, divide it in two and roll each portion into a round about 12 inches (30 cm) in diameter, if you're using a pizza stone, or into a 10-by-14-inch (25-by-35-cm) rectangle to fit a baking sheet. I find it easiest to roll the dough on a piece of parchment paper, and then either slide the round of dough off the paper onto the pizza stone, or lift the parchment paper and dough onto the baking sheet. Alternatively, oil the baking sheet and sprinkle with cornmeal and bake the dough directly on the sheet. Drizzle dough with olive oil, prick with a fork in a few places and pre-bake for 5 minutes.

Then spread with sauce, add your toppings and bake for 20 minutes.

Makes two pizzas, enough for four hungry people

FIG, ANISE, HAZELNUT AND GORGONZOLA SOURDOUGH BREAD

Adapted from blogger Bread Baby's adaptation of Nancy Silverton's original Fig Anise bread. Starter is fed 8 to 12 hours prior to beginning the recipe; the recipe then takes about 4½ hours from start to finish.

With a Mixer

Combine water-yeast mixture, starter, flour, semolina, salt, and olive oil in the mixer bowl. Mix on low speed with the paddle attachment for about 4 to 5 minutes. Change to the dough hook and knead on medium speed for about 7 to 10 minutes. The dough will be slightly tacky, but will clear the bowl of the mixer easily. Add the anise, figs and hazelnuts and mix on low speed until just combined.

By Hand

Combine water-yeast mixture, starter, flour, semolina, salt, olive oil, figs, anise and hazelnuts in a bowl and mix until ingredients are combined and it's too difficult to stir with a spoon. Turn out onto a lightly floured board; work the dough for a few minutes: draw all the edges into the centre, fold the dough in half, press the seam closed with the heel of your hand, push the dough away from you, give it a quarter turn and repeat.

Now, knead: Using one hand, fold the dough in half away from you, grab one end, lift it into the air and whack it onto the surface. Do this over and over for 8 to 10 minutes, adding just enough flour to keep the dough from sticking to the work surface. By the end the dough will still be slightly sticky but will pull away from the work surface easily.

Both Methods Continue as Follows

Transfer the dough to a covered, lightly oiled container. Proof at room temperature for 1½ to 2 hours. It will expand slightly and hold fingerprints, while only coming back slightly when touched.

1 tsp (5 mL) yeast dissolved in 1½ cups (375 mL) warm water

1 cup (250 mL) active sourdough starter

2½ cups (600 mL) all-purpose flour

2 cups (475 mL) semolina flour

2½ tsp (12.5 mL) salt

2 Tbsp (30 mL) olive oil

2 Tbsp (30 mL) anise seeds

1½ cups (350 mL) dried figs, chopped

1 cup (250 mL) toasted, chopped hazelnuts (toast in a 325F/160C oven for 10 minutes and remove skins by rubbing nuts together in a tea towel)

1 cup (250 mL) crumbled gorgonzola

Top: A bowlful of Fig, Anise and Hazelnut dough.

Middle: Shaping the dough.

Bottom: Fig, Anise, Hazlenut and Gorgonzola Bread.

Turn the dough onto a lightly floured counter and divide it into three pieces. Shape each piece into a ball or *boule*: Pull the edges into the centre and pinch them together; rotate the dough on the work surface with your hands cupped around it, guiding into a rounded shape with gentle, steady pressure. Cover the boules and let them rest for 20 minutes.

Then, working with one boule at a time: Press the boule into a flat circle with your fingertips. Sprinkle a third of your crumbled gorgonzola over the surface. Fold the near edge into the centre and tuck in the ends and turn the dough so the far edge is now the near edge, fold it into the centre, tuck in the ends and pinch the seams closed. Place seam-side up in an oiled 9-by-5-inch (23-by-13-cm) pan, and then flip over so the smooth side is uppermost and covered in oil.

If you want to make free-form long loaves, once the dough is shaped place it in a baker's "couche"—a stiff piece of canvas floured and formed into ridges. (Best to use new canvas dedicated to bread making.) Otherwise proof in the pan, covered, at room temperature until the dough has increased in size by about 50 percent, about 1½ to 2 hours.

When You're Ready to Bake

Preheat the oven to 450F (230C). Place a pan of boiling water in the oven. Slash each loaf twice with a sharp knife held at a 45 degree angle. Put into the oven immediately and bake for 8 minutes. Remove the water and bake for another 9 minutes. Now wedge the oven door open a crack and bake for a further 8 minutes, watching closely so the crust doesn't scorch.

IONE CHRISTENSEN'S SOURDOUGH HOT CAKES

The evening before you want to make hot cakes, feed the starter. Combine:

> 1 cup (250 mL) sourdough starter
>
> 2 cups (475 mL) flour
>
> 2 cups (475 mL) warm water
>
> 2 Tbsp (30 mL) sugar

After 12 hours, take out 1 cup (250 mL) of starter for the next time and return it to the fridge.

Add to starter:

> 1 egg
>
> 2 Tbsp (30 mL) melted shortening
>
> 2 Tbsp (30 mL) sugar
>
> 1 tsp (5 mL) salt

Mix all this gently, then add:

> 1 tsp (5 mL) soda mixed in 1 Tbsp (15 mL) warm water

Fold this into the batter. Bake on griddle as you would any hot cakes.

Makes twenty 3-inch (8-cm) hot cakes

Tip: Ione uses a seasoned griddle to cook her hot cakes. If you don't have a griddle, try a well-seasoned cast iron pan rubbed with butter or oil and then wiped out, and heat the pan on medium before you start. I learned by trial and error that these pancakes absorb fat easily and become heavy instead of melt-in-the-mouth velvety if there's too much fat in the pan.

HAMBURGER BUNS

About 4½ hours from start to finish.

2 tsp (10 mL) yeast

2 cups (475 mL) warm water

1 cup (250 mL) active sourdough starter

5-6 cups (1250–1500 mL) all-purpose flour, divided

2 tsp (10 mL) salt

2 Tbsp (30 mL) honey or birch syrup

⅔ cup (160 mL) skim milk powder

¼ cup (60 mL) oil

2 eggs, beaten

1 cup (250 mL) semolina, wheat germ or wheat bran

Optional:

1 egg white, beaten with 1 Tbsp (15 mL) of water (egg white wash)

¼ cup (60 mL) sesame seeds

Dissolve the yeast in warm water until bubbly, about 5 minutes. Stir in the starter and 2 cups (475 mL) flour. Allow the mixture to rise until double, about 1 hour. Stir in honey, milk, salt, oil and eggs and mix well. Add the bran or semolina and enough flour to make a soft dough. Knead until smooth and elastic, about 10 minutes, working in more flour as needed. Form into a ball.

Oil a large glass bowl, place dough in bowl and turn over to oil the top, cover and let rise until doubled, about 1 hour. Punch dough down, knead 2 minutes, divide dough in half and shape each into a 12-inch (30-cm) log. With a bread knife, slice each log into 8 equal portions and with lightly floured hands, shape into round balls.

Place on cookie sheets lined with parchment paper and flatten slightly. Brush with egg white wash and sprinkle with sesame seeds if desired; cover and refrigerate 2 hours.

Remove dough from refrigerator and allow to stand at room temperature for 15 minutes. Meanwhile, preheat oven to 400F (205C). Bake the buns for 20 to 25 minutes.

Makes 16 buns that freeze well and accommodate a 4 oz (115 gr) caribou burger very nicely

SIMPLE CARIBOU OR MOOSE BURGERS

1 lb (454 gr) ground moose or caribou

2 Tbsp (30 mL) olive oil

1 Tbsp (15 mL) dried rosemary

1 clove of garlic, chopped

1 egg, beaten

Salt and pepper to taste

Mix all ingredients together with a fork, lightly, and form into 4 oz (115 g) patties. Barbecue over medium heat, with a spray bottle handy to put out flare-ups.

Makes 4 servings

SOURDOUGH ENGLISH MUFFINS, WITH YEAST

About 3½ hours from start to finish.

Combine starter, flour, yeast and salt, then add all the rest of the ingredients and mix together until dough starts to form a ball around the spoon. Then knead the dough until it's a cohesive ball that's tacky but not sticky.

Oil a glass or pottery bowl. Place the dough in the bowl, rotate so the surface is oiled and cover it loosely. Let it sit until it's doubled in size, about 2 hours. Deflate and let rest for 15 minutes. Divide the dough into 12 pieces and form them into equal-sized disks. Dust them with flour and let rest for 20 minutes.

Heat a cast-iron frying pan on low for about 10 minutes. Sprinkle it with cornmeal and lay down as many muffins as fit without touching. Cook them on each side for 5 to 7 minutes, letting them brown but not burn. Repeat with the rest until you're done. Let the muffins cool and then split with a fork. Try them with blueberry jam and sour cream for breakfast, or toast them next day for yummy eggs Benedict. These muffins freeze well.

Makes 12 muffins

1 cup (250 mL) active sourdough starter

2 cups (475 mL) all-purpose flour

1 tsp (5 mL) dry yeast

2 tsp (10 mL) salt

2 Tbsp (30 mL) softened butter or oil

1 Tbsp (15 mL) sugar or honey

2/3 cup (160 mL) lukewarm milk

SOURDOUGH ENGLISH MUFFINS WITHOUT YEAST

Here's an alternate version, for when your starter is up and running—these could well work at Day 11 or 12 of boot camp. Try it, with some of that discarded starter. They too, freeze well; try them on Sunday morning after you've made **Smoked Salmon** (page 157) for some excellent eggs Benedict.

Sponge develops 8 to 12 hours or overnight; next day takes about 2 hours, from start to finish.

½ cup (125 mL) active sourdough starter

3 cups (700 mL) all-purpose flour

1 cup (250 mL) warm water

½ tsp (2.5 mL) baking soda

½ tsp (2.5 mL) salt

2 Tbsp (30 mL) sugar

cornmeal

Combine starter with 2 cups (475 mL) of flour and warm water. Stir, cover loosely and leave out overnight.

In the morning, add baking soda, salt and sugar to the dough and gradually add the remaining flour, 2 tablespoons (30 mL) at a time, until the dough looses its stickiness. Knead until it's a cohesive ball and let the dough rest for 20 minutes. Divide into 12 portions, form each into a ball, flatten slightly and leave to rise, covered, 45 minutes. Cook in an iron frying pan sprinkled with cornmeal, as in previous recipe, **Sourdough English Muffins, with Yeast**, from 5 to 7 minutes each side.

Makes 12 muffins

TWO-DAY SOURDOUGH BREAD, A BASIC RECIPE WITH VARIATIONS

Starter develops in 8 to 12 hours or all day, sponge develops 8-12 hours or overnight; rising time about 4 hours of second day.

Note: this bread rises once, in the pan. Use a non-reactive pan in order to avoid rusty bread!

Day 1, morning

Feed the starter:

Stir flour and water into starter, cover loosely and leave in warm place for 8 to 12 hours.

½ cup (125 mL) starter

1 cup (250 mL) all-purpose flour

1 cup (250 mL) warm water

Day 1, evening

Return ½ cup (125 mL) of your now bubbly, active starter to the fridge.

To the remaining starter, add:

> 2 cups (475 mL) all-purpose flour
>
> 2 cups (475 mL) warm water

Leave out all night, loosely covered. This is your sponge, and will form the basis of your bread tomorrow.

Day 2, morning (Making the Bread)

To the sponge, which will now be bubbly and smell nice and yeasty, add:

> 2 Tbsp (30 mL) maple syrup, birch syrup or honey
>
> 2 cups (475 mL) all-purpose flour, plus 1 additional cup (250 mL) flour— maybe more, see cautionary tale.
>
> 1 cup (250 mL) rolled oats
>
> 2 Tbsp (30 mL) salt

Once you've gotten comfortable with the basic dough, you can create your own variations.

1 cup (250 mL) pumpkin seeds

2 Tbsp (30 mL) fennel seeds

Or

¾ cup (180 mL) pitted, chopped Kalamata olives—remember to reduce salt by half

¼ cup (60 mL) sun-dried tomatoes, soaked and chopped

1 Tbsp (15 mL) dried rosemary

1 tsp (5 mL) dried sage

With a Mixer

Pour the starter into the bowl, add the maple syrup, rolled oats and 2 cups (475 mL) of flour and mix on low speed with the paddle attachment for 5 minutes, gradually adding the final cup of flour until the dough pulls away from the side of the bowl. (You might not need the whole cup of flour, and you might need more than a cup, depending on your flour, the weather and other vagaries beyond your control.)

Change to the dough hook and knead at medium-low speed for 8 to 10 minutes. Add pumpkin and fennel seeds or other options near the end of the kneading. Let the dough rest in the bowl, covered, for 20 minutes. Knead again on medium-low for 5 minutes, gradually adding the 2 tablespoons (30 mL) of salt.

By Hand

(Keep your hands and the work surface lightly floured at all times, and know that things will be sticky for a while.)

Stir the maple syrup, flour, oatmeal and optional additions into the sponge and gradually add the reserved cup of flour until the dough is too stiff to stir with a spoon any longer. Turn the dough out onto a lightly floured surface. Keep the remainder of the reserved flour handy. Work the dough for a few minutes: draw all the edges into the centre, fold the dough in half, press the seam closed with the heel of your hand, push the dough away from you, give it a quarter-turn and repeat. Then, using one hand, fold the dough in half away from you, grab one end, lift it into the air and whack it onto the surface. Do this over and over for 8 to 10 minutes, adding just enough flour to keep the dough from sticking to the work surface. By the end the dough will still be slightly sticky but will pull away from the work surface easily.

Let the dough rest on the lightly floured surface, covered with a towel, for 20 minutes.

Knead again for 5 minutes, sprinkling salt over the dough a bit at a time until all the salt is incorporated.

Both Methods Continue as Follows

Divide the dough in two. Let one piece rest while you shape the other into a ball or *boule*: pull the edges into the centre and pinch them together; rotate the dough on the work surface with your hands cupped around it, guiding into a rounded shape with gentle, steady pressure. Repeat with the second piece.

For round loaves, for the rising period I place the boule in a kitchen bowl lined with parchment paper that has been dusted with flour. Once the dough has finished rising, I either place the loaf, still in its parchment paper, onto a baking sheet (the parchment paper peels off easily when the bread is done) or, now that I've got a baking stone, slide the loaves off the paper onto the heated stone. The dough holds its shape quite well with either method.

To shape the dough to fit an 8-by-5-inch (20-by-13-cm) rectangular bread pan: Flatten the boule into a 9-inch (23-cm) circle. If you are adding Parmesan, sprinkle it over the flattened circle. Fold the near edge into the centre and tuck in the ends. Turn the dough so the far edge is now the near edge, fold it into the centre, tuck in the ends and pinch the seams closed. Place seam-side up in an oiled pan and then flip over so the smooth side is uppermost and covered in oil.

Let the dough rise in a warm place covered with a towel for 4 hours or until doubled in size.

When you're ready to bake, preheat the oven to 450F (230C). Place a pan of boiling water in the oven. Slash each loaf twice with a sharp knife held at a 45 degree angle. Put into the oven immediately and bake for 10 minutes. Remove the water and bake for another 10 minutes. Now wedge the oven door open a crack and bake for a further 5 to 10 minutes, watching closely so the crust doesn't scorch.

Turn the bread out onto a rack and let cool before slicing— it will be hard to resist having a piece right away but better for the bread in the long run.

A Cautionary Tale:

The very day I thought I had this recipe nailed, the dough acted in a way I had never seen before: during the kneading phase in the mixer it developed long, stringy strands of gluten, and seemed to want more and more flour. I added another cup and a half of all-purpose flour and kneaded a few more minutes. Then I let it rest for 20 minutes before adding the salt, and kneaded again for 3 minutes. The dough never did pull away from the bowl. I dumped it onto the counter and kneaded for a few short minutes by hand. The resting period had done its trick— the dough was fine, though stiffer than usual because of the extra flour, and the bread was as good as ever. Later I learned that the addition of salt often makes the dough get stiff and pull away from the sides of the bowl—you'll often see this happening when you add the salt after the 20-minute resting period, but not always. The lesson is, flour is unpredictable, starter is unpredictable, and the baker must be prepared to improvise. The more you work with sourdough starter and dough, the more you'll learn. Go by the look and feel of the dough and when in doubt, let it rest.

THIRTY-SIX HOUR SOURDOUGH BUTTERMILK CINNAMON ROLLS

(Breathe deeply, drink lots of water. This one is a marathon.)

Starter develops 8 to 12 hours or all day, sponge develops 8 to 12 hours or all night, next day, total rising time for dough as much as 8 hours, for shaped buns 2 to 3 hours, for a total of 10 to 11 hours.

Cinnamon rolls are ubiquitous in the Yukon. The infamous Braeburn Lodge version, on offer at this favourite pit-stop on the North Klondike Highway, weighs about five pounds (okay, that's an exaggeration) and takes an entire drive to Dawson City to consume. But it's hard to find a good cinnamon bun recipe to reproduce at home, one that gets the right balance between dough and filling, whose dough is neither leaden nor overblown, and whose filling is rich without being too greasy or too strong on the cinnamon.

By the time I finished testing sourdough cinnamon roll recipes, there was rebellion afoot chez moi. At the fourth attempt, my husband said, "I'd be just as happy to see the bulk of those leave the house." You can hardly blame him; the testing season extended from May into October. In one cold wet week in October I made four different batches. My mother, who was visiting, did not mind. When I finally found the right combination of starter, flour and other liquid ingredients, the right proportion of filling to dough, Hector agreed to be the guinea pig, one last time. I waited for the verdict as he sat at the kitchen counter, tasting, looking at the ceiling, tasting again. "You know," he pronounced, "These are heavenly." I can safely say he's right: the dough is light and billowy, the filling is rich but not too sweet or cinnamony, and the brown sugar caramelizes on the bottom of the rolls in the oven to become both chewy and crisp.

The watchword here is patience: the first rising can take anywhere from 4 to 8 hours. The second rising is much faster, from 2 to 3 hours; be vigilant starting at 2 hours to ensure the rolls don't over-proof.

Opposite: There is a resident fox in downtown Whitehorse, if you're quick you can spy him slipping over a fence.

Day 1, a.m.

Feed the starter:

> 2.5 oz/70 gr (¼ cup/60 mL) starter
>
> 2.5 oz/70 gr (½ cup/125 mL) all-purpose flour
>
> 3.5 oz/100 gr (½ cup/125 mL) warm water

Day 1, p.m.

Add to starter:

> 5.5 oz/160 gr (1 cup/250 mL) all-purpose flour
>
> 8 oz/225 gr (1 cup/250 mL) warm water

Let sit overnight, loosely covered.

Day 2, a.m.

Assemble and bring ingredients to room temperature.

2 oz/56 gr (¼ cup/60 mL) butter

4 oz/110 gr (½ cup/125 mL) sugar

2 eggs

3½ oz/105 gr (½ cup/125 mL) buttermilk

21 oz/615 gr (about 4 cups/1 L) all-purpose flour

½ oz/12 gr (1.5 tsp/7.5 mL) salt

Cream the butter and sugar until fluffy, add eggs, one at a time, then add buttermilk. Add three quarters of the flour and mix thoroughly. Add the rest of the flour gradually, during the mixing stage. If you're using a mixer, change from the paddle to the dough hook and knead for 7 to 8 minutes. The dough may pull away from the sides of the bowl, but not the bottom. Let the dough rest for 15 to 20 minutes in the bowl, covered with a tea towel, then add the salt and knead again for 2 to 3 minutes.

If you're mixing by hand keep your hands and the surface lightly floured. When you get to adding the final portion of flour, mix in the bowl for as long as you can, then flour your hands and the work surface lightly, dump the dough onto the surface and knead for 8 minutes, keeping a scraper handy to help lift the dough when you pick it up to whack it. Let rest for 15 to 20 minutes, then knead again, sprinkling the salt over the dough and incorporating it as you go.

By the time you're finished kneading the dough should be quite tacky, but shouldn't stick fiercely to your hands and the work surface.

Oil a glass, pottery or plastic bowl, dump the dough into the bowl and flip it so the surface is well oiled. Cover with a towel and let stand in a warm place until doubled in bulk. This could be anywhere from 4 to 8 hours.

In the meantime, make the filling.

Filling

Melt the butter and add the remaining ingredients, mixing well. Cook briefly over medium heat, then remove from heat, cool and beat to a good spreading consistency: not too runny. You want it to sit on the dough, not run off.

When it has doubled, punch down the dough, place it between two pieces of lightly floured parchment paper and roll out into a rectangle about 16-by-20 inches (40-by-50 cm). Spread the filling over the dough to within an inch of each edge. Press the filling lightly into the dough. Roll up tightly, starting at a long side, and seal the edge by pinching slightly. Slice evenly into 15 slices and place on a baking sheet or roasting pan lined with parchment paper. The dough will be quite floppy and you'll have to manipulate the pieces into a roundish shape. A baker's scraper is a handy tool for slicing the dough then lifting it onto the tray. You can improvise with a thick-bladed knife and a spatula.

Let rise again until nearly doubled, 2 to 3 hours. Preheat oven to 400F (205C). Bake 20 to 25 minutes; you might need to place a tray under your baking tray to catch drips. (I've started a couple of oven fires with dripping filling.)

When the buns come out of the oven brush their tops immediately with:

¼ cup (60 mL) butter

Cool on the tray for 20 minutes, then move buns, parchment paper and all, onto a rack.

The rolls are delicious with no topping at all, but if you really want to gild the lily, spread them with birch syrup glaze.

Birch Syrup Glaze

Melt the butter, stir in the birch syrup and cream and cook over low heat, stirring often, for 2 to 3 minutes. Drizzle or spread with a pastry brush over the cooled cinnamon buns. The glaze will harden somewhat as it cools.

Makes 15 rolls

½ cup (125 mL) butter

1½ cups (350 mL) brown sugar

3 Tbsp (45 mL) 35 percent cream

2 tsp (10 mL) ground cinnamon

1 cup (250 mL) currants or raisins

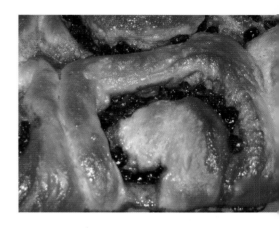

3 Tbsp (45 mL) each 35 percent cream, birch syrup and butter

CHOCOLATE SOURDOUGH TORTE

This texture of this cake is like dense and spongy fudge. The original recipe for "Italian style pudding" was posted on reluctantgourmet.com; I've substituted sourdough starter for corn starch and oil in the original, which makes it less like a pudding and more like a cake. Note that the torte changes its character depending on the size of the baking pan. Baked in a 9-inch pan it is more cake-like, and takes 50 minutes; in a 10-inch pan, it's more like a torte, and in custard cups, served warm, it's closer to a mousse. But whatever the pan size, when this cake/torte/mousse creation is still warm, the pieces of chocolate in the batter are gooey and soft. As it cools, the chocolate pieces harden and become a delicious surprise. This is the best chocolate dessert I've ever had; so rich that icing would be over the top. (But a dab of crème fraîche will never lead a cake astray, and if you choose to add some raspberry sauce I will not argue.)

½ cup (125 mL) unsalted butter

1 cup (250 mL) heavy cream

8 oz (225 gr) bittersweet or dark chocolate

¼ cup (60 mL) cocoa powder

1⅓ cups (325 mL) sugar

4 eggs at room temperature

¾ cup (180 mL) active sourdough starter; a thick starter works best

½ tsp (2.5 mL) salt

Chocolate Sourdough Torte.

Make a ganache: chop 5 ounces (140 gr) of the chocolate and put into a medium-sized bowl. Cut the remaining chocolate into small chunks and reserve. Combine the butter and cream in a small saucepan and bring to a simmer over medium-high heat. Pour the heated mixture over the chocolate, let stand for a few minutes so the chocolate melts then beat well to incorporate the ingredients. Let cool.

Sift the cocoa powder into the sugar and stir well. In another medium bowl, whisk the eggs until they're lemon-coloured and gradually add the cocoa-sugar mixture until the sugar is dissolved, then add the sourdough starter and the salt. Fold the cooled ganache into the egg mixture just until the batter is a uniform colour. Pour the batter into an oiled 10-inch (25-cm) springform pan or 12 individual ¾ cup (175 mL) ramekins. Tuck chunks of the reserved chocolate at intervals into the batter in the cake pans, or into the centre of the batter in the ramekins.

Bake the cake in a preheated 325F (160C) oven for 30 to 40 minutes, or until the edges are set and the centre still looks moist. Bake the ramekins for 25-30 minutes.

Makes one 10-inch (25-cm) cake or 12 ramekins.

Opposite: W camping in July. Wilde heroes, take

CHAPTER SEVEN

The Bush **Gourmet**

On the Land and in the Camp

Camp Cooks

"Dear Tracy,

It's going on 80 straight days of working. My body aches. My back is screwed. My brain fuzzy. My hands are sore with cuts that won't heal and a stiffness that just reverberates when they are at rest. The balls of my feet feel like pressure zones for the first hour I'm walking on them. I think this cooking job is taking its toll on me."

At the end of November, 1996, when Suzanne de la Barre wrote from camp to her sister Tracy back in civilization, she had been cooking for 45 people in an isolated mineral exploration camp in the Yukon, 12 hours a day, 7 days a week for 7 months with only one week off. "I was not well," she says now, in retrospect. And she doesn't mean just physically unwell—she means she was bushed. For the benefit of her starry-eyed interlocutor, who has always dreamed of becoming a camp cook one day, Suzanne catalogued the symptoms of being bushed:

On a clear day you can snowshoe forever.

"Paranoia, hyper-sensitivity, a tendency to overreact and, worst of all, a complete inability to visualize the future." The bizarre thing is, Suzanne was telling me all this as she readied her cook's resume to send out into the world once more. After a break of eight years, she was going back into camp that summer, and she couldn't wait.

They're a strange breed, camp cooks. They have to be, to withstand the isolation, hard work, crazy hours, lack of privacy, bears in camp, nowhere to exercise and the company of anywhere from 5 to 50 people who are working under the same conditions and are very likely to get wingy. Of course, the money's pretty good and you can't spend it anywhere, and there lies the attraction. Camp cooking is great for a quick financial fix, if you need to get out of debt, refinance a project (like buying a restaurant) or pay for an education. Most camp cooks I've met in the North have a whole other resume—Suzanne is a case in point. She has three degrees, has been a travel magazine publisher, an educator, a program officer for an international aid society…the list goes on. Joan Stickney, another pro who cooked for the workers on the South Klondike Highway that winter, is just as versatile—her resume includes stints as a stockbroker, freelance writer and office administrator. Camp cooks don't have to retreat into the bush or the highway camp for months at a time; they do it because they want to.

So what is it that pulls them in? "I'm passionate about cooking. That's what drives me," says Joan. She loved her last job because it gave her so much time to "play"—there were seven men at most, sometimes only four, and on the day we chatted, one. By playing, Joan means doing the fun stuff, getting fancy with desserts, or making little puff pastry shells and filling them with yummy things like creamed shrimp and scallops. It's especially fun to play when you have "no budget," which is code for "spend whatever you need to keep these guys happy." When camp cooks say "There was no budget on that job," they get a dreamy look, lost in happy memories of experimenting without stint, limited only by their hungry crew's willingness to go there with them.

The hungry crew is not always willing to go there—tastes can be old-fashioned in camp. Suzanne's MO was to mix the new and scary with the old standbys. When she introduced something new, like curried vegetables, she served it as a side dish with something familiar and comforting: roast chicken or pork chops. "The important thing is choice," she says. "They may want to try the new thing, but they still want the thing they're familiar with."

Gradually, the crew gets used to the kooky stuff that appears on the table now and then, and even starts to like it. "I don't know how many die-hard meat-and-potatoes guys I've turned on to spanakopita," Suzanne laughed.

Both Suzanne and Joan emphasized that their job is to create a sense of hearth and home, especially in what Joan calls a "grass roots camp," one the company builds from scratch close to the job site, and then strikes when the job is done. In those kinds of camps, often accessible only by plane or helicopter, luxuries like TV and pool tables are unheard of, and "the kitchen is the home," said Joan. "Everybody tends to congregate there, for tea and coffee and cookies and conversation." Suzanne concurred: "My success as a cook was due to my ability to create a happy, social atmosphere."

But then there are the practical skills, like setting up a kitchen in a wall tent, figuring out the intricacies of ordering—what is too much, what is too little? The best teacher is experience, like when you run out of flour and have to tell 50 people there's no dessert, Suzanne said. For five years she worked for a reforestation company in Northern Ontario, cooking for 55 vegetarian tree planters who were musicians, artists and anarchists in their other lives. She had a budget of $10 a day per person, and a working repertoire of 50 dishes—for vegetarians, you have to be smart and versatile. Her requisitioning at the beginning of the season always included a day of running around to health food stores and specialty shops for the ingredients she knew she wouldn't be able to buy locally and couldn't do without: creamed coconut, sesame oil, raspberry vinegar.

In her kitchen in Whitehorse, Suzanne held up a little green box with a yellow and orange logo. "If I didn't have this in camp I was hooped," she said. "This" is a bar of KTC creamed coconut, imported from India, available in the specialty section of most big supermarkets, and in health food stores. KTC creamed coconut is Suzanne's miracle ingredient, a little white rectangle packed with the power to transform inexpensive ingredients like potatoes, onion and chickpeas into a gorgeous Indo-Caribbean curry. Here Suzanne has provided us with both the vegetarian tree-planter and the meat and potatoes drill camp version of her bush curry.

Camp cooks live intensely. "Let's be honest," Suzanne said. "Only type-A personalities do this kind of work." From heating tin cans on an airtight stove in the Richardson Mountains in spring, to suddenly being landed with 38 extra mouths to feed in an oil and gas camp, to dealing with a bushed diamond driller who thinks you're trying to poison him, it's all grist for the camp cook's mill. Lessons learned in camp can be applied to a cook's other life— Suzanne learned this when she went back to school after a long absence and was suddenly faced with writing a paper again. "I panicked. But then I thought, 'It's okay, it's just like organizing a kitchen.' You go from the big to the small. You put the big things like sacks of flour and sugar in the bottom drawer, and then the medium-sized things like cornstarch or icing sugar in the middle drawer, and finally, in the top drawer, the details like vanilla and baking powder and spices."

And then there are the perks, like vast collections of rocks given to the cook by eager geologists. (Both camp cooks confess to forgetting the names of rocks as soon as the season is over.) Or waking up early to find that two diamond drillers have cooked breakfast for you and your assistant. Or taking a helicopter ride through a remote river valley with a pilot who has some downtime. That's the other thing about camp cooking in the North: You get to go places that most of us rarely do, unless we're geologists, or diamond drillers, or tree planters....

For authenticity, and in case you really are a camp cook heading out into the bush, Suzanne's original curry recipe is included here, along with a more recent adaptation with moose. As Suzanne pointed out the night we tested her moose recipe, when you're cooking in camp you wouldn't have moose unless it was given to you. In the Yukon it's not legal to buy or sell moose. So, deep in the bush, surrounded by wildlife, you're much more likely to eat chicken, beef or chickpeas.

The wall tent: a cozy winter retreat.

BUSH CAMP CURRY, FOR CARNIVORES AND VEGETARIANS

Ingredients for both versions

- 1 medium onion
- 2 cloves garlic
- 3 Tbsp (45 mL) butter or oil
- 2 Tbsp (30 mL) curry powder
- 1.5 tsp (7.5 mL) each garam masala and ground cumin
- 1 tsp (5 mL) turmeric
- ½ bar (9 oz / 250 gr) creamed coconut
- 1 cup (250 mL) cilantro, chopped
- Salt to taste

Tree planter version

- 2 cups (475 mL) cooked chickpeas
- 3 cups (700 mL) potatoes, chopped
- 1 cup (250 mL) snow peas
- 1 cup (250 mL) sliced red pepper

Drill Camp version

- 3 chicken breasts cut up for stew
- 1 cup (250 mL) snow peas
- 1 cup (250 mL) sliced red pepper

Sauté the onion and garlic in the butter or oil for about 5 minutes, until onions are soft. Add the curry powder, garam masala and ground cumin. When onions are thoroughly coated with the spice mixture, add the potatoes or chicken, and sauté for 5 to 7 minutes, adding water or a bit of orange juice if necessary to prevent sticking. Add the chickpeas and/or the snow peas, red pepper and chopped cilantro, stir well. Slice thin pieces from the creamed coconut bar and add them one by one, letting the sauce thicken slowly. If sauce becomes too thick, add more liquid. Let the curry simmer, stirring often, until the chicken or potatoes are cooked, about 15 minutes. Serve over rice with pappadums and **Rhubarb Chutney** (page 208).

Makes four servings

SUZANNE DE LA BARRE'S AT-HOME MOOSE CURRY WITH RHUBARB CHUTNEY

In a wide-bottomed sauce pan, heat two tablespoons (30 mL) of oil over medium heat until the surface shimmers, about 3 to 5 minutes. In batches of 10, lightly flour the pieces of moose meat by placing the flour in a plastic bag and shaking the meat inside. In batches, sear the moose meat quickly on all sides; about 1 minute in total. Important: the meat should not be cooked through.

When all the meat is seared and set aside, add more oil to the pan, sauté the onions until translucent, add the garlic and cook 2 minutes more, add spices and cook another 2 minutes. Add the water, mango juice and creamed coconut and cook for 5 to 10 minutes. When sauce begins to thicken return the meat to the pan and cook for a few minutes more, until the sauce is as thick as you want it to be. Serve immediately over basmati rice with chopped cilantro on top and Rhubarb Chutney on the side (next page).

Makes four to six servings

4–6 Tbsp (60–90 mL) olive oil for frying

4 cups (1 L) moose meat, cut into bite-sized pieces

¼ cup (60 mL) flour (you may need a bit more)

1 large onion, thinly sliced (not chopped)

3 cloves garlic, minced

4 Tbsp (60 mL) curry powder (less or more as desired)

1 cup (250 mL) water

1 cup (250 mL) mango juice

1 bar (9 oz / 250 gr) creamed coconut, shaved into thin slices (if you don't have a bar of creamed coconut, substitute coconut milk, about 2 cups / 475 mL)

1 cup (250 mL) fresh cilantro, chopped

Salt to taste

Curry Powder

2–3 dried red chilies, crushed

1 Tbsp (15 mL) coriander seeds

2 Tbsp (30 mL) fennel seeds

1 tsp (5 mL) cumin seeds

1 tsp (5 mL) ground mace

1 tsp (5 mL) white pepper

2 tsp (10 mL) turmeric

1 tsp (5 mL) ground coriander

1 tsp (5 mL) ground cardamom

¼ tsp (1 mL) ground cloves

Grind seeds together with a mortar and pestle, mix well with ground ingredients and store in a jar.

Tip: If you are not going to serve the curry immediately, cool the sauce and reserve until you are ready to finish cooking the meal. Heat sauce separately, then add meat just a few minutes before serving, and let just heat through. Moose meat will be tender if prepared in this way; it will also be tender if left to cook in the sauce for many hours, for instance if you make the curry in a crock pot and let it cook all day.

Rhubarb Chutney

1 Tbsp (15 mL) oil

2–3 cloves garlic, chopped

¼ cup (60 mL) peeled, chopped fresh ginger

½ tsp (2.5 mL) ground allspice

½ tsp (2.5 mL) dry mustard

½ tsp (2.5 mL) cinnamon

3 cups (700 mL) rhubarb, sliced into ¼-in (6-mm) pieces

¼ cup (60 mL) fresh cranberries

1¼ cups (300 mL) dark brown sugar

1 cup (250 mL) cider vinegar

¼ cup (60 mL) water

A handful of fresh mint leaves, chopped

Salt and pepper to taste

Sauté the garlic, ginger and spices in the oil over medium-low heat for 1 to 2 minutes. Add the remaining ingredients, bring to a boil, and let simmer until the liquid has evaporated, stirring often, between 20 and 30 minutes. Let chutney stand until barely warm, then spoon into a jar and refrigerate; it will thicken.

Makes about 1½ cups (350 mL) chutney

Opposite: Campfire coffee.

On The Land—Bush Cooking Methods Explored

Who in the North has not entertained fantasies of wilderness disaster? Particularly in April and May, when our seasonal hunger for adventure returns, and we dash madly onto river and lake, into bush and tundra? Examples of real-life accidents abound: the raging river and the lost canoe; the wrong turn taken on the path back to camp; the 10-day spring blizzard deep in the mountain pass. For a former city girl with a penchant for invoking calamity, possible life-threatening scenarios loom around every bend in the river. In these fevered imaginings, I leave the building of shelter or the trapping of small animals to others: it will be my job to cook. The question is, how will I pull my weight, if separated by mishap from pot and grill? One sleepless night a few years ago I realised I don't have a clue, and if I want to resemble the heroine who inhabits my daydreams I'd better bone up. Possibly others, too, could do with a quick refresher in seat-of-the-pants cuisine, hence this exploration of techniques for cooking on the land, using mostly but not exclusively the materials at hand. Disaster is not an essential ingredient: some of these methods are just plain practical in any situation.

Eldria Christiansen of the Tr'ondek Hwech'in First Nation in Dawson City, Yukon used to watch her Elders practise the hot-stone-in-water technique. Red-hot stones are placed in a pot containing water and raw meat, gradually heating the water to boiling point. As the stones cool they're replaced by hot stones fresh from the fire, until the meal is cooked. Before iron pots came on the scene, brought by European newcomers, the birchbark pot was the cooking vessel of choice for most Yukon First Nations, in response to a nomadic life and the need to travel light. Heroines and heroes, extrapolate: your vessel need not be fireproof.

However, it must hold water. Berndt Berglund and Clare E. Bolsby, authors of *Wilderness Cooking*, used a plastic tarp set in a pit, held in place at the rim with sharp sticks or heavy stones. They put supper ingredients in the tarp, filled the tarp with water, and lowered the hot stones into a basket woven from branches. The basket prevented the stones from burning holes in the tarp. While in normal circumstances few of us will dig a pit or weave a basket, especially if we're

Camping near Chuck Creek; a light-filled moment.

practising no-trace camping, the principles are transferable. How about a rain hat and a metal strainer? Or a folding dog's dish and an enamel spoon?

If you're ambitious, or in dire straits, you could make a birchbark pot, but it's tricky business for a beginner. Eldria Christiansen shared her technique over the phone. She gathers her material when the sap is running and the bark comes easily off the tree. She cuts around the tree in two places about 10 inches apart and joins those cuts with a third T-cut, careful not to penetrate the inner, protective layer. She peels off the piece of bark and with a series of origami-like folds, makes a four-sided shape—that's the hard part. She then places another piece of bark overlaid with a willow branch around the rim and stitches the whole thing together with spruce root. Eldria says the pots her Elders made were generally just big enough to cook for a small, nomadic family group. A typical meal was moose or caribou meat cut into small pieces, a lump of fat, and additions such as sage, berries, spruce needles and maybe wild onions. When I asked Eldria if she cooks with hot stones and birch bark pots these days, she hooted with laughter. "I don't think my husband wants to wait for his supper that long!" Eldria's pots usually end up on collectors' shelves.

For real no-muss, no-fuss wilderness heroine cooking, there is the mud or clay method, in which freshly caught fish or fowl is eviscerated, encased in mud and buried in coals. When the meal is ready the mud is peeled away, taking feathers or scales with it, and leaving the meat, juices intact, in a lovely steaming heap in the middle. Some sources say you don't even have to eviscerate, because the innards collect in a ball in the body cavity, won't taint the meat and can be scraped out at the end. We are also advised to look for good sticky clay or mud near rivers or another source of water, remove any stones or sticks to reduce chances of shattering, and to make a hole for the steam to escape. Berglund and Bolsby tell us to roll the clay out in a sheet, put the bird or fish in the middle, and wrap it up, sealing the seams with water—a technique similar to cooking a caribou roast in a pastry package (page 116).

One summer at a national park in Haines, Alaska I inadvertently smoked half a salmon by cooking it, skin-side down, over a very slow fire on one of those standard issue park barbecues, a half-barrel sunk in the ground with an inserted grill. The wood was green and we had no frying pan or aluminum foil but the skin acted as both cooking surface and container, holding the fish together—I didn't turn it—and the flesh was fabulous, both smoky and sweet. You can do the real thing by making a couple of tripods from thick branches and twine (spruce root if you're truly adept) and lashing a number of poles to the tripods. Hang meat or fish (skin attached) in strips over the poles. Build a fire and as coals form drag them under the marvelous structure you have made and voila! You are now smoking fish. Be careful not to burn the structure by piling coals up too close to the tripods or the poles.

In most national parks, outside of designated camp-grounds, making a fire with the wood at hand is strictly verboten; on tundra it's plain tough going. Guides who work for the Whitehorse-based Nahanni River Adventures on the Firth River in Ivvavik National Park have developed ingenious methods of coping, producing roast beef dinners, lasagnas, cinnamon rolls and chocolate cake with a few charcoal briquettes, two aluminum roasting pans and a Dutch oven. Get the briquettes burning in a tin can, then place eight briquettes in a row along the bottom of one roasting pan, in which you've made four piles of stones. Place the Dutch oven, containing your roast, the potatoes, the onions, the sage and the butter on the stones (so it won't crush the briquettes), and put twelve more glowing briquettes on top. Cover with the second aluminum roasting pan, wait an hour and a half and there you have it: a full roast beef dinner and many amazed and happy campers.

Brian Groves, who moved to Whitehorse from Ontario in the mid-2000s, swears by the reflector oven, a folding box made of sheet metal or aluminum whose open side faces the fire. Two angled surfaces reflect the fire's heat onto a cooking shelf in the middle. Access to the shelf is from above or behind. Heat control consists of moving the box closer to the fire; Brian notes that coals provide the best heat. He suggests building a three-sided fire pit, with the oven making the fourth side, and chopping wood to a consistent size. Brian makes up a dry bannock mix in quantities to last the whole trip—it becomes pizza or calzone dough, fresh-baked bread or, like the time he and his partner Garnet Muething camped in a blueberry patch, blueberry coffee cake. He presses the dough into a frying pan, places it on the shelf and watches like a hawk, turning frequently. The bannock's done when a matchstick inserted into the middle comes out clean.

All of these methods are quirky and take time to master, but with patience, you will soon produce yummy meals and earn your wilderness hero/ine badge.

BRIAN GROVE'S BASIC DRY BANNOCK RECIPE

Bannock and tea over the campfire.

1¾ cups (420 mL) flour

½ tsp (2.5 mL) salt

1 Tbsp (15 mL) baking powder

1¼ cups (300 mL) milk powder

Mix all ingredients thoroughly and store in a resealable plastic bag. When ready to bake, add:

¾ cup (180 mL) water

¼ cup (60 mL) oil

Bake in a reflector oven for 20 to 25 minutes, or in a frying pan lightly coated with oil for 20 minutes, watching closely.

Yield: One 9-by-9-inch (23-by-23-cm) pan.

GARNET MUETHING'S BLUEBERRY COFFEE CAKE

Basic bannock recipe, above, including water and oil

1 tsp (5 mL) vanilla

¾ cup (180 mL) brown sugar

½ tsp (2.5 mL) cinnamon, or more to taste

1 cup (250 mL) blueberries

Mix vanilla in with basic bannock mix. Press half of bannock mix into a 9-by-9-inch (23-by-23-cm) pan. Spread berries, sugar and cinnamon over dough. Add dollops of remaining dough on top of berries and press down. Don't worry about gaps, the blueberries and sugar will bubble up between the lumps of dough and caramelize slightly. Follow cooking instructions above, for oven or frying pan method.

Makes one 9-by-9-inch (23-by-23-cm) cake.

Survival Food

In the summer of 2009, Ed Wardle, a British cameraman and adventurer who had recently climbed Mount Everest, came to the Yukon equipped to make a *Survival*-type series with himself as the subject for the BBC and National Geographic television. He went off into the bush on his own with an array of audio-visual equipment, a sack of oatmeal and one of rice, two sachets of spice, a rifle and a Dutch oven. His goal was to spend three months with no human contact living entirely off the land. Every seven days or so he cached the week's filming in a pre-arranged spot, and hid behind a tree when the crew came to pick it up by boat or plane; the crew monitored his safety using a GPS tracking system, and his video diaries were uploaded weekly onto the National Geographic website so viewers could follow his story. After fifty days he knew he had reached his limit, and called in the crew to take him out.

His sojourn in the woods was in some ways fully supported, but because of the restraints he had put in place, he was essentially on his own. His story is singular in two ways: though fit, his bush lore was fairly minimal, so he became a kind of everyman; he could have been us. Then, as an adventurer and a skilled mountaineer he was accustomed to looking on the bright side in dangerous or stressful situations, in order to boost his own or others' morale. But for the purposes of the series, he had to play up the difficulty and the danger, he had to emphasize his own loneliness and fear, which had a debilitating effect on his morale.

On his way back home to London one day out of the bush, Ed agreed to give me the lowdown on cooking porcupine. Ed was restricted from shooting fur-bearing animals or large ungulates by Yukon hunting regulations. He could, however, shoot porcupine, and was able to catch two, one during his first week and the other a few days before he came out.

The big surprise was the porcupine liver, quite large and quite tasty, he said. He cooked the liver in the upside-down lid of his Dutch oven on hot coals, and then skewered the rest on a spit and roasted it over the fire. Not a success; the meat turned black and tough and he lost a lot of fat. The next day he stuffed the remainder in a pot with some chiming bell flowers and fireweed; Ed says the chiming bells

Labrador tea steeping on an open fire.

taste a bit like oysters, so they were good accompaniment to the fish that he caught, but they had other virtues as well. "They're not like spinach, they don't turn to mush. I boiled porcupine and oyster leaves for a good hour, and they were still like leaves. They're an amazing plant."

Ed's second porcupine, which he caught a week before he came out, he didn't bother to spit roast, but skinned, cut up and put directly into the pot. "That was much better, in terms of trying to survive out there, because there's quite a lot of fat, in a porcupine." The back legs were the best, he said. "I almost managed to convince myself they were like lamb shanks. It was like a cross between a lamb shank and a piece of rabbit that's been hanging for a few days." He made that porcupine last three days, which provided welcome relief from the daily anxiety of finding food.

Asked if he had tips for others who might find themselves in a survival situation, Ed said, "If you're in a situation where you're going to need to eat a porcupine, then go for it, don't put it off. I didn't go for the first one I saw, because I thought, 'Oh look at that unusual creature, I've never seen one before, it's quite cute.' A few days later I regretted not shooting it, because I was quite hungry. And bring seasonings with you; chilies and anything that will take the flavour away."

He noted that hunger helps you lose the feeling of disgust. He found himself swallowing small fish whole, when he would normally have thrown them back. After a while he found that when it came to eating, he had to tone down the on-camera negativity. "I almost put myself off, because I had to say on camera how awful it was, but in the end I had to stop myself and say on camera, okay, I'm going to stop saying bad things now because in a couple of minutes I'm going to have to eat it, and the more bad things I say the harder it's going to be to eat it."

There were intense rewards to feeding himself, apart from the survival aspect. "Every time I got a few fish and leaves and berries, I'd be really pleased with myself and think, I'm doing it, I'm doing it!" But a glimpse of his arms and legs, growing skinnier and skinnier, would throw him into depression again. "I'd think, 'Ah, you're great. You cooked one full meal in four days! And it's getting to the point where you can't stand up properly anymore.' I was

Ptarmigan in summer colours.

feeling really dizzy most of the time, and filling myself up with hot water."

In the end, it was time to pull the plug. "I suddenly discovered that I was starving really badly, and doing really badly, and my world kind of closed in around me. I thought, I'm weak now, and this is no place to be a weak man, you've got to get up and chop wood every day, walk a few miles, catch fish and walk back again. As soon as you've lost a certain amount of weight, it's time to get out, really. It was an interesting experience, starving, but really unpleasant in the end." That night, Ed ate a burger and drank numerous pints of beer, and the next morning he was on the plane to London.

For the record, my early edition of *Joy of Cooking* advises hanging the porcupine for 48 hours before cooking, soaking overnight in salted water in the refrigerator (a cool Yukon night would do), bringing the porcupine to a boil in the soaking water, discarding that water, placing the porcupine in cold water to cover and bringing to a boil again, and finally, cooking it with an onion, a rib of celery, three cups of water or light stock, salt and pepper, and simmering it until tender, about 2 hours and 30 minutes. And there you are, your survival rations, should you need them, and if you are lucky enough to catch a porcupine three days before you absolutely need to eat it.

MOOSE LAKE LASAGNA IN A POT

Whitehorse resident, ski instructor, hiking enthusiast and sometime wilderness guide Colleen O'Brien enjoys a reputation amongst her friends for the best low-weight, delicious and nutrition-rich hiking fare going, perfect for that 10-day trek in Kluane National Park, when you must carry on your person everything that will sustain you. Colleen notes that though it's a lot of work to make a whole lasagna, cool it, cut it into small pieces and dry it, the end result is worth it, for example on day four, when you've slogged through the willows for ten hours and have finally reached the alpine. Colleen says, "I like this lasagna recipe for two reasons. Firstly, the whole meal is in one pot and it cooks up really quickly. Secondly, it is a rather hearty looking and tasty meal. It somehow feels more fulfilling than just pasta and sauce."

1 Tbsp (15 mL) olive oil

1 medium onion, chopped small

2–4 garlic cloves, crushed

2 lbs (900 gr) of ground moose meat

2 jars (6 cups / 1.4 L) of your favourite pasta sauce (Cathy notes that you can make your own, but in the rush of getting ready for a trip those jars come in really handy.)

1 Tbsp (15 mL) brown sugar

½ tsp (2.5 mL) each of basil, oregano and marjoram

¼ tsp (1 mL) sage

Salt and pepper to taste

½ cup (125 mL) red wine

Continued on next page

Part 1 (At Home)

Preheat oven to 350F (175C).

Sauté the onions and garlic in olive oil over medium heat until the onions are nearly translucent. Add moose meat and cook until browned. Set aside.

In a large sauce pan combine the pasta sauce, brown sugar, herbs, salt and pepper and bring to a simmer. Add the moose meat and the red wine and return to a simmer for 5 to 10 minutes.

Assemble the lasagna in a 9-by-13-inch (23-by-33-cm) pan, alternating layers of sauce, noodles, vegetables and cheese.

Cover and bake for 35 minutes then uncover and bake for another 5 minutes. Remove the lasagna from oven and let stand for 10 minutes.

Cut up the whole lasagna into small pieces (approximately 1 inch/2.5 cm squares) and spread out evenly on dehydrator trays or baking trays lined with parchment paper. Colleen says, "Looks like a mess!"

Dehydrate in a food dryer or in a 150F (65C) oven until the noodles are brittle and sauce mixture is dry. Once dried, place the lasagna in an airtight plastic bag or container; 6 ounces/165 grams is generally a suitable portion for one adult.

Part 2 (In Camp)

Place dried lasagna in a pot. Add just enough water to cover and slowly bring to a simmer, stirring often to avoid sticking. Cook until noodles are rehydrated. (Add water if necessary—you are aiming for the consistency of a thick stew.) Voila, portable lasagna!

Garnish with grated Parmesan cheese.

Makes eight servings

12 lasagna noodles, cooked to *al dente* and rinsed in cold water

1 lb (454 gr) sliced mushrooms

1 large green pepper, chopped

1 zucchini, sliced thinly

8–12 oz (225 to 350 gr) mozzarella cheese, grated

Sturdy lasagna-fed hiker's calves.

BOREAL BUSH BREAKFAST

This northern-North African variation on the traditional oatmeal breakfast is an invention of former Yukoner Georgina Brown, an eager hiker and paddler who developed a fine repertoire of easy-to-make, delicious camping dishes in the decade that she lived here. Georgina was such an eager wilderness adventurer that she drove out to paddle the Takhini River once in early May and discovered that the river was still slush and barely moving. Nonetheless, she and her paddling partner put in and slogged through a few slow kilometres before admitting defeat.

1½ cups (360 mL) instant milk powder (Note: the milk powder must be instant)

¼ cup (60 mL) brown sugar

1½ tsp (7.5 mL) dried grated orange peel*

½ tsp (2.5 mL) cinnamon

¼ tsp (1 mL) salt

¾ cup (180 mL) dried, instant couscous

⅓ cup (80 mL) chopped dates

⅓ cup (80 mL) dried cranberries

Combine all ingredients except cranberries and put in a sealable bag. Pack cranberries separately.

In camp, soak cranberries in 2 cups (475 mL) water for 15 minutes, then stir in remaining ingredients and bring to a boil, stirring constantly to avoid burning the milk. Simmer for 5 to 6 minutes, remove from heat and let stand, covered, for a further 5 minutes. Then, as Georgina says, "Eat it up!"

* Georgina grates orange peel and leaves it to dry overnight. She says, "If you use moist peel and then let the bag sit for an indefinite period of time ('well, I didn't use it this trip so I'll save it for next year…') then Auntie Mould might come to visit."

Makes two to three servings

Dried Wild Cranberries or Blueberries

Dried wild berries are not as soft as the commercial varieties, which are often coated with vegetable oil to retain moisture. The wild version, after drying, tends to be quite hard, and not good for eating as is. However, dried wild berries reconstitute nicely in cooked dishes, and are therefore great staples to pack on hiking or paddling trips and throw into sweet or savoury dishes. They can start rehydrating in the cooking water while you get the rest of the meal organized.

Spread picked-over, washed berries on baking sheets lined with parchment paper and bake in a 170F (80C) oven overnight, or follow the instructions for your food dryer. The next day, let berries cool to room temperature, pour into jars and store in a cool, dark place.

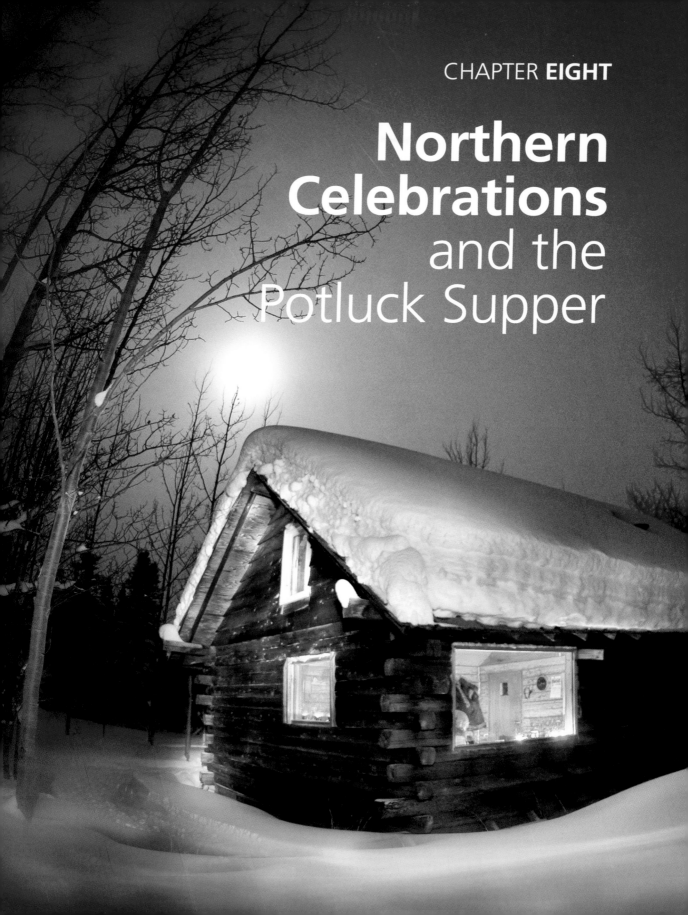

CHAPTER EIGHT

Northern Celebrations
and the
Potluck Supper

Feasts and potlucks are at the centre of social life in the Yukon. There are two reasons: first, we live far apart from each other, scattered along highways, strewn amongst suburbs and country residential enclaves and tucked away in off-the-grid homesteads. Even within Whitehorse city limits you can be separated from your posse by many kilometres of blacktop or bumpy road. Potluck suppers close the gap, especially in winter, bringing far-flung neighbours and friends together, acting as community glue. Second, we are a territory of food enthusiasts in a place where good cafés are plentiful and there are some excellent restaurants, but never quite enough to satisfy our craving for the new and the delicious. And so the feast or potluck becomes the avenue for experimentation, for discovery of unfamiliar cuisines, for flexing the culinary muscles and pulling out new tricks.

These iconic events range in size and formality from the community-wide potlatches held in First Nations halls to the shambling, steamy, woolly affairs thrown by cabin dwellers, where the entrance is clogged by Sorel boots and Salvation Army parkas and you have to clamber over four laps, three dogs and a visiting grandmother to get to your seat at the table. Sometimes we tire of potlucks, of the haphazard menus or the preponderance of fruit and berry crisps; we grow weary with the person who only ever brings tortilla chips and salsa or the one who arrives in the middle of the chaos with a bagful of groceries and says, I have to make my scalloped potatoes/moose Bourguignon/five-stage dessert here, you don't mind do you? (Recently I issued a decree: for potlucks *chez moi*, dishes must arrive plated and ready to serve. Ooh, potluck bitch-queen! But it's working....)

However, the weariness vanishes with each new invitation, with each new foray into cookbooks, magazines and the Internet as we search out the untried and the delicious with which to wow our friends. From the limited cultural perspective of someone who has attended Yukon potlucks in a smallish social circle for fifteen years, I would say the fare has vastly improved, and the level of both adventure and expertise is elevated and even intimidating. So gathered here is a collection of feast-worthy items arranged into menus, but separable as individual dishes you can be proud of when the groaning board is assembled and the hungry punters circle, plates in hand, ready to pounce.

The Vernal Equinox or Easter Celebration

Dall Sheep with Preserved Lemon, Olives and Prunes,
Baked Polenta, Eggplant Baked in the Oven, Green Salad with Mint, Cilantro
and Sesame-Miso Dressing, Birch Syrup Pie with Ice Cream or Crème Fraîche

This somewhat Mediterranean menu was inspired by the Greek practice of roasting young lamb or goat for the great Easter celebrations, when the feasting starts in the morning and carries on all day. The snowy, muddy Yukon spring bears little resemblance to the Mediterranean, with two important exceptions: the fabulous light and our soaring spirits.

DALL SHEEP WITH PRESERVED LEMON, OLIVES AND PRUNES

Whisk all marinade ingredients together and pour over sheep set in a shallow bowl. Marinate for 3 to 4 hours, turning occasionally.

Remove meat from the marinade and pat dry with paper towels. Discard the marinade. In batches, brown meat in olive oil in an oven-proof casserole over medium heat. Remove and reserve.

Reduce heat to medium-low, add the cumin, fennel, cinnamon, cardamom and juniper and sauté for 2 minutes, then add the onions, shallots, carrots and celery and sauté until vegetables are soft and slightly caramelized, about 10 minutes. Add the coriander, black pepper, ginger, nutmeg and chilies or cayenne, stir so vegetables are thoroughly coated, then add tomato paste and chopped tomatoes. Add red wine, increase heat to medium and simmer briskly until wine is reduced by half.

2 lbs (900 gr) Dall sheep shoulder or rib steak, cut into stew-sized pieces

For the Marinade:

Pulp of 1 **Preserved Lemon** (page 136)

¼ cup (60 mL) olive oil

½ cup (125 mL) white wine

1 tsp (5 mL) tomato paste

1 clove garlic, minced

2 Tbsp (30 mL) olive oil

1 Tbsp (15 mL) cumin seed

2 tsp (10 mL) fennel seed

6 whole green cardamom pods

2-inch (5 cm) piece cinnamon stick

6 juniper berries

1 medium onion, chopped

6 to 8 whole shallots, peeled

2 carrots, chopped

2 ribs celery, chopped

1 tsp (5 mL) ground coriander

Continued on next page

1 tsp (5 mL) ground black pepper

1 tsp (5 mL) ground ginger

½ teaspoon (2.5 mL) freshly grated nutmeg

2 small dried chilies, ground, or 1 tsp (5 mL) cayenne

2 Tbsp (30 mL) tomato paste

1 cup (250 mL) chopped fresh or canned tomatoes

2 cups (475 mL) red wine

1 cup (250 mL) pitted prunes

¾ cup (250 mL) pitted Kalamata or cracked green olives

1 cup (250 mL) strong meat stock

Pinch of saffron threads

1 cup (250 mL) white wine

2 bay leaves

1 **Preserved Lemon** rind (page 136), chopped

Preheat oven to 300F (150C). Add meat and all remaining ingredients to the casserole, stir, cover and return to a simmer. Place in oven and cook, covered, for 1½ to 2 hours. If the sauce is too thin, strain, reserve meat and vegetables, reduce sauce over medium-high heat, turn heat to low and add the meat and vegetables for a final heat-through. A nice way to serve is at the table, in the casserole, with a platter of Baked Polenta on the side.

Makes six servings

Baked Polenta

(adapted from Paula Wolfert's *The Slow Mediterranean Kitchen*)

Bake the polenta while the sheep is cooking.

2 cups (475 mL) coarse-grind cornmeal

8 cups (1.9 L) water

Pinch of saffron

2 Tbsp (30 mL) olive oil

1½ tsp (7.5 mL) salt

Whisk all ingredients together in an oiled, oven-proof casserole. Bake uncovered in a 300F (150C) oven for 2 hours. You don't even have to stir while it's cooking.

After two 2 hours the polenta will be thick but not solid, and will become stiffer as it cools. Either pour into an oiled 9-by-13-inch (23-by-33-cm) baking dish, let set slightly, score with a knife into serving-sized diamonds and keep warm until ready to serve, or heap in an oiled bowl or platter and pass at the table. If you choose the first route, and there are leftover diamonds, grill them on a hot, oiled barbecue for dinner the next night.

Makes eight servings

EGGPLANT BAKED IN THE OVEN

The coriander and eggplant combination, plus the hint of ginger, recalls the Middle East, Asia and Africa; the *Artemisia* brings it home to the North. Bake on the higher rack in the oven, while the polenta and sheep dishes cook on the lower rack.

Place salted eggplant in a large bowl or colander for 30 minutes. Rinse and pat dry. In the meantime, grind coriander seeds in mortar and pestle, add sage and ginger, and grind until combined. Toss eggplant in batches with the olive oil. When thoroughly coated with oil, add the spice mixture a teaspoon at a time, tossing each time to make sure the slices are evenly covered. Bake at 300F (150C) for 1 hour, until outside is crisp and the interior is soft.

Makes six servings

2 large eggplant, cut into round slices ½-in (1-cm) thick and sprinkled with salt on both sides

1 Tbsp (15 mL) coriander seeds ground in mortar and pestle

1 tsp (5 mL) *Artemisia frigida* or other sage

½ tsp (5 mL) ground ginger or ½ inch fresh ginger, chopped

¼ cup (60 mL) olive oil

GREEN SALAD WITH MINT, CILANTRO AND SESAME-MISO DRESSING

The dressing is a variation on **Miso Ginger Dressing** (page 85), but without the ginger because there's lots of ginger in this feast already.

6–8 handfuls of mixed young greens, including new fireweed shoots and very young dandelion shoots, if they have started to appear. Remove the root ends and clean thoroughly

Handful of chopped cilantro

2 Tbsp (30 mL) chopped fresh mint

For dressing:

¼ cup (60 mL) cider vinegar or ⅓ cup (80 mL) fresh lemon juice

3-4 Tbsp (45-60 mL) light miso

2 Tbsp (30 mL) dark sesame oil

½ cup (125 mL) canola or peanut oil

1 cup (250 mL) water

1 Tbsp (15 mL) toasted sesame seeds

Whisk vinegar or lemon juice and miso until smooth, whisk in sesame and vegetable oil and then add water, whisking constantly. Pour over salad, toss, sprinkle with sesame seeds and serve.

Makes six servings

BIRCH SYRUP PIE WITH ICE CREAM OR CRÈME FRAÎCHE

I admit, this Northern take on the Quebecois classic is not terribly Mediterranean, but it's seasonal. Uncle Berwyn and his crew head into the woods in late March; the first bottles of birch syrup appear in stores in late April or early May. You may have to hoard a bottle of last year's syrup if your feast occurs before then. Garnish with pine nuts for a Mediterranean touch.

Pastry

Blend the flour and salt and cut in the fat with a pastry blender or your fingertips until the mixture resembles coarse crumbs. If you're using a food processor, pulse for a few seconds at a time, checking often to make sure you're not over mixing. Sprinkle the water over the flour mixture a tablespoon at time, mixing or pulsing a few seconds, and stop adding water when the dough holds together. Dump onto a piece of waxed paper, gather together into a disk and knead a couple of times. Cut away a third of the dough and reserve for another use. Roll out the remainder between two pieces of waxed paper to a diameter of 10 to 11 inches (25 to 28 cm), for a shallow 9-inch (23-cm) pie plate. Lay the dough out over top of the pie plate and press gently into bottom and sides. Trim off excess pastry, crimp the edges and chill in the refrigerator for 30 minutes.

1½ cups (350 mL) all-purpose flour

¼ tsp (1 mL) salt

¼ cup (60 mL) cold shortening or lard

¼ cup (60 mL) cold butter

3–4 Tbsp (45–60 mL) cold water

> **Tip:** A muffin or tart tray with two-inch cups is a great tool for using up odd bits of pastry and leftover fillings. For small tarts with a pre-cooked filling, reduce the blind baking time to 10 minutes and bake for another 20 minutes at 350F (175C); for small quiches or tourtières, coat tarts with egg white first, add the filling and bake for 30 minutes at 350F (175C).

Filling

Combine sugar, syrup and cream in a saucepan and bring to the boil over medium heat. Simmer for 10 minutes, stirring often, making sure it doesn't boil over. Transfer to a bowl. Cool to room temperature then whisk in eggs, lemon juice and salt.

Preheat oven to 375F (190C). Blind bake the crust for 10 minutes and let cool to room temperature before adding the filling. Pour filling into crust and place pie on a baking sheet. Bake for 30 minutes, until pastry is golden and filling is bubbly and puffy. The filling will be quite liquid when it comes out of the oven and will set as it cools. Cool on a rack until filling is set, about 40 minutes. Serve at room temperature or if you prefer, chilled, the way my sister likes it. Serve with **Crème Fraîche** (page 150) or ice cream.

1½ cups (350 mL) brown sugar, packed

1 cup (250 mL) 35 percent cream

½ cup (125 mL) birch syrup

2 eggs, lightly beaten

1 tsp (5 mL) lemon juice

Pinch of salt

Makes one 9-inch (23-cm) pie

Circumpolar Summer Solstice Potluck:

Natalie Edelson's Gravlax, Scottish Oatcakes, Sigrun Maria Kristindottir's Beet and Turnip Bisque, Caribou Swedish Meatballs, Rhubarb Squares

Summer solstice celebrations usually happen outside, in the Yukon, and depending on one's circle, may involve drumming, poetry reading, bonfires, dancing, and staying up all night. But no matter what else, a solstice celebration always involves a potluck feast, so in true potluckian fashion, I solicited recipes from my Yukon pals and circumpolar friends and assembled them for this very northern repast.

NATALIE EDELSON'S GRAVLAX

Natalie Edelson's dad was a professional caterer and restauranteur in Ottawa, and Natalie grew up surrounded by food and helped her dad from the age of 10. Natalie moved to the Yukon in 1991, and notwithstanding her Jewish background, now enjoys a reputation as a gourmand with a particular fondness for pork. Together we are in a group of nine pals who self-identify as "The Tastebuds" and take turns hosting feasty get-togethers. Circumpolar note: my Swedish sister-in-law tells me that the use of dill recalls solstice feasts at home in Sweden, when herring plays a starring role.

Natalie says, "Homemade gravlax has come into my life recently for two reasons: First, smoked salmon is pretty much a staple for me, but also quite expensive; and second the Pacific smoked salmon we get here doesn't taste as 'authentically Jewish' as smoked Atlantic nova lox that I grew up with. It was really exciting to invest five minutes of labour (and then the two-day wait period) and be thrilled with the results. Mmm! It is magic to me, as the consistency of the fish changes from sushi-like to lox-like within forty-eight hours. While some people prefer to make the brine busier (adding orange/lemon zest, mustard, coriander seeds or vodka to the fish), I prefer the plainer salmon taste, with the exception of a hint of dill flavour.)"

Place fish in a shallow pan, flesh side up. Mix salt, sugar and pepper together and sprinkle over flesh. Pack the sprigs of dill on top, covering the entire fillet. Wrap tightly with plastic wrap. Place in refrigerator for at least 48, but less than 72 hours. (Natalie says, "I have tried leaving it for three days, and I found the fish a bit too salty for my taste.") After the waiting period, unwrap the fish. You should immediately notice a difference in consistency. Remove dill, gently rinse off excess coating and pat dry. Slice the fillet thinly at a 45-degree angle. Serve on dark rye bread or crackers* with cream cheese, garnish with capers and/or red onions. Be amazed.

*Or oatcakes!–MG

Makes 1 fillet, enough for about 100 thin slices

1½–2 lbs (680–900 gr) salmon or Arctic char fillets with skin on; fresh or frozen and defrosted

5–6 Tbsp (75–90 mL) kosher salt

1–2 Tbsp (15–30 mL) sugar

½ tsp (5 mL) ground white pepper (black pepper works too)

1 bunch fresh dill

(These proportions are approximate; what is important is that the whole top of the fillet is covered with the mixture, so that you can longer see fish underneath the topping.)

SCOTTISH OATCAKES

The Scots in my family prefer a simpler oatcake, made with just oats, flour, soda, salt and fat. However, I've experimented with numerous recipes and to my palate these are the very best. The more sugar you add, the closer the oatcakes come to Hob Nobs or digestive biscuits; great with old cheddar cheese, but not as good with salmon. I advise using the lesser amount to accompany gravlax .

1 cup (250 mL) rolled oats

½ cup (125 mL) quick oats or Bob's Red Mill Organic Scottish Oatmeal

1 cup (250 mL) all purpose flour

1 Tbsp–¼ cup (15 mL–60 mL) brown sugar

½ tsp (5 mL) baking soda

½ tsp (5 mL) salt

½ cup (125 mL) butter

¼ cup (60 mL) 10% cream, more if needed

Preheat oven to 350F (175C). Mix dry ingredients together, cut or pulse the butter in until the mixture resembles coarse crumbs and add the cream until mixture holds together. Dump mixture onto a piece of waxed paper, and with a floured rolling pin, roll out to a thickness of ⅛ to ¼ inch (3–6 mm) and cut with a three-inch round pastry cutter. Bake for 15 to 18 minutes, or until cakes are lightly browned. Cool on a rack and store in cookie tins; these will keep for months.

Makes about 20 oatcakes

SIGRUN MARIA KRISTINDOTTIR'S BEET AND TURNIP BISQUE

Sigrun, inventor of the soup, lived in southern Canada and the Yukon and wrote for the *Yukon News*. She returned to Iceland in 2005, where she is currently doing a PhD in Environment and Natural Resource Studies, focusing on sustainability, at the University of Iceland. But she remains a reporter at heart. We still miss her.

1 medium onion, chopped

1 Tbsp (15 mL) olive oil

1 large white turnip, peeled and chopped

4–6 beets, peeled and chopped

2 medium potatoes, peeled and chopped

4 cups (1 L) beef, moose or caribou stock

1 cup (250 mL) 35 percent cream

½ tsp (2.5 mL) smoked paprika, or more to taste

Salt and pepper to taste

Optional, to garnish:

A splash of gin and a dollop of **Crème Fraîche** (page 150) in each bowl

Sauté the onion in the oil in a thick-bottomed pot until golden, about 10 minutes. Add the remaining vegetables and the stock and simmer until vegetables are soft. Strain the soup into a bowl. In a food processor or blender, purée small amounts of vegetables and liquid at a time until the soup is smooth and creamy. Return to the pot, whisk in cream, smoked paprika, salt and pepper, reheat and serve. Add gin and Crème Fraîche, if using, to individual bowls just before serving.

Makes eight servings

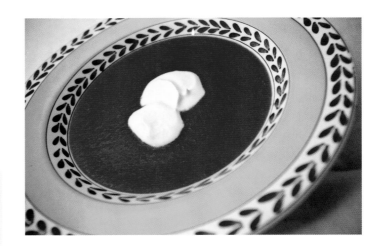

Beet and Turnip Bisque with Crème Fraîche.

Tip: The smoked paprika picks up on the earthiness of the beets and the horse-radishy bite of the turnip, but proceed with caution. The first time I made this soup I went overboard, and added a whole teaspoon of smoked paprika. Too much. Next time, I cut back to one-half teaspoon, which was just right. As the chefs at Le Cordon Bleu in Paris say, "taste, taste, taste!"

CARIBOU SWEDISH MEATBALLS

Combine all ingredients except the butter, working with a fork and using a light hand. Chill mixture for half an hour, then, again with a light hand, form into 1½-inch (4-cm) balls. Chill again for 15 minutes. Melt 1 tablespoon (15 mL) of butter in a cast-iron pan over medium heat and, in batches, brown the meatballs for 10 minutes each, adding more butter as required. Turn down the heat to medium-low if the meatballs are getting hard and crusty on the exterior. The goal is a brown exterior and a light, fluffy interior.

As each batch is cooked, remove and reserve to a baking tray lined with parchment.

¾ lb (340 gr) each ground pork and ground caribou

2 slices day-old sourdough bread soaked in ½ cup (125 mL) milk

1 egg

½ tsp (2.5 mL) salt

¼ tsp (1 mL) freshly ground black pepper

1 small onion, grated

½ tsp (2.5 mL) each allspice and grated nutmeg

2–3 Tbsp (30–45 mL) butter

Sauce

When all the meatballs are browned, add the remaining tablespoon of butter to the pan, whisk in the flour and cook for 2 to 3 minutes. Add the stock, whisking constantly, and cook over medium-low heat until the mixture is thick and the flavour developed, about 15 to 20 minutes. Add the white wine and cook 2 more minutes. Check for seasonings, add an extra pinch each of grated nutmeg and allspice, and turn the heat to low. Whisk in crème fraîche. Return the meatballs to the pan and gently heat through. Serve with **Chocolate Claim Cranberry Chutney** (page 17) and accompany with boiled new potatoes slathered with butter and sprinkled with handfuls of chives.

Makes about 24 meatballs

2 Tbsp (30 mL) flour

1½ cups (350 mL) strong meat stock

¼ cup (60 mL) white wine

pinch each grated nutmeg and allspice

½ cup (125 mL) **Crème Fraîche** (page 150)

RHUBARB SQUARES

Easy, delicious, quick. A perfect ending for a feast, or for the last-minute invite to the bonfire.

4 cups (1 L) chopped fresh or frozen rhubarb

½ cup (125 mL) sugar

Filling

Toss rhubarb with sugar and set aside. If you're using frozen rhubarb, keep frozen and toss with sugar just before assembling.

2 cups (475 mL) all-purpose flour

1 cup (250 mL) sugar

¾ cup (180 mL) chopped pecans

1 cup (250 mL) soft butter

1 egg, beaten

Crumb Mixture

Preheat oven to 350 degrees (175C). Butter a 9-by-9-inch (23-by-23-cm) baking pan. Mix dry ingredients together, then blend in the butter with a fork until mixture is crumbly, adding the egg at the end. Set aside one cup of the crumb mixture. Press remainder onto bottom of pan. Spread the rhubarb filling evenly over top, and crumble the rest of mixture over the rhubarb. Bake approximately 45 minutes, longer if rhubarb is frozen, until lightly browned. Cool and cut into squares.

Makes nine 3-inch (7.5-cm) squares

The Autumnal Feast

Cedar-Planked Salmon with Whisky, Birch and Maple Syrups Sauce, Shaggy Mane and Wild Blueberry Risotto, Carrot, Beet and Rosehip Purée, and Janet Genest's Cheesecake with Spirited Cranberry Sauce

The connection to the Pacific Northwest has always been strong in the Yukon. Before contact there were well-established trading relationships between coastal Tlingit peoples and the Northern and Southern Tutchone peoples of the interior. More recently, gold rushers travelled up the coast from San Francisco and Seattle to Skagway and from there deep into the Yukon, and now the predominantly north–south lines of communication and transport mean we're closer in many ways to British Columbia than to the Northwest Territories or Nunavut. But despite this intimate connection, the venerable West Coast tradition of cooking salmon on a cedar plank has not penetrated the territory: cedar is not found here except as building material. I never tried this simple and delicious dish until the summer of 2009, while visiting former Yukoner Janet Moore on the Opeongo Road near Barry's Bay, Ontario, a long way from the Yukon and the West Coast.

Janet rubbed the flesh of the salmon (Atlantic) with salt, pepper and granulated onion before laying the fillet out on a pre-soaked cedar plank and placing the plank on the grill of a hot barbecue. The plank caught fire and burned slowly, filling the barbecue with smoke and infusing the salmon with the flavour of smoking cedar. When the salmon was ready Janet served it forth with a bourbon and maple syrup sauce. Fabulous.

I came back to Whitehorse all enthused about this newly discovered treat. We had a ready supply of three-quarter-inch thick cedar planks in the pile of wood scraps in the backyard left over from house construction. Hector cut a plank to fit the barbecue, sanded it down and we were in business. (I've since discovered the local big box stores sell cedar planks at $4 a pop. They are thin, and good for just one use. They also tend to flame more easily, so you need to be extra vigilant with the water bottle.)

CEDAR-PLANKED SALMON WITH WHISKY, BIRCH AND MAPLE SYRUPS SAUCE

I experimented with both coho and sockeye salmon for this feast, and much preferred the sockeye; the coho didn't absorb the cedar flavour as fully, and the texture of the flesh was almost mushy. I think coho is more suited to long, slow cooking in the oven, with bright flavours to liven it up. For the sockeye, I devised a birch syrup and spruce tip marinade, to stay within the coniferous theme, but the rosemary and lemon also work well.

½ cup (125 mL) your favourite whisky (mine, for this purpose, is Scapa)

½ cup (125 mL) birch syrup

½ cup (125 mL) maple syrup

1 Tbsp (15 mL) cold butter

1 tsp (5 mL) crushed dried chili peppers or sambal oelek hot sauce

A cedar grilling plank, big enough to hold the salmon

2 Tbsp (30 mL) Dijon mustard

2 Tbsp (30 mL) birch syrup

1 Tbsp (15 L) minced spruce tips (or substitute 1 tsp/5 mL dried rosemary and 1 Tbsp/15 mL grated lemon peel)

Salt and pepper to taste

1.5 lb (680 gr) wild sockeye salmon fillet salmon with skin on

Whisky, Birch and Maple Syrups Sauce

Combine the whisky and syrups in a small saucepan and heat to a slow boil. Simmer until reduced by half, about 10 minutes. Remove from heat and beat in butter and chili peppers or sambal oelek. Set aside and keep warm.

Planked Salmon

Soak the plank in water to cover for 4 to 5 hours. Keep it immersed by placing a heavy bowl on top.

Half an hour before you are ready to start cooking, whisk together the mustard, birch syrup, spruce tips, salt and pepper. Spread mixture onto the salmon flesh and let sit at room temperature for 30 minutes.

Preheat barbecue at medium for 10 minutes. Place salmon on plank, skin side down. If the salmon overhangs the plank, fold in the thinner side to fit. Grill on the barbecue, covered, until salmon is just cooked, about 15 minutes. (As Janet says, be vigilant with the spray bottle to keep the flames down; you don't want a Burning Schoolhouse, just a slow smoulder.) Remove plank and salmon from the heat and let salmon stand on the plank for 5 minutes before serving. Place salmon on a platter, drizzle whisky sauce over top and serve additional sauce in a pitcher on the side.

Makes four servings

The Autumnal Feast: Shaggy Mane and Wild Blueberry Risotto, Carrot, Beet and Rosehip Purée, Cedar Planked Salmon.

SHAGGY MANE AND WILD BLUEBERRY RISOTTO

Remove the shaggy manes from the soaking water and pat dry. Retain one cup of the water. Heat the butter and oil in a high-sided sauté pan over medium heat until the butter foams, add the shaggy manes, sauté until golden brown, about 5 minutes, add garlic and sauté another 2 minutes. Add the rice, stirring so that all the grains are covered in butter and oil, then add dried blueberries. (Wait until rice is cooked to add fresh berries, just to heat them through. Otherwise the dish will be blue.) Add liquid to the pan a half cup at a time, waiting until all the liquid is absorbed before adding the next batch. Stir frequently. It should take about 20 minutes for the rice to cook. Reserve the last half cup of wine and add only if the rice is still al dente after 20 minutes. Add salt and pepper and keep warm over low heat until ready to serve.

Makes four servings

1 oz (28 gr) dried shaggy manes, soaked in warm water for 30 minutes

1 Tbsp (15 mL) each butter and olive oil

2 cloves garlic, minced

1 cup (250 mL) arborio rice

1 cup (250 mL) soaking water

½–1 cup (125–250 mL) white wine

½ cup (125 mL) water

2 Tbsp (15 mL) dried wild blueberries, or ¼ cup (60 mL) fresh

Salt and pepper to taste

Tip: For making risotto, a high-sided sauté pan the same size or slightly bigger than the burner you're using works best. I found that a wide, shallow frying pan tends to cook the rice in the middle but leave the outskirts raw, despite constant stirring. Even a wide-bottomed soup pot is better than a shallow frying pan. Cover the pot between stirs.

CARROT, BEET AND ROSEHIP PURÉE

Bring beets and carrots to a boil in separate pots of salted water, reduce to a simmer and cook beets for 40 minutes and carrots for 30 minutes, or until they still offer some resistance to the fork. Purée together in a food processor, place in the top of a double boiler and reheat over simmering water. Whisk in the rosehip purée and birch or maple syurp, add the cream and butter, and salt and pepper to taste.

Makes four servings

4 medium beets

6 medium carrots, peeled and quartered

½ cup (125 mL) **Basic Rosehip Purée** (page 74)

1 Tbsp (15 mL) 35 percent cream

1 Tbsp (15 mL) butter

1 Tbsp (15 mL) birch or maple syrup

JANET GENEST'S CHEESECAKE WITH SPIRITED CRANBERRY SAUCE

When my parents had dinner parties, this cheesecake was always the grand finale. We kids would hang around on the stairs, waiting until the adults returned to the living room after dessert, and then we would descend and devour. My mother used to make an apricot and strawberry jam topping; she approves of the cranberry and whisky innovation.

The abiding appeal of this cake is the two layers of filling, subtly different in flavour, colour and texture; the first layer is cheesy and rich, the second layer is creamy, smooth and slightly tangy. For the best result chill the cake for at least six hours before serving. My mother used to make it early in the day.

Crust

2¼ cups (535 mL) graham wafer crumbs

½ cup (125 mL) brown sugar

½ cup (125 mL) melted butter

Mix crumbs with brown sugar, then mix in butter. Reserve about 3 tablespoons (45 mL) of the mixture for sprinkling on top of the cake and press the rest into the bottom and sides of a 9- or 10-inch (23- or 25-cm) springform pan. Clean up the top edges by pressing down gently with the side of your thumb. Chill crust for 30 minutes.

Filling, First Layer

2 eggs, well-beaten

1 lb (454 gr) cream cheese, softened

⅔ cup (160 mL) sugar

2 tsp (10 mL) lemon juice

¼ tsp (1 mL) salt

Whisk all ingredients together until smooth and pour into crust. Bake in a preheated 375F (190C) oven for 20 minutes. Remove cake from oven and dust the top with cinnamon. Allow the cake to cool to room temperature.

Filling, Second Layer

2 cups (475 mL) thick sour cream

½ cup (125 mL) white sugar

½ tsp (5 mL) vanilla

Pinch of salt

Mix well and pour over cake. Sprinkle reserved crumbs over top. Bake in 425F (220C) oven for 5 minutes. Permit it to cool, then chill thoroughly until ready to serve.

When ready to serve, heat one cup of **Spirited Cranberry Sauce with Speyside Whisky** (page 19) over medium-low heat, and spoon over each slice.

Makes one a 9- or 10-inch (23- or 25-cm) cheesecake

The Christmas Cassoulet

Northern Cassoulet, Braised Red Cabbage and Apples, Marchpane, or Marzipan, and Cranberry Mincemeat

Two factors influenced the making of this dish: the discovery of a whole goose in the freezer, and the knowledge we were going to spend Christmas in a remote cabin, travelling on Christmas day. Christmas dinner needed to be something that would cook on top of a woodstove, and it had to be both delicious and ceremonial. I'm happy to say the cassoulet succeeded on all three counts. The long, slow preparation at home on Christmas Eve day satisfied the need for ritual so strong at this time of year. Six different kinds of meat, including confit of goose, a cooking liquid made with all the different meat juices fortified with white wine, and buttery-soft lima beans combined to create a rich, subtle and deeply satisfying version of that homey old favourite, pork and beans.

Yes, cassoulet is a farm house, peasanty kind of feast, exactly right for a four-day retreat in a cabin on the edge of the Tatshenshini-Alsek Park. This one changed with every reheating. Different flavours dominated each time: lamb, goose, fennel and orange caribou sausage, Dall sheep. In the candlelit dusk of the cabin we couldn't see the different morsels of meat, and had a great time identifying them by flavour alone. We had a jar of homemade Québécois tomato and apple ketchup as a condiment; its cool piquance was a perfect counterpoint to the cassoulet's warm and earthy flavours. The red cabbage and apple accompaniment here will provide the same piquant contrast.

Note to travellers: We hauled our supplies in on snowshoes, pulling pulks (toboggans) behind us. We simply taped the casserole lid shut and wedged it between boxes on the pulk and it survived the hilly, jolty journey from truck to cabin no problem.

Top: Janet Genest's cheesecake with Spirited Cranberry Sauce: the cheesecake that launched a thousand dinner parties.

Bottom: The cabin-dweller's bonus—a full moon over the mountains.

NORTHERN CASSOULET

Cassoulet is a great adaptor; it will take any combination of meats and become your own creation. Curnonsky reminds us that "true cassoulet" contains only beans and local sausage; freed from the need to be authentic, we can do anything we want. I assembled a northern-western medley that included homemade caribou sausage, side pork from Mission, BC, a goose from Hutterite farmers in Peace River country in Alberta, wild Yukon Dall sheep, spring lamb from Saltspring Island and pork rind from our farm-gate pig raised along the Alaska Highway.

I had both Curnonsky's *Traditional French Cooking* and Julia Child's *Mastering the Art Of French Cooking* open in front of me on Christmas Eve; between them they steered me through the many steps of preparation. The thing you have to get your head around is this: you're cooking beans and meat separately, in different stages, and then you're putting them all together at the end for a final cooking.

In this final stage, both Curnonsky and Julia tell us, the key to success is the brown crust that forms as the cassoulet cooks, which you must push down into the middle of the casserole several times. With our woodstove on the first night in the cabin we were heating a cold cabin and cooking dinner at the same time; the heat was uneven, and the crust tended to form at the sides rather than in the middle. Not that it mattered. But cassoulet cooked on a stove-top over even heat, or in the oven, will form a crust in the orthodox way.

Count on three to four hours of preparation before cassoulet is assembled and ready for its final cooking.

Rinse the soaked beans and place in a pot with water to cover.

Cook pork rind or blanched salt pork rind in simmering water for 30 minutes. Drain, cool and cut into pieces about ½-inch (1.25-cm) square. Add to pot with beans, the piece of side pork or blanched bacon, and the bouquet garni, bring to the boil, turn down the heat to low and simmer for 1 hour and 30 minutes, or until beans are nearly cooked. Remove from heat and drain, reserving liquid. Remove the side pork and reserve. Cover the beans and reserve. (The bits of pork rind will stay in amongst the beans.)

While the Beans are Cooking, Marinate the Lamb and Mutton

Place the meat in a shallow dish, whisk together marinade ingredients, pour over the meat, turn meat to coat thoroughly, cover and leave to sit at room temperature, turning every so often.

Brown the Meats and Assemble the Cassoulet

Melt the fat in a large, oven-proof casserole over medium-high heat and brown all the meat in stages. Begin with the sausages, left whole (later you'll slice them). Remove the lamb and mutton from the marinade and pat dry before browning on all sides. (Remember what Julia says: don't crowd the meat!) Brown the goose pieces briefly, leaving the skin on. As each piece of meat is browned, remove and reserve.

Reduce heat to medium-low and brown the onions in the same fat, adding more if necessary. When the onions are soft and slightly caramelized (about 10 minutes) add the garlic, tomato paste, sage and thyme, and sauté for 2 more minutes before adding wine, beef stock and returning the sausage, lamb and mutton to the pot. If the liquid doesn't quite cover the meat, add enough reserved bean cooking liquid to cover. Add bay leaves, cover and cook in a 300F (150C) oven for 1 hour and 30 minutes. Add the goose for the final 30 minutes.

2 lbs (900 gr) dried baby lima beans, soaked 8 hours or overnight (navy or Great Northern are the traditional beans, but these work beautifully)

4 oz (115 gr) pork rind (substitute salt pork rind, blanched for 10 minutes to reduce saltiness)

1 lb (454 gr) side pork (basically, unsmoked bacon. If you can't find side pork, substitute 1 lb/454 gr of unsliced bacon, blanched for 5 minutes to tone down the smoky flavour)

A bouquet garni: 3 bay leaves, 3 cloves, 1 tsp (5 mL) thyme, wrapped in cheesecloth and tied with string

2 lamb shanks, or about 1 lb (454 gr)

¾ lb (340 gr) Dall sheep rib steak or round roast (substitute moose or venison)

Marinade ingredients:

1 cup (250 mL) white wine

¼ cup (60 mL) olive oil

1 shallot, chopped

3 cloves garlic, minced

1 Tbsp (15 mL) rosemary

Olive oil, butter or melted duck or goose fat for frying

1 lb (454 gr) **Orange and Fennel Caribou Sausage** (page 111) (or substitute chorizo or Italian sausage)

1 leg and thigh and 2 wings of preserved goose (recipe follows) or substitute 2 lbs (900 gr) pork tenderloin, spread with Dijon mustard and 1 tsp (5 mL) thyme and roasted for 1 hour 30 minutes in a 325F (160C) oven—you can roast the tenderloin while the beans cook

2 medium onions, chopped

2 Tbsp (30 mL) tomato paste

Continued on next page

6 cloves garlic

1 Tbsp (15 mL) sage

1 tsp (5 mL) thyme

2 cups (475 mL) strong beef stock

1 cup (250 mL) white wine

3 bay leaves

2 cups (475 mL) breadcrumbs

4 Tbsp (60 mL) melted goose fat or
    butter

When done, remove the meat and let cool. Drain the cooking liquid into a bowl. Debone the lamb and the goose and separate the meat into serving-sized pieces. Cut the mutton into six or eight pieces. Slice the sausages into ½-inch (1-cm) chunks. Slice the side pork widthwise into pieces about ¼ inch (½ cm) thick. If you substituted pork tenderloin for the goose, slice it into ½-in (1.25-cm) thick pieces. You're ready now for the final assembly.

Line the bottom of the casserole with a layer of beans, followed by the side pork, beans, lamb and sheep, beans, goose, beans, sausage and beans. Don't worry if the layers of beans are scant in the middle, but do make sure the final layer is plentiful. Combine the bean and meat cooking liquids and pour over the beans until the liquid is just visible at the rim—don't cover the beans; liquid will bubble up during the cooking. Keep extra liquid in reserve. Tuck three bay leaves into the casserole. Cover with breadcrumbs and drizzle with goose fat or butter.

Cook the cassoulet, uncovered, in a pre-heated 375F (190C) oven, or on top of the stove over medium-low heat for about 1 hour. When the first crust forms, after 20 minutes or so, push it back down into the casserole with the back of a spoon. Turn the oven down to 350F (175C) at this point. Push the crust in two or three times. The crust may take longer to form if you're cooking on top of the stove,; count on 1 hour 30 minutes total cooking time. Serve with crusty, fresh bread, braised red cabbage and apple, with mincemeat tarts and cocoa-marzipan balls for dessert.

Makes 8 to 12 servings—2 people for 4 days

GOOSE CONFIT

This is an excellent project for a winter's day when it's too cold to go anywhere and you want to fill the house with good cooking smells.

Cut the goose into separate parts: breasts, leg and thigh, wings, leaving the skin on. Salt the goose pieces on both sides and refrigerate overnight. Save the skin and fat from the carcass and reserve the carcass to make stock for another use.

Place the skin and fat in a heat-proof casserole, and render the fat slowly over medium-low heat until the skin is shrivelled and the fat is entirely liquid. Reserve—either cool and refrigerate overnight, or put to one side while you sear the goose pieces.

Without rinsing off the salt, place the goose pieces skin side up in a roasting pan. Sear for 15 to 20 minutes in a preheated 425F (220C) oven, or until the skin is golden brown. Place the goose pieces in a casserole and cover with the melted fat, including the fat from the searing process. If the goose is not quite covered, add some of the extra fat, melted. If you don't have extra fat on hand and haven't been able to find duck fat, simply cook the goose in batches. This will extend the cooking time by a couple of hours, so plan accordingly.

Turn the heat down to 300F (150C) and cook the goose for 1½ to 2 hours, or until the meat is tender but still pink. Transfer the goose pieces to a glass or crockery container, cover completely with fat, and store in the refrigerator until ready to use. Will keep for 10 days.

One 10–12 lb (4.5–5.5 kg) goose

Extra goose fat, or duck fat, available at specialty butchers*

In the Yukon where duck fat is hard to find, the cook's best bet is to roast a duck for dinner and save the fat: frozen, it will keep for several months.

Morning or evening? In December, the question is moot.

BRAISED RED CABBAGE AND APPLES

4 cups (1 L) red cabbage, coarsely grated

2 Gala or Spartan apples, cored and chopped

1 Tbsp (15 mL) olive oil

3 Tbsp (45 mL) apple cider vinegar

2 Tbsp (30 mL) fireweed honey

Salt and pepper to taste

Sauté the cabbage in the oil over medium-low heat for 5 minutes, or until the cabbage is slightly softened. Add the apple and sauté for another 3 to 4 minutes, then add vinegar, honey, salt and pepper. Transfer to a casserole and braise uncovered for 45 minutes. Reheat, covered, on the back of the woodstove on a baffle, trivet or a couple of bricks.

A Winter's Tale: Marchpane and Mincemeat

Marzipan is not a northern ingredient, but I first encountered it here, in the Christmas treats baked by friends and neighbours of Dutch and German descent. I fell for marzipan in a big way, and then I remembered where I had come across it before.

Every Christmas or birthday until I was eleven my mother gave me a book by British children's author Rumer Godden. Rumer Godden grew up in India and moved to England as an adult; she once described herself as always longing for one place when she was in the other, an experience that will be familiar to those of us who love the North and love where we came from too.

Rumer Godden wrote about dolls, the children who owned them, and their lives together. A doll might help a misfit child fit in, a shy child gain confidence or a loud, messy child develop grace. The child helped the doll in practical ways, by providing it with a proper place to live and the right clothing, and, if the relationship was in balance, the child loved the doll and played with it, but when doll and child were really in tune, the child heard the doll's unspoken wishes, and did the right thing. As Rumer Godden said, dolls can't talk, they can only wish.

Sometimes the dolls have very serious issues—a child who neglects them, or an angry doll who makes life difficult, or worse. In *The Doll's House*, which my mother gave me for Christmas in 1966, a beautiful, wicked doll tempts a little boy doll towards a burning candle, and the little boy doll's mother throws herself on the flame to save him. She flares up and burns to a crisp while the wicked doll smiles. The wicked doll's name was Marchpane, and I never forgot it.

Last Christmas, for the first time, I iced a batch of fruitcake with marzipan, a thick confection made with almond paste, egg whites and icing sugar. Marzipan was not part of our family tradition, so I had to do some research, and in the course of reading about the history and origins of this ancient sweet, discovered that the old English word for marzipan is marchpane.

It's a gorgeous word, and a lovely name for an old-world treat—why then did Rumer Godden choose it for her wicked doll character? I went back to *The Doll's House* and found this description, provided by Tottie, a no-nonsense, penny-farthing, wooden Dutch doll who is the hero of the story. "Marchpane is a heavy, sweet, sticky stuff like almond icing, very old fashioned," said Tottie "You very quickly have enough of it."

Perhaps Tottie has a point—marchpane is best in small doses, as a thin layer on a Christmas cake, or a two-bite treat in the shape of a flower or a piece of fruit, the kind you find in European delicatessens.

Like Rumer Godden, like many northerners, marchpane is a traveller. Marchpane (or *marzapane* or *mazapán*) came to Europe from the Middle East as early as the Crusades. *Joy of Cooking* tells us that words for marchpane in other languages pay tribute to its preciousness: "a seated king," "a little box," "a stamped coin."

There are legends that place its provenance in Italy—there was a great drought, all the crops were destroyed except almonds, almond soup was invented, and so was *marzapane*. The Spanish say that during the siege of Toledo, eggs and almonds were eventually the only foodstuffs left in the walled city; someone put them together, and *listo! mazapán.*

In modern times marzipan is claimed by a number of countries as a national specialty—many websites assert the only real marzipan can be found in Lubeck, Germany. The Estonians disagree; they say *martsipani* was invented in a pharmacy in Tallinn, and the best marzipan is made by the confectionary company Kalev, located in Tallinn.

In Europe generally, marzipan was first made in pharmacies and used as a treatment for various medieval ailments. With the arrival of sugar from the New World, marzipan production moved from the pharmacy to the kitchen. In England, marchpane became an element in the creation of "subtleties," the final delicacy brought to the table at feasts in great houses. Subtleties were figures made of sugar paste and jelly, sometimes fashioned into complicated allegorical tableaux; guests at the feast had lively debates about the meaning of the allegory before dismantling the concoction and eating it.

The pharmaceutical connection provides a clue as to why Rumer Godden might have named a wicked little doll Marchpane. Sweet almonds provide relief for infections of the digestive tract and other ailments; bitter almonds contain cyanide and must be treated with caution. Some marzipan recipes call for the use of one bitter almond for every one hundred sweet almonds; more might be dangerous. Perhaps Rumer Godden's Marchpane is a sweet confection gone wrong, poisoned by bitter almonds.

In the cluttered pantry of my Christmas memories, marchpane stands next to mincemeat. My mother used to experiment with the great culinary projects demanded by the season. One year she made vast quantities of plum pudding, packed it into bowls, wrapped the bowls in red cellophane and distributed them to friends with instructions for steaming. With the plum pudding project, beef suet (the hard fat from around the kidneys and loins) entered the house for the first time. Grown used to its properties, my mother moved on to mincemeat, the real kind, with ground beef (she ground it herself), suet, apples, raisins and dates. She and my father loved it, but it was too rich for the children, and so the mincemeat experiment was not repeated.

Even now, mincemeat made with suet doesn't appeal to me, largely because of the greasy aftertaste of a cold mince tart. Fortunately there are many delicious meatless mincemeat variations out there in the world, some of them particularly suitable for a northern kitchen, where standard items are sometimes scarce. Mincemeat is forgiving; ingredients can be increased or substituted with ease and it is very amenable to the addition of northern berries. I made up the cranberry version included here; you will be safe if you follow the general guidelines and make your own substitutions.

When I was testing the recipes below, I placed a coin-sized piece of marchpane in the bottom of each tart shell before spooning in the mincemeat. I couldn't taste the marchpane, but it infused the mincemeat with something elusive, like memory, like the mysteries of this season.

Christmas Pudding

MARCHPANE, OR MARZIPAN

This is a two-stage recipe, starting with an almond paste and proceeding to marzipan.

4 cups (1 L) blanched almonds

2 cups (475 mL) sugar

1 cup (250 mL) water

6–8 Tbsp (90–120 mL) cognac, orange juice or kirsch

Tip: I have found it easier to add the almonds to the syrup, rather than the other way around; hence the instruction for a roomy saucepan. Put the pot on a damp tea cloth for stability, and whisk the almonds into the syrup a few spoonfuls at a time, changing to a wooden spoon when the mixture stiffens. Work quickly while the syrup is still warm.

2 egg whites

4 cups (1 L) almond paste, at room temperature

½–¾ cups (125–180 mL) icing sugar

Almond Paste

Grind the almonds very fine, stopping just before the oil separates from the nuts and you have almond butter. Mix sugar and water in a saucepan big enough to accommodate all the ingredients (see tip), bring to the boil and cook at high heat until the temperature reaches 240F (120C), the "soft ball" stage. Watch carefully once the thermometer registers 220F (110C); heat rises quickly at this point.

Cool the syrup to 110F (43C), add the ground almonds and the cognac or other flavouring and stir vigorously until ingredients are creamy. Refrigerate for 12 hours. Dust a flat surface with icing sugar, turn the almond paste out and knead it as you would bread dough, sprinkling icing sugar as needed to keep it from sticking. Stop kneading when the paste becomes easy to handle but still liable to stick to the counter if you let it sit. The almond paste is perfectly useable (and delicious) at this point, for use in stollen or other Christmas treats. Or you can carry on and make marzipan, slightly sweeter and a little more malleable.

Marzipan

Whip egg whites until they hold stiff peaks and mix into almond paste. Sift the sugar into the mixture and mix thoroughly. Sprinkle icing sugar on the counter and knead the marzipan until it is pliable and yet firm enough to hold its shape.

For cocoa marzipan balls, pinch coffee spoon-sized pieces of marzipan with your fingers and roll them into balls between the palms. Sift cocoa powder onto a plate, and roll each ball until thoroughly coated. Harden overnight, uncovered, in the refrigerator, and then store in cookie tins or add to Christmas cookie baskets.

CRANBERRY MINCEMEAT

Combine all ingredients in a saucepan with a heavy bottom. Cook uncovered over low heat, stirring often, until apples are tender about 45 minutes. Mincemeat can be stored in the fridge for up to a week, and in the freezer for three months. For canning, pack while hot in hot, sterilized jars, seal with two-piece metal lids and immerse in a boiling water bath for 5 minutes. Store in a cool dark place.

Makes about 6 cups (1.5 L)

To make mincemeat tarts, follow the instructions for **Short-crust Tart Shell**, page 20. Roll pastry out between two pieces of waxed paper, and use a 4-inch (10-cm) round pastry cutter to cut out 12 tarts, and fit them into the cups of a muffin tin. Chill pastry for 30 minutes, then pre-bake for 10 minutes at 375F (190C). Cool to room temperature and fill shells with mincemeat, about 2 cups (475 mL) in total. Bake for 30 minutes, or until pastry is golden.

Makes 12 tarts

2 lb (900 gr) baking apples (such as Ambrosia, Gala or Spartan), cored, peeled and chopped in small pieces

1½ cups (350 mL) fresh or frozen wild cranberries

1 cup (250 mL) golden raisins or chopped dried pear

1 cup (250 mL) Thompson raisins

1 cup (250 mL) chopped toasted pecans

½ cup (125 mL) packed brown sugar

¼ cup (60 mL) birch syrup or molasses

⅓ cup (80 mL) brandy

¼ cup (60 mL) unsalted butter

¼ cup (60 mL) apple juice or cider

2 Tbsp (30 mL) lemon juice

2 tsp (10 mL) grated lemon peel

¾ tsp (3.5 mL) ground ginger

½ tsp (2.5 mL) ground cloves

½ tsp (2.5 mL) grated nutmeg

Pinch of salt

Lynx in winter.

Sources and Suppliers

Birch Syrup and Spruce Tip Syrup
Uncle Berwyn
www.yukonbirch.ca / uncleberwyn@yukonbirch.ca
P.O. Box 1735 Dawson City, Yukon Territory, Y0B 1G0
Visit Uncle Berwyn's website to see pictures of the syrup-making process, find great recipes and learn about the difference between birch and maple syrups.

Birch Boy Products
www.birchboy.com / birchboy@aptalaska.net
P.O. Box 637 Haines, Alaska, USA, 99827
Tel: 1-877-769-5660 / (907) 767-5660
In addition to birch and spruce tip syrups Birch Boy Products makes all kinds of other syrups from indigenous trees and fruits.

Fireweed Honey
There are a number of producers of fireweed honey and jelly in the Yukon, including
Yukon Wild Things
http://yukonwildthings.com / yukonwildthings@yahoo.com
Location: Km 261.4 Klondike Hwy., Yukon Territory, Canada
Mailing address: PO Box 31535, Whitehorse, YT Y1A 6K8.
Tel: (867) 456-2477
Yukon Wild Things specializes in wild products including honey, Arctic char, jellies and syrups, dried morels and wild teas.

Fireweed Jelly
Aurora Mountain Farm
http://auroramountain.yukonfood.com / auroramountain@yahoo.ca
Mailing address: Box 20228, Whitehorse, YT Y1A 7A2.
In addition to fireweed jelly, Aurora Mountain Farm produces a range of other products including dandelion and yarrow jellies.

Goat Cheeses and Meat
Lendrum Ross Farm
lendrumross@northwestel.net
Brian Lendrum & Susan Ross, Box 31531 Whitehorse, Yukon Y1A 6K8
Tel: (867) 633-4201

Herbal Teas
Aroma Borealis Herb Shop
www.aromaborealis.com
504-B Main St., Whitehorse, YT, Y1A 2B9
Tel: (867) 667-HERB (4372)
In addition to herbal teas, Aroma Borealis supplies skin care and aromatherapy products inspired by the northern boreal forest.

Highbush Cranberry Products
Birch Boy Products
See under Birch Syrup and Spruce Tip Syrup for contact information.

Yukon Wild Things
See under Fireweed Honey for contact information.

Morels and Other Dried Mushrooms
Mitobi Enterprises Ltd.
www.mitobi.com / mail@mitobi.com
Tel: 250-537-2335

Pacific Rim Mushrooms
pacrimmushrooms.com / info@pacrimmushrooms.com
Tel: (604) 568-6033

Yukon Wild Things
See under Fireweed Honey for contact information.

Smoked Salmon
Taku Wild Product
www.takuwild.com / sales@takuwild.com
Box 335, 1 Taku Drive, Atlin, BC, V0W 1A0
Tel: 1-888-551-8258
Taku Wild sells smoked wild sockeye from the Taku Rriver and the business is owned and operated by the Taku River Tlingit.

Soapberry Jelly
Yukon Wild Things
See under Fireweed Honey for contact information.

Sourdough

www.carlsfriends.org

If you send a stamped, self-addressed envelope to the address provided on the website you'll receive a packet of Carl Griffiths Oregon Trail 150-year-old starter, free of charge. Volunteers continue Carl Griffiths' tradition of giving free sourdough to anyone who requests it.

Other Products

Yukon Farm Products and Services is a comprehensive list published by the Yukon and Canadian governments, available in book form or online at www.farmproducts.yukonfood.com. The website is updated regularly.

References and Recommended Reading

Aidells, Bruce, and Denis Kelly. *Bruce Aidells' Complete Sausage Book: Recipes from America's Premier Sausage Maker*. Berkeley: Ten Speed Press, 2000.

Allman, Ruth. *Alaska Sourdough*. Portland: Alaska Northwest Books, 2003.

Beranbaum, Rose Levy. *The Bread Bible*. New York: Norton, 2003.

Berglund, Berndt, and Clare E. Bolsby. *Wilderness Cooking: A Unique Illustrated Cookbook and Guide for Outdoor Enthusiasts*. New York: Scribner, 1973.

Child, Julia, Louisette Bertholle and Simone Beck. *Mastering The Art of French Cooking, Volumes One and Two*. New York: Knopf, 2009.

Curnonsky. *Larousse Traditional French Cooking*. Toronto: Doubleday Canada, 1989.

Dufresne, Francine. *Cooking Fish and Game, French Canadian Style*. San Francisco: 101 Productions, 1975.

Esquivel, Laura. *Like Water for Chocolate: A Novel in Monthly Installments, with Recipes, Romances, and Home Remedies*. New York: Anchor Books, 1995.

Fireweed Community Market Society. *Celebrate Yukon Food: Seasonal Recipes*. Whitehorse: Fireweed Community Market Society, 2006.

Gray, Beverley. *Gathering Wild Wisdom: Medicinal and Edible Plants of the Northern Boreal Forest*. Yukon: Aroma Borealis Press, 2010.

McKimm, Margo. *Everday Gourmet: A Collection of Family Favourites*. Privately published. Smith Falls: Performance Printing, 1995.

Rombauer, Irma S., and Rombauer Becker, Marion. *Joy of Cooking: The American Household Classic Newly Revised and Expanded with Over 4500 Recipes and 1000 Informative Illustrations*. New York: Scribner, 1995.

Silverton, Nancy. *Nancy Silverton's Breads from the La Brea Bakery*. New York: Villard, 1996.

The Scottish Women's Rural Institutes Cookery Book (Tenth Edition). Edinburgh: The Scottish Women's Rural Institutes, 2002.

Turner, Nancy J, and Adam F. Szczawinski. *Edible Wild Fruits and Nuts of Canada: Canada's Edible Wild Plants Series, Vol. 3*. Ottawa: Fitzhenry and Whiteside/National Museum of Natural Sciences, 1988.

University of Alaska, Fairbanks, School of Natural Resources and Agricultural Sciences, Agricultural and Forestry Experimentation Station. "Morels: A Morsel After the Fire." *Agroborealis*, 37.1, summer 2005. Available online: www.uaf.edu/snras/afes/pubs/agro/Agro37-1.pdf

Wolfert, Paula. *The Slow Mediterranean Kitchen: Recipes for the Passionate Cook*. New Jersey: John Wiley & Sons, 2003.

Useful Websites

I learned much about spruce tips from Alaskan cook Laurie Helen Constantino, who writes a blog called "Mediterranean Cooking in Alaska"(*medcookingalaska.blogspot.com*) and is a fearless and inventive forager.

For more information on wilderness cooking methods (with a minimum of posturing) see *wildwoodsurvival.com*.

For more Yukon fishing lore, and the occasional recipe, visit Dennis Zimmerman's website *fishonyukon.com*

For instructions on how to build your own reflector oven, go to *www.blazingpaddles.ca/outdoor_cooking/reflector/index.htm*.

For sourdough advice and inspiration, visit *thefreshloaf.com*, *sourdo.com* and *wildyeastblog.com*.

Au revoir et bon appétit.

Index

Professional freelance photographer **Cathie Archbould**, based in Whitehorse, Yukon Territory, captures the essence of the land and people north of 60. Cathie brings 20 years of excellence to her assignments for corporate, commercial and industrial clients. She photographs the North with a passion that could only come from doing what she loves—living large in one of Canada's last frontiers. Cathie is also an accomplished hunter and cook, and donated generous amounts of wild meat for *The Boreal Gourmet* cooking experiments.

Laurel Parry is thrilled to be a part of this project. Drawing, while not a vocation, has always been part of her life, and some of her happiest memories are of sitting at the kitchen table working out how to draw things, first with her two brothers and then her two sons. Illustrations of kitchen scenes, utensils, ingredients and other oddball subjects have been a pleasure to create for this book. Both the drawing and the extensive tasting, in the name of "research," have been a riot.